Breaking the Silence!

Breaking the Silence!

The Voiceless Victims of Physical and Emotional Violence

Dr. Kim Yancey James

Copyright © 2010 by Dr. Kim Yancey James.
Cover Design by Betty Saby—Butterfly Ministries www.butterflyministries4u.org

Library of Congress Control Number:		2010902333
ISBN:	Hardcover	978-1-4500-4855-2
	Softcover	978-1-4500-4854-5
	Ebook	978-1-4500-4856-9

All rights reserved. No part of this book may be reproduced or transmitted in any form or by any means, electronic or mechanical, including photocopying, recording, or by any information storage and retrieval system, without permission in writing from the copyright owner.

This book was printed in the United States of America.

For workshops, seminars and book signings, please contact the author at:

Rev. Dr. Kim Yancey James
kyanceyjam@msn.com
973-624-6614 option #3

To order additional copies of this book, contact:
Xlibris Corporation
1-888-795-4274
www.Xlibris.com
Orders@Xlibris.com

Contents

Prologue xi

Acknowledgments xiii

Dedication xv

Introduction 1

Chapters

    1. Ministry Focus 3

        The Making of A Healing Vessel 4

            My Career Path 5

        Context of Ministry 8

            The Economy 8

            Demographics 9

            Education 10

            Community Organization and Services 10

            The Paradise Baptist Church 10

            The Church History 12

            Affiliations 14

        Synergy 17

2. The State of the Art 18

    Violence Against Women in America Today 18

        Terms and Definitions 22

        Violence 23

        Victim-Survivor 23

        Battering and Nonphysical Abuse 27

        Child Sexual Abuse 28

        Confidentiality 28

        Silence 29

        Woundedness 32

        Healing 34

    Forgiveness 35

    Pastoral Care and Counseling 36

    The Role of the Church in the Field of Violence Against Women 37

        Leadership 39

3. Theoretical Foundations 41

    Historical Foundation 42

        Women as Slaves in the United States 51

        The Black Nationalist Movement 53

        The Civil Rights Movement 55

        Sexual Harassment of African American Women 57

>
> Biblical Foundations 63
>
> Theological Foundation.. 74
>
>> The Theological Aspect of the Black Church 81
>
> 4. Methodology 89
>
>> Treatment Hypothesis.. 89
>
>> Intervention.. 89
>
>> Research Design... 89
>
>> Measurement.. 91
>
>> Instrumentation.. 91
>
> 5. The Ministry Model.. 93
>
>> Designing the Research Project.. 93
>
>>> Focus Group 93
>
>> Surveys 94
>
>>> Pre-test and Post-test Surveys 94
>
>>> Interviews... 94
>
>>> Narratives 94
>
>> Implementing the Research Project 94
>
>>> Evaluating the Research Project 97
>
>>> Pre-test Survey Results... 98
>
>>> Post-test Survey Results 102
>
>>> The Interviews and Narratives 106

    6. Reflection, Summary, and Conclusions 107

        Summary of Research Project.. 107

            The Collaborative... 107

            The Interviews and Narratives 107

            How the Silence was Broken... 108

            How the Participants Inform and Protect Their Children.... 109

            Healing and Pastoral Care and Counseling........................ 109

            Education and Transformation.. 109

            Suggested Changes 112

            Modified Research Project... 113

            Recommendations for Further Research............................ 113

Appendix

    A. Power and Control Wheel... 115

    B. Five Kinds of Abuse 116

    C. Pre-test Survey Questions... 117

    D. Interview Questions... 127

    E. Post-test Survey: Questions and Results 129

    F. Women of Divine Destiny Conference Flyer............................... 135

    G. Women's Fellowship and Summer Bible School Flyer
       Lesson I—Jesus' Relationships with Women............................ 136

    H. Women's Fellowship and Summer Bible School:
       Lesson II The Broken and Abused Woman................................ 147

I. Women's Fellowship and Summer Bible School:
Lesson III The Guilty Woman 158

J. Women's Fellowship and Summer Bible School:
Lesson IV The Labeled and Misunderstood Woman................. 166

K. Women's Fellowship and Summer Bible School:
Lesson V The Stressed and Worried Woman............................ 175

L. Women's Fellowship and Summer Bible School:
Lesson VI The Transformed and Triumphant Woman............... 185

M. Women's Fellowship and Summer Bible School:
Certificate of Achievement 194

N. Violence Against Women Community Awareness Day:
Flyer and Registration Form 195

O. Violence Against Women Community Awareness Day:
Donation Request Letter 198

P. Violence Against Women Community Awareness Day:
Program 201

Q. Participant Interviews and Narratives 206

Bibliography 229

Prologue

The journey of life has pointed me in the direction to passionately and spiritually address the issues surrounding the silence of the church and community concerning violence against women. The historical, biblical, and theological lenses that are employed provide the reader with an in-depth understanding as to the magnitude of the phenomenon and how violence impacts the lives and relationships of abused women. It is a global concern that has not been limited by time, space, race or religion. The book offers definitions of terminology associated with abuse: physical, verbal, emotional, psychological, and spiritual along with materials that may be used for workshops and conferences.

This study outlines a model of ministry that has proven effective in breaking the silence of abuse while providing a safe and nurturing environment in which those who have suffered abuse may begin the lengthy process of healing. The context for this ministry is the Paradise Baptist Church located in Newark, New Jersey.

The women who courageously participated in the research describe their victimization in such detail that it brings the reader into the heart of the wounded party. They are open and honest, candidly expressing their challenges. Yet, their voices have become messages of strength and hope. Thus, in the process of healing they become instruments of healing for others.

Men and women alike, stand to gain much needed insight through exploring the multifaceted issues surrounding violence against women. The research conducted in the ministry context indicates that a majority of the female members of the church have either experienced abuse directly or indirectly through female family members. We found that we are somehow associated with a woman who is currently in an abusive relationship and/or is a survivor of violence and abuse. Once I began to speak publicly about this subject, countless women have shared their stories, many of which include childhood sexual abuse. Yet, because of the shame associated with this victimization, there are many who remain silent. The message that is often spoken to them is that they should "forgive and forget." Failure to do so often results in a feeling of guilt and a sense of inadequacy, which if unaddressed, leads to more pain and more silence.

Therefore, the church can no longer remain silent concerning violence against women, who represent a large part of the congregations, attending church Sunday after Sunday—they suffer in silence. The church must encourage women to speak out concerning their pain, as naming the pain and the source begins the process of the plan to bring about change.

The love of God is made manifest when the church serves as agents of change through caring for the wounded and broken persons in the church, as well as in the world.

It is through intentional sharing and caring that we encourage women to break the silence—we must open the door for dialogue and collaboration that focuses on this crisis that continues to plague our communities.

Acknowledgments

It is with humble and sincere gratitude that I acknowledge the friends, colleagues, peers, and church community that supported, encouraged, and prayed with me through this process. The Paradise Baptist Church and the Women's Ministry have been there from the beginning, affirming my ministry gifts—"and for this I wish you love."

To my husband, Bishop Jethro C. James, Jr., who trusted that God was leading me in this ministry project and helped me to "work out my soul salvation." Your personal sacrifice, commitment to the ministry of the Gospel, and prophetic vision have been exemplary.

To my father, James Weldon Yancey, who has always been supportive and proud of my accomplishments.

I greatly appreciate Rev. Dr. Edward L. Hunt, Dr. Jackie Baston, and Rev. Dr. Sharon Ellis Davis for sharing their time and expertise. You are the best!

To my United Theological Seminary friends and colleagues who prayed together and stayed together; Dr. RoyEtta P. Quateka-Means, Dr. Stephanie Jordan, Dr. Ralph Williamson, Dr. Betty Harris, Dr. Clarence Burke, Dr. Joseph Jones, Dr. Edward Davis, Dr. Donna Curry, and Dr. William Dixon, I love you much!

To Rev. Dr. Weldon McWilliams Jr., your words of encouragement and wisdom will never be forgotten.

My dear context associates, I could not have done this without you. You did the work.

And finally to my mentors, Dr. Harold A. Hudson and Dr. Daryl R. Hairston, who are mentors par excellence. Thank you for your dedication, commitment, and assistance in the completion of this project.

Dedication

In loving memory of the women on whose shoulders I stand; Louise Yancey, Jacqueline Hinton, Dorothy Watson, Mabel Bland, Antoinette Stevens, and Valerie Dade.

To my children, Terrill, Tanisha, and Danielle, may life bring you much love, joy, and happiness. And to my grandson, Isaiah Nathaniel, and Grandma Kim's Taylor Jewel, *you are the sunshine of my life.*

Introduction

Violence against women and the devastating effect on their lives continues to be endemic in the world today. My concern is that the failure on the part of the Black church to minister to those who are victimized will not only hinder the process of healing, but also add further stress and anxiety.

Abused persons who attend church could well benefit from messages and messengers who are sensitive to their needs, are equipped to provide care, supply information, and make appropriate referrals for services. I believe that openly addressing and providing care for female victim-survivors of violence and abuse will be instrumental in breaking the silence concerning their abuse and assist in the process of healing.

Chapter one presents my educational, professional, and spiritual experiences as they relate to the ministry project. Additionally, this chapter delineates the ministry context, my passion for the project, and the goals that were set in order to implement the model of care.

Chapter two explores the work of professionals whose field involves the care of abused persons. It is here that specific terminology is examined and various kinds of abuse are defined. Additionally, the field of pastoral care and counseling is discussed as an instrument of healing.

Chapter three examines the theoretical foundation of violence and abuse while exploring the historical, biblical, and theological starting points for the project.

Information is shared concerning the history of violence against women as it relates to racism and patriarchy. This is followed by biblical history to the present day as I have engaged the work of Black and womanist theologians who provide insight into the position of the church concerning the subjugation of women.

Chapter four describes the design of the project, methods, instruments of measurement, and the evaluation of the project. This chapter gives details as to the purpose of the chosen instruments and methods. It is important that the methodology; *how* we do ministry, is appropriate for the ministry setting.

Chapter five presents the analysis of the project. It is in this chapter that I delve into the data that was collected and closely evaluate the responses of the participants. The women who participated in the ministry model openly share the details of their victimization in a manner that draws the reader into their hearts—it is life changing! The success of the project is evaluated and determined based upon results found in the data, bearing in mind that the process is as significant as the data.

Chapter six provides the summary of the research project with a critical analysis of the outcome. This chapter suggests changes and revisions in the model. In addition, I discuss my personal growth and enlightenment as a result of my involvement in the development of the ministry project.

Chapter One

Ministry Focus

The ministry project, a model of care for female victim-survivors of violence and abuse, is an area of ministry, which has the potential to positively impact the lives of church and community. After reflecting on the numerous wonderful, challenging, educational experiences that life has presented I was certain that God had orchestrated my steps in preparation for the design of this ministry model.

I bring to this project many years of experience by providing services to vulnerable adults and have been certified[1] by the State of New Jersey as a social worker since 1995. Additionally, in order to become further equipped in the area of Christian counseling, I have taken the following courses offered by the American Association of Christian Counselors: Surviving Sexual Abuse, Overcoming Depression, Divorce Recovery: Starting Over Again, Psychiatric Care and Medications, Anger Management and Guilt: Love's Unseen Enemy.

As required in the field of ministry, social workers must learn to listen, respond to crisis, identify needs, offer encouragement, provide care, have knowledge of corresponding community services, make referrals to appropriate care professionals when necessary, and provide follow-up services as required by the client population.

Licensed to preach in 1999 and ordained in 2005, I graduated from New York Theological Seminary with a Master of Divinity degree. The seminary, which has a focus in urban ministry, served to further equip me as a preacher of the gospel and as an advocate for the people. The field of supervised ministry provided the opportunity to observe and learn from experienced church leaders while pastoral care and counseling provided insight, further enhancing my social work skills.

As the president and founder of Women of Divine Destiny, Inc., a non-profit corporation that organizes women's conferences, I continue to collaborate with women's ministries in the New York/New Jersey area. Since

---

[1] The State of New Jersey requires certified Social Workers to complete continuing education courses in order to maintain their status.

1999, I have also been the facilitator of the Women's Fellowship and Summer Bible School at the Paradise Baptist Church in Newark, New Jersey. The class is attended by more than one hundred women from churches in the community, some traveling from the State of New York. I have been invited to minister by numerous churches in the New York Tri-State area and beyond as a preacher and workshop facilitator.

The Making of a Healing Vessel

I was born to Jacqueline Stevens and James Yancey who were twenty-one and twenty-two years old, respectively, at the time of my birth. They never married and when they experienced problems in their relationship, they decided to separate, leaving me, their eight-month-old child to live temporarily with my paternal aunt. Unfortunately, neither of my parents was able to assume the responsibility of taking care of a child. So Dorothy, my aunt and eldest sister of my father, raised me from the ripe age of eight months old to adulthood and was, indeed, my mother. It was Dorothy who made sure that I attended both Sunday school and church regularly at the Mount Olive Baptist Church in Hackensack, New Jersey. I remember, as if it were yesterday, the booming voice of the deacon, who would chant every Sunday: "I was glad when they said unto me: let us go into the house of the Lord. Our feet shall stand within thy gates, O Jerusalem." The choir would then immediately march in singing, "We're marching to Zion." My spiritual journey began as a young child who loved the church, the music of the church, and loved to sing.

The family, comprised of Dorothy, soul mate; Thomas, and her adult daughter; Mabel, moved to Paterson, New Jersey when I reached the age of five. This move was somewhat disheartening because I had just entered kindergarten and had to be transferred to a new school. There was no church affiliation in Paterson until I reached the age of nine, when I met a lady in the neighborhood named Della Savington, who was a gifted musician and singer. "Ms. Della" immediately recognized my ability to sing and spent a great deal of time cultivating my vocal talent, often teaching me the hymns of the African Methodist Episcopal Zion Church. Ironically, Ms. Della was a musician for a Baptist church to which I traveled with her Sunday after Sunday, singing in the choir and participating in church programs. I was baptized at the age of twelve and became a member of the Shiloh Baptist Church in Paterson, New Jersey, where Rev. Alfred Blakely was the pastor. I always enjoyed the worship services and was a devoted choir member.

Having been a good student throughout the early childhood education years, I was always encouraged to attend college and did so, despite the challenge of becoming a mother at the age of sixteen. Dorothy, being the good mother that she was, along with Mabel and my paternal grandmother;

Louise, did not hesitate to help in caring for my son. Determined to continue my educational pursuits, I enrolled at Howard University in Washington, DC, graduating early in three and a half years. My chosen major was political science with a concentration in pre-law. Further educational studies included communication arts at William Paterson University with a focus in television production.

It was during the early 1980s that I became interested in biblical studies as a member of the Canaan Baptist Church in Paterson, New Jersey. Serving as an assistant choir director gave me the opportunity to study the ministry of music, which led to a closer walk with God. Music ministry became a focal point, which gave rise to singing with various community choirs as well as live performances in the Off-Broadway play, *Mama I Want To Sing*.

Several years later upon answering the call to preach, I earned a Master of Divinity from New York Theological Seminary.

My Career Path

I lived in Silver Spring, Maryland for a year following graduation from Howard University and was employed in retail management. I later returned to Paterson, New Jersey where I was employed by the CETA (Comprehensive Employment and Training Act) program as a planner and grant writer. The CETA program provided training and job opportunities for individuals in the community who were unemployed and impoverished. It was my responsibility to complete statistical reports and to review requests for proposals from community-based organizations who sought to provide services and employment training to this population.

Subsequent employment included a position as an advertising sales representative for a local newspaper. This required meeting with retail stores and the local chamber of commerce to plan sales promotions. It also involved designing or arranging for the design of retail advertisements and scheduling the same to appear in the newspaper.

For the past twenty-four years, I have been employed by the Passaic County Board of Social Services in Paterson, New Jersey. The board of social services is the provider of numerous social services, which include, but are not limited to, cash assistance, Medicaid, food stamps, emergency assistance, and child support services to eligible clients in Passaic County. I have held the following positions including: income maintenance worker, child support worker, social worker, and currently, life skills educator/senior training technician. Fourteen of my twenty-four years of employment with the agency were in the position of social worker in Adult Protective Services, which provided services to vulnerable adults in the community who were homeless and/or victims of self-neglect, caretaker neglect, physical abuse, psychological abuse, and personal or financial exploitation. This position often involved crisis intervention, emergency housing arrangements, and nursing home placements, all of which required collaboration with coworkers, community-based organizations, mental health services, alcohol and drug rehabilitation centers, federal agencies, law enforcement officers, and the judicial system. As such, I have come to value this experience as essential to urban ministry, which is descriptive of the current ministry context.

I count it as a blessing that my occupation and vocation came together and culminated into the present position of life skills educator/senior training technician. Both my occupation and vocation present situations where men and women are in need of nurturing through spiritual direction and words of encouragement. Although I am not able to preach the gospel in the work setting, the gospel is lived out in each presentation.

The classes are open to both men and women; however, as a result of the composition of the low-income population consisting of public assistance recipients, many of the participants are women. Several of the class exercises are designed to help the students to identify their strengths and weaknesses. Goals are identified followed by a plan to achieve them. There is a "Who I Am and Where I Want to Go"[2] exercise in the training manual, which presents the opportunity for participants to share their stories, many of which involve their experiences of physical, emotional, and sexual abuse. The students are advised that they are not to share anything that they are not comfortable with discussing. However, on several occasions women have chosen to share their intimate stories claiming they had never told anyone or those whom they told did not believe them.

It was the various experiences in these settings that caused me to identify and raise a level of consciousness that many female survivors of violence and abuse suffer in silence. Thus, I began to look at the ministry context in light of the same, questioning how many congregants have experienced abuse and suffer in silence. I grew concerned and interested in a model of ministry that would break this silence and provide care, which would aid in the often lengthy process of healing. I was aware of a few congregants who had experienced abuse, but intuitively, knew that there were many others. The subject was mentioned during a women's ministry planning committee meeting at Paradise Baptist Church which was attended by approximately ten women. Three of the ten women acknowledged that they had been sexually abused as children at which time I knew that a ministry of care and healing was needed.

---

[2] Caroline Manuele Adkins, Winthrop R. Adkins and Myriam Belloch-Cort, *Adkins Life Skill Program Career Development Series*, 3rd ed., 10 vols., vol. 1 (New York: Institute for Life Coping Skills, Inc., 2000), 8-12.

I proceeded to discuss this topic with the pastor, who agreed and granted permission for the study and development of a ministry model of care for female victim-survivors of violence and abuse. The concerns about the project were confidentiality, counseling, and crisis intervention for those who may experience emotional trauma as a result of breaking their silence. I assured the pastor that confidentiality was paramount and each participant would receive careful consideration during the implementation of the project.

Context of Ministry

This project's ministry context is the Paradise Baptist Church in Newark, New Jersey, where my husband has served as pastor for twenty years. I had served as a minister of music for eighteen years, director of women's ministries for nine years, and currently as executive minister.

Newark is the county seat of Essex County and the largest city in the state.[3] The city is divided into five political wards, which are the North Ward, East Ward, West Ward, Vailsburg, and Central Ward. Paradise Baptist Church is situated in the Central Ward of Newark, which was directly impacted by the 1967 race riots as many of the businesses, which were looted and destroyed were in the Central Ward. According to members of the congregation who resided in Newark during this time, shopping has never been the same. As a result of the rioting and looting, 13 percent of the businesses closed followed by another 19 percent within a year.[4] This area is now predominantly inhabited by indigent African Americans.

Poverty continues as a problem within the city of Newark. Despite revitalization plans, a large number of people live below the poverty line. The area where most of the devastation occurred during the 1967 riots still remains one of the poorest areas of the city. The riots began when a black man named John Smith was brutally beaten by police.[5] Angry mobs outside the police station were told that he was dead and thus began to burn, loot, and destroy property in the area. The area has been rebuilt, but the poverty, anger, and violence remain. The city recently remembered the forty-year anniversary of the devastating riots that changed the lives of all of the residents.

The Economy

Despite the poverty and violence, businesses, insurance, and financial centers have remained in the city. "Newark is a trade, insurance, financial, and

---

[3] Love To Know Classic Encyclopedia, *Newark, New Jersey-Love to Know*; available from http://www.1911emcyclopedia/org/Newark,_New_Jersey/ (accessed August 24, 2007).

[4] Brad Parks, "*Crossroads Pt.3:* After the Riots, Change Is Slow to Come" "[4 Part Series] (July 10, 2007 3:10AM accessed); available from http://blog.nj.com/ledgernewark/2007/07/crossroads _ pt _ 3.html/ (accessed September 1, 2007).

[5] Brad Parks, "*Crossroads Pt.2:* 5: Days That Changed a City" (Newark Star Ledger, accessed Posted July 9, 2007); available from http://blog.nj.com/ledger/2007/07/crossroads _pt _ 2.html/ (accessed September 1, 2007).

transportation center."[6] Prudential and Horizon Blue Cross and Blue Shield, which are two of the nation's largest insurance companies, have offices in Newark.[7] Prudential, Mutual Benefit Life, and The American Fire Company are headquartered in Newark.[8] In addition, one of the country's largest cargo ports and truck terminals is located in Newark.[9] The Newark International Liberty Airport is one of the busiest in the nation and is one of three major airports in the New York metropolitan area.

Demographics

According to the 2000 census, the demographics are as follows:

> African Americans comprise 53.5 percent of the population, whites 26.5 percent, Asians 1.2 percent, Native Americans 0.4 percent, native Hawaiians, and other Pacific islanders less that 0.1 percent. The balance of the population includes those of a mixed heritage or did not indicate race. Hispanics are counted as 29.5 percent. The total population according to the 2000 census is 273,546. It was estimated at 280,666 in 2005.[10] There are 140,845 females and 132,701 males. The median resident age is 30.8 years; the estimated median household income is $30,665 compared to $61,672 for the state of New Jersey. The median home value is $242,600 compared to $333,900 for the state and the median gross rent is $769 and 24.8 percent of the residents live in poverty. About 57.9 percent of the population aged twenty-five and above have high school diplomas and above while only 9 percent have a bachelor's degree or above. There are eight registered sex offenders living in the city according to early 2007 research, which is smaller than the state average comparing the number of residents to the number of offenders.[11]

---

[6] MSN Encarta Premium, *Newark (New Jersey)*(accessed); available from http://encarta.msn.com/encyclopedia _ 761566779/Newark_(New_Jersey).html/ (accessed August 22, 2007).

[7] Ibid.

[8] Love To Know Classic Encyclopedia, *Newark, New Jersey-Love to Know 1911*(accessed); available from http://www.1911encyclopedia.org/Newark, _ New _ Jersey./ (accessed August 22, 2007).

[9] MSN Encarta. Premium/ (accessed August 22, 2007).

[10] Ibid.

[11] City-Data.com, *Newark, New Jersey*; available from http:www.city-data.com/city/Newark-New-Jersey-.html/ (accessed August 31, 2007).

Education

The following postsecondary educational institutions are located in Newark: Rutgers University—Newark, the New Jersey Institute of Technology (NJIT), Seton Hall University School of Law, the University of Medicine and Dentistry of New Jersey (UMDNJ), and Essex County College.

The Newark Public Schools are located in the Abbott District and has been taken over by the state of New Jersey. Despite the fact that the schools are run by the state of New Jersey, students still score low on standardized tests.

Community Organizations and Services

In 1968, the New Community Corporation ("NCC") was organized by a group of community leaders, who responded to the need to rebuild and revitalize this community that was the scene of the 1967 riots. The riots resulted in twenty-six deaths and $10 million in damage to property.[12] The first housing development was opened in 1975.[13] Since then, senior citizen housing and low-rise, low-income housing have been built in the Central Ward. The five-story building is adjacent to the church building and the low-rise building is directly across the street. The senior citizens' building is approximately one and a half blocks away.

NCC has expanded its services from housing units to child care service, health care services, and human services, which include counseling, education, substance abuse program referrals, job placement, neighborhood recreational center, and after-school activities for youth.[14]

The Paradise Baptist Church

The Paradise Baptist Church Constitution and By-Laws are set forth below in the following paragraphs. A church mission statement is important to inform and educate the congregants what the church is supposed to do and what the members have agreed to do. A church constitution should be reviewed periodically to insure that it is designed to meet the needs of the

---

[12] Brad Parks, "Crossroads Pt. 2: 5 Days That Changed a City" (Newark Star Ledger, Posted July 9, 2007; available from *http://.nj.com/ledger/2007/07crossroads_pt_2.html*, (accessed September 1, 2007).

[13] Ibid.

[14] *New Community Corporation*, [History] (accessed); available from http://www.new community.org/main/htm/ (accessed September 1, 2007).

church community, which is constantly changing. It should not be a document that is set in stone, never to be changed or amended. The Paradise Baptist Church documents were revised and ratified at the annual church meeting in November 1997, at which I was present.

> Mission Statement: The mission statement of the Paradise Baptist Church is to be a Bible-based ministry of excellence whose purpose is to evangelize the community, equip and teach its members in the ways of Christ and promote family devotion, edify the Body of Christ through preaching and teaching the Word of God.[15]

> Preamble: The church is a community of all true believers of Jesus Christ. It is the redeeming fellowship in which the Word of God is preached by persons divinely called. The sacraments are duly administered according to Christ's own appointment. Under the discipline of the Holy Spirit, the church seeks to provide for maintenance of worship, the edification of believers, and the redemption of the world. As part of the Body of Christ, the Paradise Baptist Church of Newark, New Jersey exists to save souls that none may be lost.[16]

> Article I: The name of the church is Paradise Baptist Church. The church is a non-profit (501c3) corporation registered with the federal government and state of New Jersey. The officers and agents of the corporation are elected by the church body. The church must register with the state each year in order to remain a non-profit, tax exempt entity. The Paradise Baptist Church is and shall remain a sovereign entity in and of herself in all legal matters and is not to be confused with or under any jurisdiction, organization, or convention. The preamble and article I are included with the mission statement to further express the purpose of the ministry and the autonomy of the congregation.

---

[15] Jethro C. James, "Church Mission Statement," Paradise Baptist Church, 1997). This statement is included in the revised constitution which was ratified by the church during the annual church meeting which is held on the second Saturday in November each year.

[16] This information is taken directly from the revised church constitution which was ratified by the church body during the annual church meeting of 1997, held on the second Saturday in November.

The Church History

The Paradise Baptist Church history was duplicated in part from the church records,[17] as follows:

In the year 1943, the late Rev. Robert Mead called several persons together to form a Mission Circle and from this group came what is now known as the Paradise Baptist Church. In October 1944, the Mission Circle obtained a religious church charter and registered as such with the State of New Jersey.

It held its first service in a store front at Seven Charlton Street in the City of Newark, New Jersey. The noise of the church disturbed the neighbors to such an extent that they were asked to move. Having little funds, the pastor moved the church to Livingston Street into a building known as the Evangelical Garden. However, due to the extreme cold, only a few services were held there.

It looked like the church would not survive, but the late Rev. J. W. Caldwell, pastor of the Little Friendship Baptist Church, located at 186 Charlton Street, opened the doors of his church allowing Paradise to worship with them. It was not long before the church saw an opportunity to purchase a small building at 134 Charlton Street. Unfortunately, the church was unable to meet the financial obligations. However, they did not give up and were soon able to purchase a building at 158 Chestnut Street.

Pastor Mead, who suffered from chronic asthma, resigned as pastor due to his illness. Soon after, the church called Rev. Frank Hardwick, who had been serving as assistant pastor. The church members worked hard and with less than twenty active members burned two mortgages and purchased new pews along with other key renovations. The church also purchased a parsonage at 189 Leslie Street in Newark.

In October 1962, the church moved to 332-336 New York Avenue in Newark. The basement and sidewalk was paved, the kitchen was remodeled and new bathrooms were installed. The church also owned the adjacent house, which was aluminum sided. Rev. B. F. Hardwick, after serving for thirty-four years, retired on the first Sunday in May 1984 and moved to Texas. He left the church free of debt.

Rev. Wilbert Constance Eural was called as pastor of the church in September 1984. During his pastorate, the building at 334-336 New York Avenue was sold and the property at 348-352 Fifteenth Avenue was purchased.

---

17 Elfreida Hardie, "Church History," (Paradise Baptist Church, 1993). Information was obtained from public legal documents, Mother Minnie Berrian, who was the only living charter member and Deacon Walter Robertson. The original document continues to be updated.

The property had an old building with three vacant lots. Reverend Eural began renovating the old building with plans to relocate the church to Fifteenth Avenue. However, the congregation grew unhappy with some of his business and financial dealings, which resulted in his resignation.

When Reverend Eural left, a few dedicated members continued the worship services at New York Avenue inviting different ministers to preach on Sunday. Despite the fact that the church only had fifty active members, they were of one accord; united in purpose. The membership decided to cease the renovation of the old building at Fifteenth Avenue and have it demolished with the intent of building a new edifice.

Rev. John Sharpe was called to the pastorate of the church in early 1990, but soon left to become the pastor of Shiloh Baptist Church in Newark. Paradise was disheartened, but learned to "Trust in the Lord with all thine heart and lean not unto thine own understanding. In all thy ways acknowledge Him and he shall direct thy path." Although the membership remained united, having weekly Bible study and prayer meeting as well as fiery services on Sunday, they realized the need for a pastor. So they began to pray that God would send one.

In October 1990, Rev. Jethro C. James Jr., accepted the leadership of the church with much faith and enthusiasm. Soon the parsonage at Leslie Street was sold and a groundbreaking service was held at the new church site at 348-352 Fifteenth Avenue. A new edifice was built, fully furnished with new pews and pulpit. The church also obtained another house valued at $70,000 through a grant written by Pastor James. Pastor James, not wanting to be installed until the new church was built, was installed on the day that the congregants marched into the new building; July 25, 1993.

In 1997, the Paradise Community Development Corporation, Inc. was formulated and obtained 501c3 non-profit status. The church consistently makes capital improvements on the property which includes paving the parking lot, which accommodates seventy cars, remodeling the kitchen, the fellowship hall as well as new furnishings for the pastor's study, the deacon's room, and the trustee room. The basement was recently remodeled with additional office space and seating to accommodate overflow from the main sanctuary.

In the summer of 1999, Pastor James announced the Minnie Berian Scholarship Foundation in honor of our founding church mother, which would provide funds to all student members who are attending their first year of college. In addition, there is a scholarship funded by Ms. Helen Ford in the name of my mother, Dorothy Watson.

In July 2000, the church purchased a forty-seven-passenger coach that is used to transport the members as the congregants share in fellowship with other churches as well as other church community functions.

The following ministries were organized under the leadership of Pastor James: The Men's Ministry, the Women's Ministry, the Praise Dance Ministry, the Youth Ministry, the Minnie Berian Scholarship Fund, the Dorothy Watson Scholarship Fund, the scholarship ministry, the tutorial program, and the Pastor's Love Ministry. Existing ministries have grown in number and in effectiveness. Pastor James continues to serve as a gifted teacher, preacher, and advocate for the people in the community. The church, through his leadership is at the forefront of issues that impact the lives of Newark residents. Most recently, Paradise participated as a site in the gun buyback program, which offered money to those who turned in guns to the police department.

Affiliations

The Paradise Baptist Church is a member of the American Baptist and National Baptist Conventions. The pastor is the president of Newark/North Jersey Committee for Black Clergy, a non-denomination group of ministers who identify and address the socioeconomic concerns of the church and community. He is also a member of the Newark Police Chaplaincy Unit, the New Jersey State Police Chaplaincy Unit, the Governor's Gangland Security Task Force, and the Essex County Legal Ethics Committee. A true advocate for people in the community, Pastor James consistently opens the church to those who provide valuable services to church and community.

As I reflected upon the relationship that the church has with the community, it is apparent that many of its members have been or are currently residents of the Central Ward, which is sometimes called New Community. The sound of gunshots is a common occurrence in this community, which has resulted in police barricades. On May 7, 2007, many members were stopped by the police as they attempted to attend church. The street had been closed because a young man, the husband of one our members, was murdered on the previous Tuesday night.

In 1990, when my husband came to the congregation, there were forty to fifty active members. There are now approximately four hundred active members. The "original" fifty members are not Central Ward residents and thus have not had the recent life experiences of living in poverty. Many of them share stories of growing up poor in the rural South, often speaking of how everyone shared what they had with their neighbor. The atrocities of life in the inner city for many congregants include: living in a crowded housing project, smelling the stench of urine in the hallways and on the elevators, parents and children using drugs and seeing your friends gunned down in the street.

The makeup of the congregation is approximately 85 percent women, many of whom are in recovery from substance abuse or have been sexually molested, physically and/or emotionally abused. Certainly, there are those who have experienced abuse and have not lived in poverty. However, I see a connection with being black, female, and poor. In addition, there is also a connecting point with being a black, poor, female, sexually abused, drug abuser. Each one of these areas present challenges and when compounded makes difficult seem impossible. The ministry at Paradise Baptist Church seeks to nurture those who are in difficult places in their lives. The ministry celebrates every victory, reading report cards of children as well as adults who may have just received their high school diploma. Recently, a female member came to me and said "I just celebrated one year of being clean from drugs." This was a great accomplishment!

Paradise has the reputation of being a place where one is free to worship without the typical stigma, which has been associated with the African American Baptist Church. The church does not have a particular dress code. Although there are ladies who wear "church hats," all are welcomed even if they do not have one. The pastor is generous and is concerned about the needs of the membership as well as the community. He is an advocate for people in the community opening the church to provide services. A First-Time Home Buyers workshop was held at the church every Saturday. Paradise is also among the first churches in Newark to have a defibrillator. Our nursing staff was trained by the University Hospital of Medicine and Dentistry (UMDNJ). Paradise has served as the largest Volunteer Income Tax Assistance (VITA) site in the city of Newark with volunteer tax preparers from the Internal Revenue Service available to the church and community free of charge during the tax season. The people in the community know the pastor and he knows many of them. He is very active in the political affairs on both local and state levels as an advocate for the "least of these." In essence, he is the right person for pastorate in this context and the church has embraced the vision given to him by God.

The congregation expects the pastor to be available to meet with them, pray with them, and to visit them when they are hospitalized. He is respected as a spiritual leader who cares for the flock. Most recently, in recognition of his leadership and guidance to the ecclesiastical community, Pastor James was consecrated as Bishop James.

Serving as executive minister and director of women's ministries, it has been my responsibility to assist in facilitating programs and services. Having been an integral part of the ministry for twenty years has provided opportunity and insight as to how to conduct collaborative ministry in this context. It has been a continual and interesting learning process, which has transformed both church and community.

During the time that the congregation was planning the move from the Ironbound section (East Ward) of Newark to the present location, I recall hearing the officers speaking of moving up "on the hill" to make a difference. Since I never lived in Newark, I did not have any idea what this meant. However, shortly after the church arrived, I realized that we were in "the hood." Everything had to be burglar proofed by installing alarms, double and triple-locks at the church, as well as to the cars in the parking lot. The church had to beware of reckless drivers of stolen cars as well as carjackers. Although I grew up in "the hood," I had not lived there in many years.

Newark, as most urban centers, lives with the daily threat of the loss of life as a result of gang violence. This is a reality that has touched the lives of the community and congregation. In 2007, the execution-style murder of three college students and the attempted murder of a fourth has further devastated and outraged a community struggling with the increasing incidents of gang related murder and violence.[18] One of the fatally wounded victims of this vile attack was a female, whose face was cut in such a manner that her skin was detached. I question the reason for the assailants' decision to disfigure the female after shooting her in the back of the head.

Gang violence continues to plague the community, which has caused Newark to receive nationwide attention. Rev. Jessie Jackson has visited the city to address the gun violence. Mayor Corey Booker, sworn in at the age of thirty-six, is a young man who faces challenges that were present when he took office after Sharpe James had been mayor for sixteen years. He has endured the scrutiny of peers and elders, some of whom feel that he has brought in "outsiders" to fill key positions in his cabinet. Although there is a large contingency of voters who wanted an African American police chief, Mayor Booker felt that a Caucasian was more qualified for the job. There was also a layoff of 130 city workers in an attempt to balance the budget. Mayor Booker, an attorney by trade, admitted to providing information that resulted in the indictment of former mayor and State Senator Sharpe James. Statistics indicate that the murder rate has declined beginning in 2008. Yet there is an increase in over all crime statistics. The decrease in the murder rate may be attributed to how the statistics are categorized. Some questioned whether or not Booker will be a long-term mayor. He has chosen to seek

---

[18] Janet Frankston Lorin, "Shootings Renew Mayor"s Sense of Purpose" (8/23/2007 accessed); available from http://examiner.com/a-887966 _ Shootings _Renew _ Mayor _ s _ Sense _ of Purpose.html/ (accessed August 23, 2007), 1-6.

re-election in May of 2010. The last three mayors; Addonizio, Gibson, and James held office for three terms.

Synergy

Like most, I was somewhat fearful during the call to ministry. Yet like the prophet Isaiah, I was willing to go. However, after a few years of ministering at the church under the leadership of my pastor/husband, we both experienced a spirit of restlessness. Despite these feelings, I always knew that there should be no move without God's direction and approval, but I still had to deal with my feelings.

God is so awesome, because in the midst of this trial God spoke through the words of Eugene H. Peterson's, *Under the Predictable Plant: An Exploration in Vocational Holiness.* My husband and I shared in the reading of this book and it has helped tremendously in understanding the importance of flourishing where one is planted.

It is as a result of introspective self examination that I have gained an understanding as to my passion for women's ministry; particularly to those who are survivors of violence and abuse. My biological mother; Jacqueline, was a victim-survivor of physical abuse and the woman who raised me; Dorothy, was a victim-survivor of child sexual abuse. I came to know Dorothy's story through other family members and have seen Jacqueline's bruises and black eyes as a result of the hands and fists of her boyfriend, August Felisbret. Despite the fact that he is no longer living, thoughts of him still produce anger. I do not remember that anyone shed tears at his funeral including my youngest sister, who is his daughter. When I received the call that he had died while sleeping I was relieved. My first thought was that my mother was finally rid of him and would not be beaten again. When my sister, who was sixteen years old at the time, heard that her father died, she was afraid that my mother had killed him.

My elder sister, Antoinette, who died in February 2006, lived for twenty-eight years as a paraplegic. This was as a result of a stab wound in the back that severed her spinal cord. She was left in a closet to die. It is believed that she was attacked by a male known to her. This was never proven nor was the perpetrator tried for the crime because she was so traumatized that she could not remember the event. Neither of these women ever spoke to me about their feelings or the pain and humiliation associated with these traumatic events. I am not aware that they ever spoke to anyone.

They suffered in silence. Thus, this book serves to break the silence of abuse, provide aftercare for survivors, as well as to honor the memory of Dorothy, Jacqueline, and Antoinette.

Chapter Two

The State of the Art

Violence Against Women in America Today

Domestic violence, sexual assault, child sexual abuse, and sexual harassment; all forms of victimization, affect the lives of every woman.[19] The home, a place where one would hope to find safety, is the least safe place for women and children, with battering being the "major cause of injury to adult women."[20] One of three females in the United States and one of seven males are sexually abused.[21] According to reported cases, a woman is raped every six minutes, and when one takes into account the unreported incidents, the FBI estimates that a woman is raped in the United States every two minutes.[22] Violence against women has become an epidemic as it is estimated that between three and four million women in the United States are battered by intimate partners.[23] I am aware that men are also victims of violence. However, since the ministry project involves a model of care for female victim-survivors, this review of literature focused on the state of the art for intervention with women.

These previously mentioned alarming statistics speak to the peril that women face in their daily lives, many while juggling the responsibility of managing households, raising children, and maintaining employment. Therefore, it is important that employers are educated concerning violence against women in hopes that it will assist them in recognizing behaviors that may indicate abuse and services that are available for victims.

---

[19] Marie Fortune and Carol J. Adams, ed., *Violence against Women and Children* (New York: The Continuum Publishing Company, 1995), 15.
[20] Ibid.
[21] Ibid.
[22] Ibid.
[23] Ruth A. Brandwein, ed., *Battered Women, Children and Welfare Reform*, ed. Claire M. Renzitti and Jeffrey L. Edleson, Sage Series on Violence against Women (Thousand Oaks, CA: Sage Publications, 1999), 18.

For twenty years or more, those who advocated for the rights of women and spoke out concerning violence against women persistently held rallies and developed programs, which provided services for abused women.[24] This advocacy opened the door for discourse concerning the victimization of women, which resulted in the Violence Against Women Act (VAWA), enacted by the United States Congress in 1994.[25]

According to the statutory provisions of VAWA, "violence against women is defined primarily as acts of domestic violence and sexual assault."[26] As a result of the enactment of VAWA, the federal government has assumed the responsibility to insure the safety of women through sanctions that promote arrest and prosecution of offenders.[27] Non-citizen women have also benefited from the enactment of this law, having been able to obtain legal classification, which would have been sabotaged by an abusive spouse.[28] The government is assisted in this effort by a diverse group of professional experts and paid consultants, who are involved in influencing the decisions to fund programs that provide services to victims.[29] The Office of Violence Against Women provides funding and has implemented a system, which requires the collaboration of local law enforcement, prosecutors, and courts to work together in response to domestic violence and sexual assault.[30]

However, despite the progress of the anti-violence movement in this country, which is based in feminism, there are concerns that it has not addressed the particular concerns of the African American female.[31] Beth E. Richie provides a black feminist perspective of violence against women. Richie posits that "violence against women of color is deeply embedded in issues of structural racism and poverty."[32] She raises a valid argument in that the movement has made great strides in raising awareness that any and every woman could be a victim of violence. However, in adopting the "everywoman" paradigm for developing and implementing services,

---

[24] Gail Garfield, *Knowing What We Know* (New Brunswick: Rutgers University Press, 2005), 1.

[25] Ibid., 2.

[26] Ibid.

[27] Ibid.

[28] Michael L. Penn and Rahel Nardos, *Overcoming Violence Against Women and Girls* (New York: Rowman & Littleton Publishers, Inc., 2003), 177.

[29] Garfield, *Knowing What We Know*, 1.

[30] Ibid.

[31] Natalie J. Sokoloff and Christina Pratt, ed., *Domestic Violence at the Margins: Readings on Race, Class, Gender and Culture* (New Brunswick: Rutgers University Press, 2005), 51.

[32] Ibid., 50.

"everywoman" evolved as "a white middle-class woman who could turn to a private therapist, a doctor, a police officer, or a law to protect her from abuse."[33] She adds that when women of color are victims of abuse, the problem is labeled as something other than victimization. Richie's argument is supported by referencing the increasing numbers of incarcerated women as a result of drug abuse, gang-related activity, and substandard housing in low-income dangerous neighborhoods.[34] Gang related activity and drug abuse are often the result of an underlying problem, which if investigated would more than likely reveal a history of physical and/or emotional abuse.

Research literature reveals that victims of domestic violence are "five times more likely to attempt suicide, fifteen times more likely to abuse alcohol, nine times more likely to abuse drugs, and three times more likely to be diagnosed as depressed or psychotic."[35]

I have experienced the reality of this as an employee of the Passaic County Board of Social Services (PCBSS). The agency has implemented a domestic violence initiative to provide services to victims of domestic violence in the form of referrals to women's centers and emergency housing assistance. The initiative came about through the work of Dr. William Curcio who, prior to his retirement, had been my supervisor. His dissertation involved a study of the welfare recipients and domestic violence. Curcio completed a survey with a sample of 846 women receiving welfare who were enrolled in an eight-week life skills class. During the two-year study, it was found that 15 percent of the samples reported that they were current victims of physical violence, and 25 percent reported that they were currently verbally or emotionally abused.[36] This caused Curcio to gain more understanding and concern for the clients, which was represented in his support of clients as well as the life skills educators whom he supervised.

Realizing the importance of informing the client population about services available to abused women, I also arranged for a representative from the Passaic County Women's Center to address each life skills class that I facilitated. The representatives shared information about the services and educated them concerning the different kinds of abuse. The responses to the presentation vary with each class. Some students will reveal that they are in abusive relationships and request further information.

Advocacy for victims of abuse through PCBSS was the precursor to my exploration of the need for the same in the ministry context. I have

---

[33] Ibid., 53.
[34] Ibid.
[35] Jody Raphael, *Saving Bernice: Battered Women, Welfare and Poverty* (Boston, MA: Northeastern University Press, 2000), 85.
[36] Ibid., 27.

known, intuitively, that many of the women in the context congregation are victim-survivors of abuse, and have silently questioned how the same affected their lives. As a result of interaction with abused women, it became clear that this would be a place of integrating my secular occupation and spiritual vocation. It has become apparent that violence against women should be addressed in both church and community.

Funding has become available, as a result of VAWA, to organizations that will provide training for courts and law enforcement officers, supervised visitation, and transitional housing. Faith-based communities are positioned to apply for funding and to be instrumental in the dissemination of information and the provision of services to those who may be in need of emergency assistance.

The goal and mission of the church, which is a faith-based community, should involve reaching out to all who are in need.[37] Dietrich Bonhoeffer's discussion of Christian fellowship defines the church as a community of believers united through and in Jesus Christ.[38] The keywords are "believers united," which indicates that the church should have concern for the well-being of all members of the community. The responsibility rests upon the church to speak to the needs of all of the members through sermons, teaching, and dissemination of applicable information. Kenneth Pohly posits that "there is a long and close relationship between social work and pastoral work, both being referred to frequently as helping professions."[39]

As one scans the congregations of churches representing various denominations, the majority of the persons in attendance are women. When the church does not address victimization associated with violence against women, it may further perpetuate a sense of despondency and hopelessness. Women may "remain in church—torn, disoriented, and self-hating—or they reject the God and the religion, which seem to be obstacles to the struggle to heal and reclaim their identity and integrity."[40]

> Andrew Sung Park addresses this in *From Hurt to Healing*.
> In the pews, we find all kinds of people. On any given Sunday, the preacher could be looking out at oppressors, exploiters, aggressors, invaders, abusers, rapists, murderers, and more. At the same time,

---

[37] Teresa L. Fry Brown, *God Don't Like Ugly* (Nashville, TN: Abingdon Press, 2000), 29.
[38] Deitrich Bonhoeffer, *Life Together* (New York: HarperCollins, 1954), 35.
[39] Kenneth Pohly, *Transforming the Rough Places*, 2nd ed. (Franklin, NY: Providence House Publishers, 2001), 52.
[40] Elizabeth Schussler Fiorenza and Mary Shawn Copeland, ed., *Violence against Women* (Maryknoll, NY: Orbis Books, 1994), 9.

however, the preacher is likely to be confronted with the victims of these sins, so that those who have been oppressed, exploited, injured, invaded, abused, raped, and bereft—as well as their families and friends—are also waiting to hear a word from God.[41]

Therefore, the goal of this project was the development of a model of care, which will aid in the spiritual and emotional healing of females who are victims and/or survivors of violence and abuse. During the review of literature for this project, I examined material, which provides information about the lives of victims; their thoughts, feelings, fears, and anxieties, as well as interventions employed by care providers in an effort to promote the process of healing. I have also taken into consideration the culture of the ministry context, which involves race, ethnicity, socioeconomic class, denominational, and theological traditions.[42] It has proven instrumental in understanding how things were done in years past, and how to best proceed with the implementation of the model of ministry. The state of the art for this project involves a study of terms and definitions associated with abuse. In addition, I have explored other projects and methods of intervention, employed by those who have provided care for abused women. Many of the referenced writers are victim-survivors whose experience of pain, suffering, and quest for wholeness in the lengthy process of healing lead them to explore and develop care models that would benefit others. It was imperative for me to glean from the expertise of those who have provided care and counseling to female victims of violence and abuse, in an effort to extract information that would prove instrumental in the model of care for this project.

Terms and Definitions

The state of the art for this project involves a study of terms and definitions associated with abuse; violence, victim-survivor, battering and nonphysical abuse, child sexual abuse, and confidentiality. Additionally, I explored silence, woundedness, healing, forgiveness, and pastoral care and counseling as they pertain to violence against women.

Terms and definitions used as descriptions of violence against women continue to evolve as the phenomenon is examined through the eyes of the victims, the law, and professional consultants.[43]

---

[41] Andrew Sung Park, *From Hurt to Healing* (Nashville, TN: Abingdon Press, 2004), 9.

[42] Jackson W. Carroll, Nancy T. Ammerman, Carl. S. Dudley and William McKinney, ed., *Studying Congregations* (Nashville, TN: Abingdon Press, 1993), 82.

[43] Nancy A. Crowell and Ann W. Burgess, ed., *Understanding Violence against Women* (Washington: National Academy Press, 1996), 9.

Violence

The controversy surrounding the subject concerns whether to define the term violence or to consider the more broad term "violence against women" as actions that "adversely and disproportionately affect women."[44] Researchers in the fields of social work, psychology, and mental health consider violence as covering a wide scope of behaviors, which include physically and emotionally harmful acts.[45]

> The Task Force on Male Violence Against Women of the American Psychological Association defined violence as physical, visual, verbal, or sexual acts that are experienced by a woman or a girl as a threat, invasion, or assault and that have the effect of hurting her or degrading her and/or taking away her ability to control contact (intimate or otherwise) with another individual.[46]

It is important to understand violence as not being limited to physical assault as trauma caused by nonphysical violence is painful and devastating to the victim. It is essential to identify nonphysical behavior as a form of violence, and that this information be shared with the community, many of whom may be victims or abusers, who are not aware of the many forms of violence against women. As one reflects on the definition of violence against women given by The Task Force on Male Violence Against Women, it is interesting to note that any behavior that results in pain and degradation is also seen as having the potential to render the victim as powerless to control contact with another. In essence, the abused person is subjected to whatever the abuser chooses to do, and either has no control or has been threatened and coerced into believing that they have no control. The life of an abused person may very well involve constantly seeking the means to survive. Those who have experienced abusive relationships have a clear understanding of what is involved in survival. They have "walked on eggshells" so as not to upset the abuser. They have tried to find ways to please the victimizer for fear that they would be physically and/or verbally abused.

Victim-Survivor

I first examined the term, *victim-survivor* through the lens of Traci West, who used the term to "remind us of the dual status of women who have

---

[44] Ibid.
[45] Ibid., 10.
[46] Ibid.

been both victimized by violent assault and have survived it."[47] It has been important in the implementation of the project that close attention be given to the strengths and limitations of the victim-survivor. Strength is revealed in the fact that they endured the emotional, psychological, and physical pain that is associated with abuse. Limitation is sometimes revealed in their trepidation, which is the result of the abuse. Abusers engage in behavior that is intended "to control and subjugate another human being through the use of fear, humiliation, and verbal or physical threats."[48] Leaving an abusive relationship does not always end the violence, but often causes the abuser to escalate the violent behavior.[49] The fear of retaliation may often emotionally paralyze the victim, making it difficult for them to make rational decisions.

I experienced this firsthand with a client who was battered by her boyfriend who actually lived with another woman. The abuser was a gang member who was often in and out of jail. However, despite his absence, there were other gang members who would watch her daily activities and if he received an unfavorable report there would be a beating upon his release from jail. She had an aunt who lived on the West Coast of the United States who was willing to open her home to the client and her two children. The writer was able to arrange for payment of the relocation. The client stated that she would need to prepare for the move over the weekend, but she did not return to class. I saw her in passing several months later. She had apparently chosen to stay in the abusive relationship. Lenore Walker, who founded the learned helplessness theory "posits that women stay because they are so abused and eventually the abuse strips them of their will to live."[50] Sharon Ellis Davis adds that this theory does not address the economic, social, and cultural dynamics, which involves the fear of retaliation and being shunned by family and community.[51] The aforementioned client did express that she felt that her life was ruined. She was also concerned that her victimizer would harm the Father of one of her children who, according to the victim, was a nonviolent, working-class man. She remained on good terms with him and he had expressed concern about her abuse and on one occasion did confront the abuser. She also had a bad relationship with her

---

[47] Traci C. West, *Wounds of the Spirit* (New York: New York University Press, 1999), 5.
[48] Beverly Engel, *The Emotionally Abused Woman* (New York: Fawcett Books, 1990), 10.
[49] Brandwein, *Battered Women, Children and Welfare Reform*, 35.
[50] Sharon Ellis Davis, "Hear Our Cries: Breaking the Gender Entrapment of African American Battered Women," (Ph.D. diss., The Chicago Theological Seminary, 2006), 26.
[51] Ibid., 27.

mother and stepfather and was living on the second floor in a home that was owned by them. Her stepfather had sexually molested her as a child and her mother did not believe her story. Also, her stepfather admitted that he didn't like one of her children who was of a darker complexion, fathered by an African American man. Despite the difficulties within this family, the victim expressed a desire to have a loving relationship with her mother. Therefore, the social, cultural, and family dynamics affected her ability to leave.

I have heard African American women voice their reluctance to contact the police when they are physically battered out of concern that their abuser may be brutalized by the law enforcement officers. Davis posits that African American women live with constant reminders of how institutions have been used as a means to "destroy African American communities."[52] It is not uncommon to hear an African American male abuser berate the victim for calling "the white man" and for the mother of the abuser to do the same because the victim had her son "locked up."

Many women are also trapped in abusive relationships because they are financially dependent on the abuser. I have experienced this through contact with welfare clients who are victims of intimate violence. Receiving public assistance has helped those who are impoverished. However, it is extremely difficult to raise a family on a welfare grant and food stamps.

Battered women are often reluctant to either report the abuse or leave the abuser. I recall an experience involving a church member who became tearful at the prospect of reporting her physically abusive husband to the police. She considered leaving her husband, but could not afford to live on her own. This abused woman has no family support as a result of years of drug abuse, which she now understands came as a result of child sexual molestation and the extreme physical abuse of her first husband. Despite the fact that she has not used drugs in more than fourteen, her familial relationships are strained.

Fear and anger as a result of abuse also present difficulties in personal relationships. It is not uncommon for survivors of violence to have difficulty in the workplace because they fear a reoccurrence of victimization.[53] Survivors often exhibit repressed anger that they were afraid to express while they were in the abusive relationship.[54] I have encountered this in client or students who have had angry disagreements with each other in the life skills classes at PCBSS. As I had the opportunity to learn more about them, it is often revealed that they are currently or have been victims of violence. They appear angry

---

[52] Ibid., 59.
[53] Raphael, *Saving Bernice,* 79.
[54] Ibid., 78.

from the first day of class and present a tough exterior. However, when one enters into a private conversation with them, they often begin to cry. Many victim-survivors who do not receive counseling may for many years live with dysfunction, depression, difficulty with sustenance of relationships, trying to numb the pain with drugs and alcohol, as well as abusing their children.[55] This will be further discussed in the interviews with victim-survivor context associates, some of whom express their thoughts concerning fear and its impact on their personal relationships. The select group of context associates cannot represent all female victim-survivors because though experiences may be similar, responses are unique.[56]

The dichotomy between the terms victim and survivor are interesting in that some individuals prefer to view themselves as survivors as opposed to victims.[57] Persons who are victimized often live in a state of consciousness that results in the expectation of victimization and exploitation, which may cause them experience powerlessness concerning what happens in their lives.[58]

Paul Hansen, a therapist who has worked with survivors of sexual abuse and also offers workshops for couples employs the terms, victim, survivor, and thriver offering a detailed description of each. Victims often live their lives in a manner that confirms them as victims, frequently complaining and blaming others, which may result in depression.[59] Others may sense their feeling of powerlessness and take advantage of them.[60]

A survivor, on the other hand, is unwilling to submit to victimization and "has made a commitment to heal from the abuse."[61] The victim appears to seek relationships that maintain her identity as an injured party, and may not have embraced the possibility that she has choices. The survivor, though wounded, realizes that they have been oppressed and has emerged as one who is willing to fight for freedom. The thriver has achieved a level of success where the abuse has faded into the background and while never totally forgotten it does not negatively impact their daily life.[62]

---

[55] Lori S. Robinson, *I Will Survive* (Emeryville, CA: Seal Press, 2002), 59.
[56] West, *Wounds of the Spirit*, 6.
[57] Copeland, *Violence Against Women*, 9.
[58] Paul A. Hansen, *Survivors & Partners: Healing the Relationships of Sexual Abuse Survivors* (Longmont, CO: Heron Hill Publishing Company, 1991), 2.
[59] Ibid.
[60] Ibid.
[61] Ibid., 3.
[62] Ibid.

Battering and Nonphysical Abuse

Battering is abusive and intimidating behavior that is used as a means to establish authority and maintain control of the battered partner.[63] Violence is used as a means to control the victim and for the abuser to assure that everything will be done in accordance with the rules that have been established by the abuser. Unfortunately, the victim is not able to follow the rules to the letter because they may not be revealed until there is an offense, or the rules change according to the mood of the abuser.

The Power and Control Wheel[64] (see appendix A) identifies the behaviors of an abuser toward their victim. Often individuals do not realize that they are abused until they examine the information on the wheel. The wheel suggests that abusers are concerned with power and control of the victim. They will employ the tactics that have the best results. Physical battering and nonphysical abuse, which includes psychological, verbal, and economic abuse, are all represented on the Power and Control Wheel because they are all means of controlling and intimidating the victim.

Women's indoctrination to the acceptance of physical abuse is the result of a continuous and "vicious cycle of violence against women,"[65] which has been in existence for many generations.[66] It is not uncommon to hear stories of how women have advised each other to stay in abusive relationships especially if the man is a "good provider." I have encountered several women who have endured abuse for many years because they did not understand that they were abused and/or did not feel that their experience was uncommon. The acceptance of the age old cliché that "men will be men" has served to excuse the abusive behavior of men as well as to indoctrinate women into acceptance of the same. It is extremely important that this cycle be broken. It begins with women speaking out, educating themselves, sharing information,

---

[63] Pamela Cooper-White, *The Cry of Tamar* (Minneapolis, MN: Fortress Press, 1995), 102.

[64] The Power and Control Wheel was developed by battered women in Duluth who had been abused by their male partners and were attending women's education groups sponsored by the women's shelter. The Wheel used in our curriculum is for men who have used violence against their female partners. While we recognize that there are women who use violence against men, and that there are men and women in same-sex relationships who use violence, this wheel is meant specifically to illustrate men's abusive behaviors toward women. The Equality Wheel was also developed for use with the same curriculum.

[65] Copeland, *Violence Against Women*, 9.

[66] Ibid.

teaching the youth, both male and female to recognize, reject, and abstain from abusive behaviors.

Child Sexual Abuse

It is an "act of violence, hatred, and aggression," which usually results is both physical and psychological injuries.[67] This involves any act that is sexual in nature that is done by one individual to another without consent. Child sexual abuse is in this category because children are not able to give consent. For this reason, a sexual act with a child is called statutory rape. The age of consent varies according to the state law.

As I engaged the writings of the various authors, the common thread which was identified is that all of the victims continued to suffer pain long after the abusive relationship or incident ended. Those who experienced abuse as children and those who are abused as adults go through life asking the same question, "why me?"[68]

The Children's Division of the American Humane Fund completed a study in 1969 involving 1,100 incidents of child sexual abuse in Brooklyn, New York. The study found that 75 percent of the offenders were acquainted with the children and their families. Around 27 percent lived in the same household and 11 percent were relatives who did share the same home. The average age of the victimized child was age eleven and in 41 percent of the cases studied, the sexual abuse had taken place for a period of seven years.[69] Offenders are able to abuse their victims for many years because the child has been silenced. It is horrifying to imagine the impact that these events have on the daily life of the victim. The silence surrounding child sexual abuse is one of the most damaging aspects because it causes the victim to endure the atrocity without telling anyone—and worse, it permits the abuse to persist unchecked.[70]

Confidentiality

Confidentiality means that counselors are not to share information that has been told in confidence. This may be extremely difficult because pastors and

---

[67] Marie M. Fortune, *Sexual Violence the Sin Revisited* (Cleveland, OH: The Pilgrim Press, 2005), 4.

[68] Hansen, 48.

[69] Sandra Butler, *Conspiracy of Silence*, Updated ed. (Volcano, CA: Volcano Press, 1996), 13.

[70] Laura Davis, *The Courage to Heal Workbook* (New York: HarperCollins Publishers, 1990), 234.

counselors have a tendency to "unburden"[71] themselves with what they have experienced. This rule does not apply when someone may present danger to themselves or to others.[72] It is advisable that one not share information with their spouse who is not bound by the same professional ethic as the pastoral counselor.[73]

There was a concern that the privacy of the context associates be protected and for this reason, I chose those whom, I believed, would remain discreet. One cannot assume that because an individual is a victim-survivor and is a part of a group that is addressing this sensitive matter that they will not talk to individuals outside of the group.

Silence

Silence may be defined as not telling the story of abuse, not reporting the details to anyone, keeping the secret within the family, and suffering alone. It is a phenomenon that plagues our society, and it is the norm that many victims of violence keep silent. Statistics report that the majority of individuals, who were traumatized by sexual molestation and incest as children, reach adulthood "with their secret intact."[74]

Writers, Tillie Olsen, Virginia Woolf and feminists have seriously considered the role of silence among women.[75] Silence does not indicate that one has nothing to say, but rather suggests a muted message of oppression.[76] Mary Belenky and coauthors of *Women's Ways of Knowing* view silence as a part of the initial stage of development in young girls and women who have not found their voice or have been "silenced by their families, communities, or both."[77]

Elaine J. Lawless offers a different view of these "culturally shaped responses to violence"—the silence that is practiced by women in order to survive, silences that may prevent further abuse.[78] In essence, women remain silent for fear of retaliation. This is one of the levels of silence that

---

[71] Emma J. Justes, *Hearing Beyond the Words* (Nashville, TN: Abingdon Press, 2006), 76.
[72] Ibid., 77.
[73] Ibid.
[74] J. Lebron McBride, *Spiritual Crisis: Surviving Trauma to the Soul* (New York: The Haworth Pastoral Press, 1998), 19.
[75] Elaine J. Lawless, *Women Escaping Violence* (Columbia, MO: University of Missouri Press, 2001), 79.
[76] Ibid., 82.
[77] Ibid., 83.
[78] Ibid.

is addressed in the ministry model. The other level of silence speaks to the lack of response on the part of community and clergy as well as the failure to educate youth. Breaking the silence of abuse requires that the community, law enforcement, and the church form an alliance to intervene on behalf of women who are abused and to prevent others from victimization. When victims are aware that there is a supporting community available to provide assistance and protection, it is possible that they will cry out for help when needed. The decision to leave an abuser is difficult and it is common for the victim to return to the abuser several times before the final separation. Nevertheless, there should be supports in place for women who desire to escape abusive relationships.

No young girl should be told that a boy is hitting her because he likes her or is just trying to get her attention. Children should be taught about inappropriate touching from an early age and be encouraged to report any improper behavior to a parent or authority figure. The silence is broken when the people openly speak of the victimization of women in the community as well as in the church with the expectation that it will positively impact the lives of the victim. I posit that many women have entered into and remained in abusive relationships because they were unable to recognize the signs of an abusive person or once in the relationship did not know that they were abused. When women find that their stories are common it could translate into a norm, while those who are in loving and affirming relationships are the exception. How often has it been stated that "a man will be a man?" or "a half of a loaf is better than none." How often have women taken the blame for a man raping them because the woman was not dressed properly? Statements of this kind are a result of a cultural environment, which says that women must expect and accept abuse, which would lead to silence, shame, and self-blaming.

Charlotte Pierce-Baker, author of *Surviving the Silence*, is a research professor of English and women's studies at Duke University. She refers to her writing as a "book of voices,"[79] which breaks the silence with which many women have lived, in order to protect themselves from criticism, their families from disgrace, and the men whom they believed were "brothers."[80] Pierce-Baker, a survivor of rape, writes from her experience, telling and soliciting the stories of women who have been silent; some for many years. She explores the cause and effect of silence as it pertains to the lives of African American women. The telling of the stories is powerful as the women seem to be in conversation with each other though they are not in the same space.

---

[79] Charlotte Pierce-Baker, *Surviving the Silence* (New York: W.W. Norton & Company, 1998), 18.
[80] Ibid., 19.

The writers, Ellen Bass and Laura Davis; *The Courage to Heal,* Patrick Fanning; *Self Esteem,* and Diana Russell; *The Secret Trauma,* address the devastation that women experience as a result of sexual abuse by male family members and neighbors whom they trusted.[81] Added to the trauma of the abuse, the girl is "cautioned not to tell."[82] This forces the victim to suffer in silence, sometimes feeling that no one cares. One of the context associates for the project, who was molested, first by her uncle (father's brother) and then by her father says that her uncle threatened to kill her family if she told. When she was molested by father she felt that her mother knew. She never discussed the incidents with her mother until she was an adult. Her mother gave no response. Unfortunately, this is not uncommon. In many instances, victims are accused of either lying and are punished for telling. Joyce Meyer, a renowned author and televangelist experienced the pain of what she calls betrayal by her mother.

> I was about eight or nine when I told my mother what was going on between my father and me. She examined me and confronted my dad, but he claimed that I was lying—and she chose to believe him rather than me. What woman would not want to believe her husband in such a situation? I think deep down inside, my mother knew the truth. She had just hoped that she was wrong. When I was fourteen years old, she walked into the house one day, having returned earlier than expected from grocery shopping and actually caught my father in the act of sexually abusing me. She looked, walked out, and came back two hours later, acting as if she had never been there. My mother betrayed me.[83]

The phenomenon of silence among girls, in general, has been the subject of research, which concludes that girls "could speak, but for the most part felt that few cared or listened to what they had to say. Having a 'big mouth' often got them into trouble, but silence, the slow slipping into a kind of invisible isolation, was also devastating."[84]

Taylor, Gilligan, and Sullivan, authors of *Between Voice and Silence,* posit that it helps girls to speak when the experiences of older women are shared with them. However, when their mothers, grandmothers, and aunts are not able to speak of their own pain, the process is then aborted.[85]

---

[81] Lawless, *Women Escaping Violence,* 82.
[82] Ibid., 83.
[83] Joyce Meyer, *Beauty for Ashes,* Revised and Expanded ed. (New York: Warner Faith, 2003; reprint, 2003), 16.
[84] Lawless, *Women Escaping Violence,* 83.
[85] Ibid., 84.

The practice of women, sharing their stories, is essential to the process of educating young women about abuse, hopefully serving as a measure of prevention and in cases where there has been victimization, aiding in emotional healing. Telling is a part of the healing process for victim-survivors; a process, which is lengthy. The pain of wounds associated with abuse is as a result of an event or series of events that has left the victim traumatized.

Woundedness

Prior to the work conducted by feminists during the 1970s, it was thought that PTSD (post-traumatic stress disorder) was only experienced by men who had fought in a war as opposed to civilian victims of violence.[86] Persons who suffer from PTSD may have flashbacks, nightmares, and difficulty sleeping.[87] PTSD has been used as a means to systemize "some of the more serious psychological responses in women survivors of domestic violence," as well as rape and incest.[88]

The diagnosis of PTSD has its basis in "three categories of symptoms."[89]

1. Reliving or reexperiencing the trauma, dreaming about it, having flashbacks or feeling that the trauma is happening again, or being upset at events or experiences that remind the survivor of the trauma.
2. Avoidance or numbing of responses, diminished interest in usual activities, feeling distant, having a sense of impending doom, or not expecting to have a long life, career, or family.
3. Increased arousal or hypervigilance as demonstrated by inability to go to sleep or to stay asleep, irritability, inability to concentrate, extreme watchfulness, or hair-trigger response.[90]

These challenges may alter the person's ability to interact with others, which results in difficulty in relationships. I once spoke with a Latina female client/student who has been diagnosed with PTSD. She stressed that she does not trust men at all, often has nightmares, panic attacks, and awakens at night in fear. Despite stating that she does not trust men, her closest

---

[86] Kristen J. Leslie, *When Violence Is No Stranger* (Minneapolis, MN: Fortress Press, 2003), 49.
[87] Monica A. Coleman, *The Dinah Project* (Cleveland, OH: The Pilgrim Press, 2004), 65.
[88] Raphael, *Saving Bernice*, 84.
[89] Ibid.
[90] Ibid.

friend is a male. Judith Herman posits that repeated trauma in the life of an adult eats away the already formed personality while repeated trauma experienced by a child "forms and deforms the personality."[91] It appears that she is afraid of intimacy with a man, but does not have difficulty with a platonic relationship.

She has a strong desire to obtain her high school diploma, to further her education, and secure full-time employment. However, she admits that she has not been able to keep a job for more than six months due to her condition. Her story of violence dates back to early childhood as a foster child who was sexually molested and beaten. Later returned to the custody of her mother, subjected her to being molested by her mother's boyfriend. When she told her mother, she did not believe her and as a result she kept silent about further incidents. She later became involved with a boyfriend who battered her frequently and continued to physically abuse her when she ended the relationship. She is currently seeing a therapist who has prescribed medication. She was able to receive help after a series of panic attacks resulted in hospitalization.

When one considers that many victim-survivors suffer in silence, it is quite possible that the symptoms of PTSD are not shared with family, friends, and medical or mental health care professionals. Revealing the symptoms may require telling a story that has never been shared. The shame, fear, or guilt, which promotes silence, continues to operate and thus the suffering continues without relief.

> Andrew Sung Park describes this intense pain as *han*.
> Han is the abysmal experience of pain. It has two aspects: active and inactive. Active pain is closer to aggressive emotion, while inactive han is similar to an acquiescent spirit. Of the two, inactive han is more common to the human experience.[92]

The acquiescent spirit that Park speaks of may be interpreted as silence and complicit behavior, which comes as a result of fear and feeling that there is no hope. Hopelessness and despondency has the potential to interfere with the daily functions of the victim. The danger of the acquiescent spirit is that the individual may not acknowledge their pain and thus not ask for help. Just as with any diagnosis, the illness must either present by itself or be presented by the infirmed or a caring party. When neither of these conditions is present, the possibility for healing becomes dismal.

---

[91] Judith Herman, *Trauma and Recovery* (New York: Basic Books, 1992), 33.
[92] Andrew Sung Park, *The Wounded Heart of God: The Asian Concept of Han and the Christian Doctrine of Sin* (Nashville, TN: Abingdon Press, 1993), 15.

Healing

Pierce-Baker stresses that "healing is a continuous process,"[93] a reality, which I have encountered during counseling sessions with context associates and survivors of violence, in general. The work of Pierce-Baker has been instrumental in the further development of my understanding of the effect of silence in the life of the victim-survivor. Pierce-Baker devotes the first four chapters to a detailed description of her assault and insight as to how it impacts relationships, both personal and professional, for many years. According to Pierce-Baker, counseling may be instrumental in the healing process, but is not a once and for all, fix-it. Having been told that she suffered from PTSD, she thought that her recovery would take place after a few counseling sessions.[94] It did not. This stresses the need for ongoing support for victim-survivors, and while breaking the silence is a part of healing, continued care is essential.

I also found *The Courage to Heal Workbook* by Laura Davis, coauthor of *The Courage to Heal,* instrumental in the discussion of breaking silence. The workbook provided several questionnaires that may be used by victim-survivors to explore reasons that the silence should be broken, how it may be accomplished, what one may expect as a result, and the importance of sharing discriminately.[95] The exercises were useful and effective in the implementation of the ministry project as my context associates, four of whom are victim-survivors of child sexual abuse, indicated that they benefited from their participation.

It was also important to glean information provided by Christian mental health professionals who offered method and approach to pastoral care and counseling—this is essential as the ministry context is the church.

I encountered one member of the church who is resistant to pastoral or professional counseling. She is a survivor of sexual child abuse and rape. She has nightmares and is afraid to sleep in the dark. Her husband does not want anyone to know "their business," so she was not "allowed" to participate in the project as a context associate. He also convinced her that she could possibly "lose her mind if she opened that can of worms." In my opinion, this is another form of abuse as her husband has placed his pride and ego above her need for emotional support, care, and healing. During the few conversations that I had with this abused woman, she also stressed that she has had difficulty forgiving her childhood abuser. She was happy when he died and has felt guilty about her thoughts toward him.

---

[93] Pierce-Baker, *Surviving the Silence,* 69.
[94] Ibid., 61.
[95] Davis, *The Courage to Heal Workbook,* 234.

Forgiveness

Forgiveness is a struggle for one who has been hurt, be it physically or emotionally by another individual. Christians are taught to forgive others in order to be forgiven of sins. Therefore, if a Christian has difficulty with forgiveness, there is often a feeling of guilt and questioning whether or not one is a true Christian.

In *From Hurt to Healing*, Dr. Park suggests that forgiving does not require that one forget, but indicates that one should not allow the harmful incident control over their life.[96] Forgiveness, a part of the healing process, is a process within the process.

Experts in the field of recovery from the trauma associated with abuse stress that mourning is a part of the process, but some survivors refuse to give into mourning due to fear or pride.[97] Anger is also a part of the process, which cannot be experienced unless the wounded person is able to cry out.

Beverly Flanigan, a social work professor and author of *Forgiving the Unforgivable*, suggests several steps toward healing and recovery: name the injury, claim the injury, blame the one who injures you, balance the scales, and choose to forgive.[98] The Stanford University Forgiveness Project found that knowing how to forgive "improves our physical and emotional health."[99] I posit that persons who have been traumatized by abuse, recover and are able to let go, but are never able to forget. It is the remembering that may allow anger to resurface. Monica A. Coleman, Ph. D., founder of the Dinah Project, a ministry for rape victims and an ordained elder in the African Methodist Episcopal Church expresses her personal challenge with forgiveness.

> When I faced him during our legal proceedings, I honestly said to him: 95 percent of the time, I have forgiven you. But oh, that 5 percent! That 5 percent creeps in when I hear about how he is doing now or when the anniversary of the rape rolls around. I am full of bitter, angry, furious, and full of hate. I see this man as the cause of my pain, anguish, tears, and broken relationships. When I look in the mirror, I can almost see steam coming out of my ears. In my eyes, he is evil incarnate.[100]

---

[96] Park, *From Hurt to Healing,* 87.
[97] Herman, *Trauma and Recovery*, 188.
[98] Park, *From Hurt to Healing,* 85.
[99] Ibid., 86.
[100] Coleman, *The Dinah Project,* 90.

Pastoral Care and Counseling

The true essence of pastoral care and counseling is assisting those who are troubled in bringing their "woundedness, struggles, doubts, and anxieties into dynamic healing contact with the God who is known by his people as the wonderful counselor."[101]

Pastoral counseling is spiritually directed as the goal is always to lead the individual into a closer relationship with God.[102] The pastor is required to do more than a Christian counselor in that he or she is not able to limit their contact with the person to the times which are scheduled.[103] Pastoral counseling involves response to crisis as pastors often receive calls in the middle of the night from a distraught mother whose child has died or a child whose mother has died. These incidents require immediate response and while they know that there is nothing that the pastor can do, they are looking for someone who can reach out to God in their behalf. The spirit is crying out for help, which is why we must allow those who are in pain to lament.

Howard Clinebell offers an interesting perspective on the relevance of pastoral counseling.

> Traditionally, the task of the church has been divided into four functions—*kerygma* (proclaiming the good news of God's love), *didache* (teaching), *koinonia* (the establishing of a caring community with a vertical dimension), and *diakonia* . . . Caring and counseling can be ways of communicating the Gospel by helping them to open themselves to a healing relationship. Until they have experienced accepting unearned love in a human relationship, it cannot come alive in them.[104]

There must be structure with pastoral counseling. It is important to be with others in their struggles, but at the same time be able to set rules and boundaries.[105] Failure to do so may render the counselor overwhelmed and the counseled overly dependent.

David Benner, a distinguished professor of psychology and spirituality gives a definition of pastoral care and counseling.

---

[101] David G. Benner, *Strategic Pastoral Counseling*, 2nd ed. (Grand Rapids, MI: Baker Academic, 2003), 40.
[102] Ibid., 23.
[103] Ibid., 25.
[104] Howard Clinebell, *Basic Types of Pastoral Care & Counseling*, Revised ed. (Nashville, TN: Abingdon Press, 1984), 66.
[105] Benner, *Strategic Pastoral Counseling*, 28.

> Pastoral counseling involves the establishment of a time-limited relationship that is structured to provide comfort to troubled persons by enhancing their awareness of God's grace and faithful presence, and thereby increasing their ability to live their lives more fully in light of these realizations.[106]

Pastors and clergy can be instrumental in the healing process by letting the abused person know that it is okay to cry out to the Lord. This is an important part of the process of moving from victim to survivor with the understanding that surviving the tragedy or atrocity is a part of their identity.[107] The Psalms of lament are in opposition to our tendency to disallow individuals to express the intensity of their pain and grief.[108] People are expected to forgive without talking about the things that they have experienced that make forgiveness necessary.[109] How often does the church make people feel guilty about their anger? How often are people told that they need to get over it? When one considers the silence that is associated with abuse, many victims have never talked about it and if they did, no one believed them. Some may have been afraid to speak about it. They come into the church and are told that God hears and answers prayer, but don't cry over this thing too much—you need to "lose it and let it go!" Lament is not an act of mourning, but on the contrary, it is an act of protest.[110]

As life presents problems, which may not be resolved, humanity wrestling with the unresolved challenges can count on the presence of God (Ps. 46).[111]

The Role of the Church in the Field of Violence Against Women

The church, which is the context for this ministry project, must provide an environment, which represents a safe space and a safe haven for victim-survivors of abuse. The church should also teach children; both male and female, about the importance of self-respect and respect for others. Pastors and clergy have continuous access to captive audiences and should use this time to encourage, uplift, and teach about the importance of respect for women. Pastors are preachers as well as educators and must be prepared

---

[106] Ibid., 40.

[107] Patrick D. Miller and Sally A. Brown, ed., *Lament* (Louisville, KY: Westminster John Knox Press, 2005), 7.

[108] Ibid.

[109] Ibid., 8.

[110] Ibid., xv.

[111] Michael Card, *A Sacred Sorrow* (Colorado Springs, CO: Navpress, 2005), 71.

to seize the teaching moment. Samuel DeWitt Proctor did just that in a conversation with a young lady on an elevator at Rutgers University. The young lady entered the elevator that was already occupied by Dr. Proctor and he immediately removed his hat. She apparently thought this strange and chuckled while making the remark that he was living in the Victorian age. Dr. Proctor responded that he was not a Victorian, but would explain further if she would get off the elevator with him, which she did. Dr. Proctor then explained his actions.

> I'm not a Victorian, I said, but some things stay in place from one generation to another and certain manners stand for values that I hold dear. I believe a society that ceases to respect women is on its way out. Women bear and raise our children, they are bound to them in early infancy; they need our support and security in this process. When we forget that, the keystone of family and home is lost. When we neglect and abuse women, the family falls apart and children are less well parented, and they fill up our jails and are buried in early graves. I believe that respect for women is the linchpin of the family and society. Therefore, when you entered the elevator, I wanted you to have automatic, immediate, unqualified assurance that if the elevator caught fire, I would help you out through the top first. If a strange man boarded and began to slap you around and tear your clothes off, he would have to kill me first. If the elevator broke down and stopped between floors, I would not leave you in here. If you fainted and slumped to the floor, I would stop everything and get you to a hospital. Now it would take a lot of time to say all that, so when I removed my hat, I meant all of the above.[112]

The church is positioned to make a difference in the lives of victim-survivors of abuse and to offer spiritual underpinning to the healing process.[113] Monica A. Coleman posits that the church can educate social service agencies and other professionals concerning sensitivity to faith issues in counseling, which will result in a "more integrated model of spiritual and psychological counseling."[114]

I have embraced this thought in the implementation of the ministry project, understanding the importance of the clinical and spiritual aspects of healing.

---

[112] Samuel DeWitt Proctor, *The Substance of Things Hoped For* (Valley Forge, PA: Judson Press, 1995), 151-152.
[113] Coleman, *The Dinah Project*, 51.
[114] Ibid.

The Dinah Project uses a therapy group model as opposed to a support group. The therapy group was closed after a period of time, which did not allow for new members to come into the group.[115] I chose to use a support group methodology as opposed to a therapy group, the difference being that therapy groups are led by therapists. The expertise of therapists and professionals was obtained through consultation when needed. I worked closely with two licensed clinical social workers and a professional associate who is a professor of pastoral care and counseling at New York Theological Seminary. They have provided further insight into post-traumatic stress syndrome and the methods by which clinical and spiritual care may integrate.

The church is a place where one would hope to receive loving support in difficult times, praying with and for one another, as a show of concern for the well-being of a troubled sister or brother. The relationship of love and care is essential to the process of healing the wound. Judith Herman expresses similar sentiments in terms of psychological trauma stating that "recovery can only take place within the context of relationships, it cannot occur in isolation."[116]

The combination of the spiritual, clinical, and legal issues that surround abuse of women have substantiated the necessity for collaboration. Therefore, I collaborated with clergy, social services, and law enforcement in the implementation of this project. As I observed the churches in the community at-large, there were few that addressed violence against women, which is why it is so important to educate pastors and clergy members; the church leaders. I assert that most, if not all, victim-survivors of violence and abuse can benefit from professional counseling. In the words of Carmen Diaz Cuevas, LCSW, a friend and coworker "If you don't deal with your pain, it will deal with you."

Leadership

According to sociologists, the most introverted person influences ten thousand people during a lifetime.[117] It is my hope that this statement will be applied to this project. I have endeavored to establish fellowship with sister churches and women's ministries in the community that will result in transformation and empowerment.

As I explored the collaborative leadership component of the ministry model, it was necessary to seek ways in which to engage local pastors.

---

[115] Ibid., 90.
[116] Herman, *Trauma and Recovery*, 33.
[117] John C. Maxwell, *Leadership 101* (Nashville, TN: Thomas Nelson Publishers, 2002), 71.

social service agencies and law enforcement were already involved in the work. However, many of the pastors have not been involved in ministry for abused women, which may be due to a lack of awareness, insensitivity and in some instances, they may be abusers. Unfortunately, some wives of ministers have silently endured physical and emotional abuse. Despite their own pain they have concern that telling their story will tarnish the image of the abuser and bring shame to the church. In essence, she becomes the protector of her abuser.

Most of the churches have women's ministries, some of which are headed by the pastor's wife. I did not anticipate that the pastors would initially be involved in a project that involves women breaking the silence of violence and abuse. However, I did expect that speaking to them would prove influential, informing their decision to encourage women in their congregations to attend ministry events. This has worked quite well.

The healing process for victims of abuse takes time, as will the ability encourage pastors to address the abuse of women in the congregations. The process has begun in my ministry context and will undoubtedly spread beyond. "When Jesus set out to change the world, he chose only a dozen people to work with—not a cast of thousands."[118]

---

[118] Laura Beth Jones, *Jesus, CEO*, Reprinted ed. (New York: Hyperion, 1993), 76.

Chapter Three

Theoretical Foundations

The focus group with which I was engaged as a Doctor of Ministry student at United Theological Seminary was Collaborative Leadership in the Twenty-first Century. During this process, I embraced the thought that persons who are survivors of violence and abuse require the continued support of church and community. Those whose current situation is that of abuse need to know that help is available. Those who are survivors need to be nurtured through the healing process. This ministry focus provided the opportunity to explore and implement a model of ministry, which fosters a collaborative relationship between the church, social service agencies, mental health professionals, and law enforcement officials, all of which will prove instrumental in providing services to female victims and survivors of violence and abuse in our community.

The ministry model involved breaking the silence for women in the church who are survivor-victims of abuse; physical, sexual, verbal, psychological, and spiritual. I have, for the past eleven years hosted a women's conference, which is attended by women from numerous churches in the community as well as a six-week Women's Fellowship and Summer Bible School of not less than 125 participants. Serving as executive minister of the Paradise Baptist Church and director of women's ministries has provided ample opportunity to encourage women to be healed as they participate in the healing process of others.

It was important to seek opportunities to collaborate with other church leaders as a learning tool, which further equipped me to engage clergy, laity, and community as participants in the ministry project, which will be further described in this writing. God, with infinite wisdom, unites us with persons who are like-minded and Christ-centered. Hence, in the year 2006, I met Deaconess Margaret Lewis, director of The New Hope Baptist Church Women's Connection. The first Women of Divine Destiny Conference was held in 2006, as a collaborative endeavor with Paradise Baptist Church (Rev. Dr. Jethro C. James Jr.), The New Hope Baptist Church (Pastor Joe A. Carter); both of Newark, New Jersey, and First Baptist Church (Rev. Dr. Weldon McWilliams Jr.) of Spring Valley, New York. It has since grown to include other ministries, seminars, workshops, and revivals. Our first Women of Divine Destiny Essex County-Wide Revival was hosted by Pastor Joe A. Carter at The New Hope Baptist Church in Newark and was followed by the Passaic County-Wide Revival hosted by Canaan Baptist Church of Paterson, New Jersey; Rev. Dr. Gadson L. Graham, pastor. These various ministry events have developed and strengthened relationships between women in the church and community as we are drawn into a closer relationship with God. Women of Divine Destiny, Inc. has since become a non-profit corporation, which strives to equip and empower women for church and community leadership. Our members represent various church denominations, which are comprised of ordained ministers as well as lay members. We address the various needs of women in the church and surrounding community, which includes mentoring, counseling and referral services, ministerial training, education, and scholarship. The organization looks to further collaborate with churches, community-based organizations, caregivers; professional and spiritual as well as legal service providers. Together, we can more effectively provide information, protection, nurturing, and financial support to women whose lives have been altered by violence and abuse. The experience has been that there is strength and power in unity of purpose. As in a choral ensemble, the voices are different; soprano, alto, tenor, baritone, and bass, but the song is the same—women must break the silence and stop the violence.

Historical Foundation

The following speaks to the historical aspects of the abuse of African American women and the response of the church community concerning the same.

The patriarchal society, in which we live, has its roots in a belief system, which stresses that God intends for men to dominate women.[119] The creation story, which is told in Genesis 1 clearly expresses that men and women were created equal; both in the image of God and with dominion over the creation.[120] However, the teaching of the church in regard to marriage, family structure, leadership in church and society has been based on the Genesis 2 account. Despite the fact that the text does not support subservience of women, it is used to uphold the belief that men should dominate and women should submit. [121] God, upon completion of creation announced

---

[119] Catherine Clark Kroeger and James R. Beck, ed., *Women, Abuse, and the Bible* (Grand Rapids, MI: Baker Books, 1996), 16.
[120] Ibid., 29.
[121] Ibid., 17.

that it was very good, which indicates equality in goodness.[122] However, the Old Testament indicates that the father was the supreme authority in the household while the wife/mother was subordinate.[123]

It is my thought that when one is given or assumes dominance over another, there is an ever-present potential for abuse of power. Further, when one believes that power and dominance is their God-given right, they will do whatever is required to maintain power and control—violence and abuse are often employed as the means by which this is accomplished.

David M. Sholer posits that there is a connection between abuse of women and the Bible which he views as having "at least two dimensions" within Christian tradition.[124]

> First, many men who abuse their wives appear to feel that the alleged biblical teaching of "male headship" is warrant, at least in some degree, for their behavior. Second, many abused women, especially those who have been taught the biblical principles of male headship and female submission, have understood the abuse they have received as either God's rightful punishment for their sins or God's will for their lives, even if it involves suffering unjustly.[125]

Cain Hope Felder writes that Phyllis A. Bird has noted that as one peruses the genealogies written in the Old Testament, that it is obvious that the mention of women is rare. He quotes Bird as stating, "The biblical world is a man's world, for the genealogies are fundamentally lists of males, in which women do not normally appear."[126]

When mentioned, women were spoken of as weak and responsible for the Fall of humanity. The early church fathers, who were among the first interpreters of the Gospel expressed "misogynism in their writings."[127] Tertullian wrote:

> You are the Devil's gateway. You are the unsealer of the forbidden tree. You are the first deserter of the Divine Law. You are she who

---

[122] Emilie M. Townes, ed., *A Troubling in My Soul* (Maryknoll, NY: 1993), 189-190.
[123] Cain Hope Felder, *Troubling Biblical* Waters (Maryknoll, NY: Orbis Books, 1989), 152.
[124] Kroeger and Beck, ed., *Women Abuse and the Bible*, 29.
[125] Ibid., 33.
[126] Felder, *Troubling Biblical Waters*, 140.
[127] Elizabeth Schussler Fiorenza and Mary Shawn Copeland, ed., *Violence against Women* (Maryknoll, KY: Orbis Books, 1994), 51.

persuaded him whom the devil was not valiant enough to attack. You destroyed so easily God's image, man. On account of your dessert, that is death, even the Son of God had to die (Tertullian, *De Culta Fem. I. I*).[128]

Saint Augustine, one of the great theologians of the early church, wrote in terms which purport male dominance and female subservience. Sholer quotes Augustine's reflection on Genesis 3.

> That a man endowed with a spiritual mind could have believed the [the lie of the serpent] is astonishing. And just because it is impossible to believe it, a woman was given to man, woman who was of small intelligence and who perhaps still lives more in accordance with the promptings of the inferior flesh than by superior reason.[129]

Humanity has used scripture as a means to depict women as the lesser vessel; one who, beguiled by Satan, led humanity into transgression. These interpretations have fostered the belief that the woman is without self-control or discipline—as a result, male dominance has been promulgated and promoted since Eve was blamed for causing Adam to sin. Adam, himself, attempted to make an excuse for his disobedience by telling God that it occurred because of the woman that God gave him. Eve's response that she was tricked could easily be interpreted as evidence that the woman is easily misled when it would be more appropriate to note that Satan is extremely cunning.

> The man said, "The woman whom you gave to be with me, she gave me fruit from the tree, and I ate." Then the *Lord* God said to the woman, "What is this that you have done?" The woman said, "The serpent tricked me, and I ate." [130]

Interpretation of scripture has not produced information concerning the details of Adam and Eve's marital relationship, as the only information that has been presented is that they had children. However, considering Adam's response to God, referring to Eve as "the woman" and God's statement that Adam would rule over her, I am inclined to believe that Eve had a difficult

---

[128] Ibid.

[129] Kroeger and Beck, *Women, Abuse and the Bible,* 33.

[130] Gen. 3:12-13. Unless otherwise stated all scripture references are from the New Revised Standard Version.

life. Eve may have been continuously reminded that it was because of her error that humanity worked hard, women bear children in pain and have a monthly menstrual cycle, which has been referred to as "the curse." Eve was one who needed to be controlled and ruled, which, if taken literally, would violate "and they become one flesh." There is agreement and unity of purpose in oneness, but in headship, as has been interpreted by some Bible scholars; the male is the leader and the woman is the follower; a relationship interpreted by many to be ordained by God.

Charles Ess points to Augustine as "the single most important source in Western tradition for the image of Eve as (sexual) temptress and cause of sin."[131] Augustine's interpretation of Genesis 2-3 becomes fundamental to his work on the doctrine of original sin. As a result, it serves to justify the subordination of women as agents of chaos who would threaten male headship.[132] However, revisiting the text in light of the Jesus movement and consideration that earlier interpretations may have reflected the social and political climate of that time may reveal that Eve was a victim of male violence.[133]

Women in the Old Testament were often characterized as Eve, Jezebel, Rahab, or Tamar (widow of Er and Onan) who were depicted as sinful, wicked, adulteresses, harlots, or seductresses.[134] As late as the nineteenth century, women who spoke in public were called "disobedient Eves or Jezebels."[135] Women were clearly second-class citizens whose hope of liberation was in God, who is just and has no respect of persons.

The marginalization of any group of individuals in the church and oppression by another violates and distorts the image of God, giving the impression that there is not equal access to the Creator. J. Deotis Roberts says:

> Any denial of dignity and equality of persons in the divine creative act is a sin against creation. It is a form of self-glorification and idolatry. Humans who consider themselves as being superior to others because they are "male" seek, as it were, to become Gods. As creatures, they would usurp the prerogatives of the Creator. This is the original pride, the cause of the first fall.[136]

---

[131] Carol J. Adams and Marie Fortune eds., *Violence against Women and Children* (New York: The Continuum Publishing Company, 1995), 100.

[132] Ibid.

[133] Ibid.

[134] Felder, *Troubling Biblical Waters*, 140.

[135] Agnes Ogden Bellis, *Helpmates, Harlots and Heroes* (Louisville, KY: Westminster/John Knox Press, 1994), 3.

[136] J. Deotis Roberts, *The Prophethood of Black Believers* (Louisville, KY: Westminster/John Knox Press, 1994), 79.

Roberts further postulates that "sexism is a sin against grace."[137] He is mindful of the equality of men and women as both are created by God and are "equally in need of repentance and forgiveness before God."[138] Considering women as less than equal and to deny their equality in dignity is to contradict the creative plan of God.[139]

It is clear that the subjugation of women began with the interpretation of biblical accounts of the creation story, which were written and redacted by men. The incidents in the creation stories, which speak to the "Fall of humanity" actually identify the root of misogyny, which is sin.

Andrew Sung Park has an interesting view of sin, which he says exists on at least two levels, which are individual and collective. Park defines individual sin as an offense against God and humanity, which presents itself as selfishness, superiority pride, exclusive ethnocentrism, and nationalism. According to Park, collective sin is more structural tolerant capitalism, racism, classism, and sexism, which for the oppressed, are the root of structural *han*.[140]

> Han is an Asian, particularly Korean, term used to describe the depths of human suffering. Han is essentially untranslatable; even in Korean, its meaning is difficult to articulate. Han is the abysmal experience of pain. It has two aspects: active and inactive. Active pain is closer to aggressive emotion, while inactive *han* is similar to an acquiescent spirit. Of the two, inactive han is more common to the human experience.[141]

Scriptures have been interpreted to benefit those in power and to control those who are powerless. Kenneth Cauthen says these interpretations of scripture are what he calls the Law of Infinite Hermeneutical Adaptability, which results in the interpretation of scripture in a way that supports any conceivable doctrine and the Phenomenon of Total Surprise. He also speaks of this phenomenon in its "Lo and Behold" form, which says: "When individuals and groups find the Word of God in the Bible, the

---

[137] Ibid., 81.
[138] Ibid.
[139] Ibid., 80.
[140] Andrew Sung Park, *From Hurt to Healing* (Nashville, TN: Abingdon Press, 2004), 32.
[141] Andrew Sung Park, *The Wounded Heart of God: The Asian Concept of Han and the Christian Doctrine of Sin* (Nashville, TN: Abingdon Press, 1993), 15.

results, lo and behold, turn out to be identical to what they themselves believe!" [142]

Christians have a canon within a canon, which means that one favors particular passages of scripture, which minister to them personally and support their theological stance. However, growing in understanding of God requires that one approach the text openly with awareness that the hermeneutic of the reader as well as that of the writer is subject to bias.

Considering the aforementioned, I am aware that many of the biblical interpretations and commentaries have been written from a male hermeneutic. This makes it extremely important to reflect the work of womanist theologians who capture the voice of the African American female, giving voice to biblical and modern day women who would otherwise remain silent.

Lot's daughters are an example of two women who were to be sacrificed by their father to men who were told that they could do with them as they pleased. This is a direct reflection of the value of a woman in the eyes of a man, which would certainly raise questions as to how these women would see themselves. Their view of themselves may have become distorted. If their father is willing to sacrifice them to be raped by men, then their value is determined by their service to men. Their purpose is defined by their relationship to men and the ability to produce what is expected and desired of them. Lot had no regard for their feelings or the fact that they may be violated and emotionally traumatized by the sexual abuse. Clearly, his goal was to protect the men, who were on the inside of his house, satisfy the depraved lust of the men, who were on the outside of the house, by sacrificing two innocent women.

It was common in Eastern countries that a man who took guests into his home would have been responsible for their safety, even if it cost him his life.[143] However, his respect for hospitality apparently superseded his obligation as a father.[144]

> Look, I have two daughters who have not known a man; let me bring them out to you, and do to them as you please; only do nothing to these men, for they have come under the shelter of my roof.[145]

---

[142] Kenneth Cauthen, *An Essay on Using the Bible with Integrity* (accessed November 15 2003); available from www.frontier.net/kenc/bibint.htm./ (Accessed November 15, 2003).

[143] *Adam Clarke's Commentary* (Seattle, WA: Biblesoft, 2001).

[144] *Keil and Delitzsch Old Testament Commentary* (Seattle, WA: Biblesoft, 2001).

[145] Gen. 19:8

Lot was clearly willing to "pimp" his daughters, which aids in the understanding of why they would, in Genesis 19:30-36, conspire to preserve their father's seed by bearing his children. They matched their father in desperation, which was precluded by a mental and emotional devaluation of their personhood. This may have relegated them as sexual beings whose purpose was defined by an earthly father who was so thoughtless that he offered them to be sexually abused by the sodomites.[146]

The history of the Hebrew people clearly reflects that daughters were not valued as highly as sons.[147] Leviticus 27:1-4 delineates the difference between the value of a male and the value of a female.

> The *Lord* spoke to Moses, saying: Speak to the people of Israel and say to them: When a person makes an explicit vow to the *Lord* concerning the equivalent for a human being, the equivalent for a male shall be: from twenty to sixty years of age the equivalent shall be fifty shekels of silver by the sanctuary shekel. If the person is a female, the equivalent is thirty shekels.

According to Levitical Law (Lev. 12) a woman was ceremonially unclean after the birth of a son, but was unclean for an even longer period of time after the birth of a daughter. There is no reason given for this distinction, which seems to imply that the female child is inferior to the male, and by virtue of the same would cause the birth mother to remain unclean for an extended period.[148] The girl child came into the world with a stigma attached to her that her gender rendered her mother unclean for a longer period of time than if she had been a male child.

Girls were expected to obey their fathers without question and if married, to obey their husbands in the same manner.[149] Due to an innate sense that something was inherently wrong with the subservient demeanor, which has been expected of women in society and in the church, I struggled with the acceptance of this at a very young age.

When scholars address the Fall of humanity it is often spoken of as disobedience to the instruction given by God to humanity. However, one

---

[146] Albert Barnes, *Barnes' Notes on the Old and New Testament* (Seattle, WA: Biblesoft, 2001).

[147] M.C. Tenney and J. I. Packer, eds., *Illustrated Manners and Customs of the Bible* (Nashville, TN: Thomas Nelson Publishers, 1980), 414.

[148] Ibid., 449.

[149] Ibid., 420.

must not overlook the, not so obvious, immediate result, which was a broken relationship with each other.

Humanity, created in the image of God (Gen. 1:27), has God's image of holiness within us.[150] David R. Blumenthal posits that the holiness within humanity enables humans to talk about and with God.[151] The Fall of humanity temporarily interrupted the communication on the part of humanity, but was soon initiated by God, who sought Adam (Gen. 3:9).

It is likely that the "Fall" changed Adam and Eve's relationship as Adam assumed the role of ruler over his wife. As I compare their lives before the "Fall" to life after the "Fall," it is highly probable that Adam struggled with the appropriate use of the new power, which was driven by this sin nature caused him to focus more on his personal concerns than those of Eve. Eve may have very well been an abused woman, who though created an equal partner, was relegated to a role of subservience; a victim of male privilege.

Cheryl B. Anderson, in *Women, Ideology, and Violence*, examines the construct of gender in the Book of the Covenant (1200-1000 BCE) and the Deuteronomic Law (640-609 BCE).[152] Anderson posits that according to these laws, the female body surrenders to male authority, is made to have sex with males, and is meant to bear children.[153] Thus women's roles in the home and society were set and determined by male exertion of power and privilege. The structure of the family was based upon the total and unquestionable authority of the father who ruled his wives and his children as his property.[154] He had the authority to sell his daughters as slaves, have disobedient children killed, divorce his wife at will and was not required to support her. The wife, on the other hand, could not leave her husband because she was his property as were the sheep and the goats. Women were not able to inherit property and thus the widow was often also poor.[155]

Women in the United States challenged the laws governing domestic relations in the nineteenth century during an unprecedented meeting led by

---

[150] David R. Blumenthal, *Facing The Abusing God* (Louisville, KY: Westminster John Knox Press), 7-8.
[151] Ibid., 8.
[152] Cheryl B. Anderson, *Women, Ideology and Violence* (New York: T&T Clark International, 2004), 1.
[153] Ibid., 69-72.
[154] E. W. Heaton, *Everyday Life in Old Testament Times* (New York: Charles Scribner's Sons, 1956), 69.
[155] Ibid.

Elizabeth Cady Stanton, the daughter of a judge.[156] "Until 1874, it was legal in the United States for husbands to beat their wives."[157]

The ancient custom of honor killings, which allows males to kill female family members who are suspected of having sex prior to marriage or outside of the marriage, is still practiced today.[158] Reports indicate that in 1997, at least three hundred women in a province of Pakistan were victims of honor killings and in 1999 more than two-thirds of the deaths in the Gaza Strip of Palestine and the West Bank of Jordan were like honor killings.[159] The victimizers are said to be under the age of eighteen and are honored as heroes in their communities.[160]

The Mormon Church, which espouses strong family value, has roots in patriarchy. Cathy Ferrand Bullock, who conducted a study of domestic violence in Utah and in the Latter Day Saints Church, found that 70 percent of the state's population belongs to the Mormon Church.[161] However, the structure of the family as well as the church is patriarchal in that the men alone hold the office of the priesthood and "the authority to act in God's name."[162]

Patriarchy, defined as an "unequal distribution of power and privilege,"[163] is endemic in the social structure of America. The public and religious spheres continue to be run disproportionately by men.[164] The truth of the matter is that power rests with white men; a state of affairs which has been in existence since white men "discovered" America. Abigail Adams, wife of John Adams, cautioned her husband during the writing of the Declaration of Independence, to "remember the ladies."[165] Yet law making and application of the law has largely been done by men "who made assumptions about women rather

---

[156] Mary Welek Atwell, *Equal Protection of the Law?* (New York: Peter Lang, 2002), 4.
[157] Carol J. Adams and Marie Fortune eds., *Violence against Women and Children* (New York: The Continuum Publishing Company, 1995), 175., 1995), 175.
[158] Michael L. Penn and Rahel Nardos, *Overcoming Violence Against Women and Girls The International Campaign to Eradicate a Worldwide Problem* (New York: Rowman & Littlefield Publishers, Inc., 2003), 87.
[159] Ibid.
[160] Ibid.
[161] Cathy Ferrand Bullock, "Framing Domestic Violence Fatalities: Coverage by Utah Newspapers," *Women's Studies in Communication* 30, no. 1 (2007) : 3.
[162] Ibid.
[163] Atwell, *Equal Protection of the Law?*, 4.
[164] Ibid.
[165] Ibid., 12.

than by women who could draw on their own experience."[166] Mary Welek Atwell, writer of the book, *Equal Protection of the Law?*, elaborates on how the same has fostered a system of inequality of women.

That these assumptions may have become more enlightened during the last two hundred years is no doubt true, but that women did not speak for themselves in the legislature and courts is also true. To acknowledge the fact is not to blame or "bash" individual men for women's legal inequality, but to understand the history and the consequences of a system that may have been intended to be "for" women, but was definitely neither "by" women nor "of" women . . . women have constitutionally protected liberties, and those liberties belong to them as individual citizens, not as female relatives of male citizens.[167]

White male supremacy was exhibited in the Declaration of Independence, which states that "all men are created equal." Abraham Lincoln, in the Gettysburg Address stated that "this nation, under God, shall have a new birth of freedom—and that government of the people, by the people, for the people . . ." Yet this government has oppressed and denied rights to women and enslaved an entire race of people.

Women as Slaves in the United States

Women in the United States have historically been denied the rights and privileges that have been given to men. African American women have been denied because they are not men and because they are not white, which presents a double jeopardy.

Deborah Gray White posits that it is not possible for an African American woman to identify with race without identifying with her sex and vice versa.[168]

> In fact, black women did not experience sexism the same way white women did. Owing to their color, white men saw black women differently and exploited them differently . . . The rape of black women, their endless toil, the denial of their beauty, the inattention to their pregnancy, the sale of their children were simultaneous manifestations of racism and sexism, not an extreme form of one or the other. For black women, race and sex cannot be separated. We cannot consider who black women are as black people without considering their sex, nor can we consider who they are as women without considering their race . . . Black and white womanhood

---

[166] Ibid.
[167] Ibid.
[168] Deborah Gray White, *Ar'nt I a Woman? Female Slaves in the Plantation South* (New York: Norton, 1999), 6.

> were interdependent. They played off one another . . . White women were mistresses *because* black women were slaves. White women had real power over enslaved women because black women were really powerless. Black and white women had so little in common, because the sexism they both experienced kept them apart.[169]

Certainly, African American men were demoralized as slaves, abused and stripped of a sense of pride that may be associated with manhood. The master sexually abused their women, sold their children, as a result of which they experienced a deep sense of pain and frustration due to their inability to provide protection for their families. The sense of family unity and love was thwarted by constant violence and separation, which was inherent in the slavery system—violence and the threat of violence was a daily occurrence. This history of African Americans is replete with accounts of women who were raped, children beaten and separated from their families while men were also beaten into submission by white masters.[170]

It was common for women to be placed in the auction block with their bodies exposed during which they were physically examined to "determine their capacity for child bearing."[171] Women brought from Africa on slave ships were not shackled as the men, but were kept above on the quarter deck. This arrangement caused them to be further traumatized as a result of sexual assault and abuse.

> Male and female slavery was different from the very beginning. As noted previously, women did not generally travel the middle passage in the holds of slave ships, but took the dreaded journey on the quarter deck. According to the 1789 Report of the Committee of the Privy Council, the female passage was further distinguished from that of males in that women and girls were not shackled . . . This policy had at least two significant consequences for black women. First, they were more easily accessible to the criminal whims and sexual desires of seamen, and few attempts were made to keep the crew members of slave ships from molesting African women. As one slave reported, officers were permitted to indulge their passions at pleasure and were *sometimes guilty of such brutal excesses as disgrace human nature*.[172]

---

[169] Ibid.

[170] Carlyle Fielding III Stewart, *Soul Survivors* (Louisville, KY: Westminster John Knox Press, 1997), 26.

[171] White, *Ar'nt I a Woman? Female Slaves in the Plantation South*, 32.

[172] Ibid.

It was common for female slaves to suffer physical and sexual violence. Sexual relations between slave masters and female slaves were an acceptable practice that was not considered adultery or abuse of the slave.[173] The autobiography of Harriet Jacobs, written under the fictitious name of Linda Brent, tells how she had to remain silent about the sexual advances of her master, Dr. Flint, upon threat of death.[174]

Despite the humiliation and disgrace that these women endured, they were not passive and from the time that they arrived in America in 1619, have rebelled against their enslaved condition.[175]

I acknowledge the pain and suffering of African American men. However, this study speaks to the abuse and suffering of African American women, which began during slavery and has continued, not only at the hands of "Massa," but by African American men, as well. This violence may well have been a learned behavior taught by "Massa" and "overseer" as the means to control the slaves. Slaves were not treated with respect or asked their opinion concerning work assignments—it was "obey the master or else . . . !"

Unfortunately, the oppressed often take on the social and behavioral policies[176] of the oppressor, which in this case would be violence, abuse, lack of respect, disregard for personhood, and inhumane treatment. Hence, as they have been socialized to do, many African American men exhibit some level of this behavior toward the women with whom they have casual or intimate relationships.

The Black Nationalist Movement

The Black Nationalist movement of the 1960s was one in which women were expected to support men in the struggle, but often at the expense of losing their identity, submitting to abuse thus subordinating their hopes and dreams of the future to those of men. Amiri Baraka (aka Leroi Jones), a native of the ministry context, Newark, New Jersey, authored prose and plays that expressed the vision of the movement. Traci West discusses one of his plays:

> *Madheart (A Morality Play)* presents the black woman and the black man working out their destiny. At one point, the black woman

---

[173] Adams and Fortune, *Violence Against Women and Children*, 268.
[174] Ibid., 269.
[175] Dolores S. Williams, *Sisters in the Wilderness* (Maryknoll, NY: Orbis Books, 1993), 136.
[176] Walter Brueggemann, *The Prophetic Imagination* (Minneapolis, MN: Fortress Press, 2001), 27.

assertively tells the black man that in order to find his future, he'd better leave the white woman and return to her. In response to this insolent attitude, the black man hits her repeatedly across the face. He continues to slap her as she cries and pleads for him to stop. The black man tells her, I want you woman, as a woman. Go down. (He slaps her again.) Go down, submit, submit . . . to love . . . and to man, now, forever. Finally, after he abuses her further, finally she announces her willingness to submit, they kiss, and she declares: "I am your woman, and you are the strongest of God. Fill me with your seed." [177]

This is, undoubtedly, the role which African American women were expected to fill—subordinate, submissive, a sexual slave who wanted to be impregnated by the man who abused her. It is interesting to note the connection that Baraka makes between abuse, love, and sex, which is at the core of sexual abuse and intimate violence. The psychological trauma creates a state of anxiety and instability for the victim as they never know what to expect.[178] Judith Herman, a psychiatrist, posits that "methods of establishing control over another person are based upon the systematic, repetitive infliction of psychological trauma."[179] It also creates confusion because the victim may define love based upon their mate's anger and level of violence. I have heard women say, "He beats me because he loves me." A childhood memory recalls the experience of a teenage friend who loved her boyfriend so much that she allowed him to beat her. She believed that the violence proved his love for her and for many years (they married when she was sixteen) she lived with verbal, physical, and psychological abuse, which did not end until he was incarcerated with a very long prison term. I remember that this young lady wanted so much to please him that she wanted to "be filled with his seed." When this did not occur, she became so obsessed that she experienced what is known as a psychosomatic pregnancy. She actually appeared to be at least seven months pregnant!

Eldridge Cleaver, a leader of the Black Panther Party and spokesman for the revolution acknowledges rape of white and African American women stating that he practiced on black ghetto girls before moving up to white women. He later came to disapprove rape, seeking to deal with the issues that would cause the African American man to take out his anger on white

---

[177] Traci C. West, *Wounds of the Spirit* (New York: New York University Press, 1999), 126.

[178] Mary Susan Miller, *No Visible Wounds* (New York: Random House Publishing, 1995), 46.

[179] Judith Herman, M.D., *Trauma and Recovery* (New York: Basic Books, 1992), 77.

women. However, he fails to address issues concerning the violence against the black ghetto girls.[180]

Huey Newton, also a leader in the Black Panther Party, reportedly was supportive of the abuse of a female member by her boyfriend. Elaine Brown reported that she was in a relationship with a man whom she called Steve. He accused her of sleeping with another man and as a result physically assaulted her throughout the night, only pausing to urinate, rest, returning to continue the beatings with even more rage. When she was able to get away from him, she went to Huey Newton with hopes that he would protect her and punish Steve. Instead, he blew it off and agreed with the other men present that "it was about time" she "got her ass kicked, because she was "an arrogant bitch."[181] This woman subsequently left the Black Panther Party, physically and emotionally abused by the men whom she had honored and supported as leaders whom, she thought, were fighting for liberation of all Blacks. She may have been considered arrogant because she was intelligent, articulate, and outspoken, which usually results in an African American female being referred to as an arrogant bitch.

Obery Hendricks addresses this in the novel, *Living Water*.

> Men nowadays have the sad idea that women aren't suppose to be *nephesh*, to have as much life, as much spirit, as a man, because men need to feel in control of things. I guess a brave girl child makes them afraid they might lose that control.[182]

The Civil Rights Movement

Dwight Hopkins posits that both Dr. Martin Luther King and Malcolm X "suffered from the male chauvinist environment that permeated the mid 1950s to the late 1960s."[183] This is evidenced by the absence of female leadership in the movement despite their work and support in the struggle. Despite the contribution of women; Septima Clark, Daisy Bates, Diane Nash, Ella Baker, Fannie Lou Hamer, and Marian Wright, they were not seen working alongside Dr. King.[184] The women were present at the meetings and church services serving as "foot soldiers in demonstrations and marches."[185]

---

[180] West, *Wounds of the Spirit,* 127.
[181] Ibid., 129.
[182] Obery Hendricks, *Living Water* (New York: HarperCollins Publishers, Inc., 2003), 56.
[183] Dwight N. Hopkins, *Shoes That Fit Our Feet* (Maryknoll, KY: Orbis Books, 1993), 191.
[184] Ibid., 192.
[185] Ibid., 193.

Many of these women were Christians whose "faith in God translated to deeds," which were inspired by God.[186] Ella Baker, who was the national director of the Southern Christian Leadership Conference (SCLC) and founder/advisor of the Student Nonviolent Coordinating Committee (SNCC), remembers her mother, Geogianna Ross Baker as an active member in the Black Baptist missionary movement.[187] Ella Baker remembers that her mother and the women of the church put their faith into action through serving in a manner, which addressed the social needs of their people; particularly the women. The women were faithful and committed organizers, who were capable of holding their own meetings, managed their own funds and experienced what may be recognized as autonomy in the Black Baptist church.[188]

Julian Bond remembers Ella Baker's "More Than a Hamburger" speech as she admonished the young people to move beyond the lunch counter sit-ins.[189] It was during this weekend at Raleigh, North Carolina, that SNCC was organized.[190]

Barbara Ransy speaks of Ella Baker as a behind-the-scenes organizer and quotes Evelyn Brooks Higginbotham.

> Black Baptist women encouraged an aggressive womanhood that felt personal responsibility to labor no less than men, for the advancement of salvation of the world (and) . . . their evangelical zeal fervently rejected a fragile, passive womanhood or the type preoccupied with fashion, novels, and self-indulgence.[191]

It is not uncommon for educated and intelligent African American women to suffer rejection by both men and women when they "cross the line," as if they don't know "their place." African American females have been socialized to place the needs of their men and African American men in general, first. Failing to do so may often result in enduring the wrath of the community.

---

[186] Bettye Collier-Thomas and V.P. Franklin, eds., *Sisters in the Struggle* (New York: University Press, 2001), 45.
[187] Ibid., 44.
[188] Ibid., 45.
[189] Steve Fayer and Henry Hampton, *Voices of Freedom* (New York: Bantam Books, 1991), 63.
[190] Ibid., 64.
[191] Collier-Thomas and Franklin, *Sisters in the Struggle*, 45.

Sexual Harassment of African American Women

The Equal Employment Opportunity Commission (EEOC) defines sexual harassment "as a form of gender discrimination that is in violation of Title VII of the 1964 Civil Rights."[192] Both men and women are victims of sexual harassment. A telephone poll conducted by Louis Harris and Associates on 782 workers indicated:

> Around 31 percent of the female workers reported that they had been harassed at work, 7 percent of the male workers reported they had been harassed at work, 62 percent took no action, 100 percent of women reported the harasser was a man, 59 percent of men reported the harasser was a woman, 41 percent of men reported the harasser was another man.[193]

African American women are often accused of race betrayal when they report being harassed by an African American male. Anita Hill, in her accusations concerning Clarence Thomas is an example of a woman who was accused of lying and betraying her race. According to many African Americans, not to mention Caucasians, there was absolutely no reason for her to attempt to ruin Thomas' chance of an appointment to the United States Supreme Court. The community was clearly more concerned about the hope of an African American male appointment to the court than the possibility that he sexually harassed Anita Hill. Men have been sexually harassing women for years without consequence and women have been victims; socialized and conditioned to believe that this is acceptable—"men will be men." Anita Hill may have suffered more as a result of the hearings than one can imagine and may not have realized that she would be disbelieved by African Americans and Caucasians.

The Amsterdam News in New York City published a letter from a reader as documented by Traci West. It appeared in an article entitled, *Why Didn't Our Black Leaders Defend Thomas?*

> I believe a "black" woman, overly ambitious and self-centered, decided to lie, deliberately, to destroy a decent black man. As an African American woman, I am ashamed . . . Clarence Thomas was

---

[192] Sexual Harassment Support, *Sexual Harassment in the Workplace* (accessed December 4 2007); available from http://www.sexualharassmentsupport.org/SHworkplace.html./(Accessed December 4, 2007).

[193] Ibid.

lynched publicly and with blacks fashioning the noose . . . Anita Hill was and is a liar.[194]

Carol J. Adams writes concerning Catharine MacKinnon's theory of sex inequality states that "women's words about sexual victimization become oral pornography."[195] MacKinnon had the following description of the Thomas hearings:

> The more silent he is, the more powerful and credible. But the moment she opens her mouth, her credibility flounders [sic]. Senators said they were offended by her; President Bush said he felt unclean. The dirt and uncleanliness stuck to her. When she spoke truth to power, she was treated like a pig in a parlor. He said these things, but she was blamed. Once you are used for sex, you lose your human status. Your testimony becomes live oral porn in a drama starring you.[196]

Toni Morrison posits that if both, Anita Hill and Clarence Thomas had been white, there would have never been hearings concerning this matter. Morrison argues that the accusation would have disqualified a white candidate, no proof required. Morrison viewed this as another opportunity to "ponder the limits and excesses of black bodies."[197]

Clarence Thomas's appointment to the court is evidence that Anita Hill's story was not believed. It is interesting to note that there was a question as to the absence of support from African American leaders for Clarence Thomas. However, the same cannot be said for Mike Tyson.

I remember the climate in the African American community concerning the Thomas and Tyson incidents, There were often long heated debates concerning Tyson's innocence or guilt. I am still amazed and appalled by the mind-set of numerous African American men and women who felt that Desiree Washington should not have been in Mike Tyson's hotel—after all, "what did she expect?" It certainly was not to be humiliated, raped, and discarded as a piece of rubbish!

In this case, the African American religious community supported the victimizer and not the victim. Baptist clergy joined forces with the Nation of

---

[194] West, *Wounds of the Spirit*, 125.
[195] Adams and Fortune, *Violence Against Women and Children*, 19.
[196] Ibid., 187.
[197] Ibid., 373.

Islam; the former circulated petitions, organized prayer vigils, and participated in a "welcome home" rally for Mike Tyson.[198]

Rev. T. J. Jemison was, at the time of the trial, president of The National Baptist Convention. The nation's largest Baptist denomination is reported to have said that "the church has great respect for Black Womanhood . . . However, I am concerned about the Black Male and his plight."[199]

Rev. Al Sharpton, who occasionally finds himself fighting the cause of the dishonest, supported Tyson and defended Jemison's request that Washington drop the charges. He justified this by stating that Jemison was "concerned about the image of Black people."[200]

Jill Nelson notes that many African American churches participated in a rally held in Harlem to celebrate the prison release of convicted rapist, Mike Tyson. Nelson, who is a survivor of domestic violence attempted to organize church and community leaders to oppose the celebration. With the exception of Rev. Dr. Calvin Butts, pastor of the Abyssinian Baptist Church, she received a calloused and unconcerned response.[201]

Just a few years ago, Don Imus, a radio "shock jock," who has the reputation of bluntly expressing his opinion, referred to the African American players of the Rutgers University women's basketball team as "nappy-headed hos and as a result was fired from his job."[202] However, eight months later, on Monday, December 4, 2007, Imus returned to the airwaves, hired by WABC-AM radio.[203] I never doubted that he would be hired by another radio station. However, it was disappointing that it occurred so quickly and without regard for the humiliating and devastating effect that this may have on the lives of the young women.

Kia Vaughn, one of the basketball players, filed a defamation lawsuit against Imus, which also named various media sources that broadcast the Imus show. Vaughn withdrew the lawsuit choosing to "focus on her education" as a student at Rutgers University in New Jersey where she is journalism major and a player on the basketball team.[204] I was disappointed when the lawsuit was

---

[198] West, *Wounds of the Spirit*, 142.
[199] Ibid.
[200] Ibid.
[201] West, *Wounds of the Spirit*, 143.
[202] Clyde Haberman. "Back on Air, Imus Vows to Play Fair," *The New York Times*, December 4, 2007.
[203] Ibid.
[204] The Associated Press, "Rutgers Player Withdraws Imus Lawsuit" [News Article] (ABC News, accessed December 3 2007); available from http://abcnews.go.com/entertain,emt/wire/story?id-3589766./(Accessed December 3, 2007).

dropped, as it may have given the impression that Imus' behavior is excusable. There is no amount of money that would remove the sting of the insults of these young women. However, those who employ such individuals may be forced to consider the liability incurred as a result of engaging their services.

Yet ironically, money seemed not to be an issue when Madison Square Garden was ordered to pay "$11.6 million in punitive damages" to Anucha Browne Sanders.[205]

Isiah Thomas, then head coach of the New York Knickerbockers basketball team, was found guilty of sexually harassing Anucha Browne Sanders, a former executive of the team. There is no report that Thomas was reprimanded as a result. Thomas eventually lost his job. However, as I anticipated, it had nothing to do with the sexual harassment lawsuit. He was fired as a result of the New York Knickerbockers humiliating losing streak.

Various opinions surrounding the case of Sanders have indicated disbelief of her accusations based upon her appearance as well as to question lack of racial solidarity since both, she and Thomas are African American.

Many African Americans demonstrated misplaced loyalty by confusing racial solidarity with moral justice. Women have suffered humiliation, violence, and abuse as a result of a social construct, which places the guilt on the victim because she reported the abuse to "the white man." Cornel West makes it clear that the African American community needs to replace "racial reasoning with moral reasoning."[206] Unfortunately, the response of the African American community to violence against women and children has been unheard. This failure to respond may not necessarily be as a result of acceptance, but a sense of shame, fear, and misplaced racial loyalty.[207]

The failure of the black church to address violence, abuse, and subjugation of women exists for a few reasons: (1) as Cornel West states: confusing racial reasoning with moral reasoning,[208] (2) church leaders lack training in responding to domestic violence,[209] (3) focus on preaching a gospel of forgiveness of perpetrators while failing to care for the wounds of the victim—"forgive and forget."[210]

John M. Johnson conducted a study from 1981 to 1982 concerning the response of the church to domestic violence.[211] The denominations

---

[205] Richard Sandomir, "Jury Finds Knicks and Coach Harassed a Former Executive," *The New York Times,* October 3, 2007.
[206] Adams and Fortune, *Violence Against Women and Children,* 374.
[207] Ibid., 187.
[208] Ibid., 374.
[209] Ibid., 418.
[210] Park, *From Hurt to Healing,* 9.
[211] Adams and Fortune, *Violence Against Women and Children,* 412-420.

represented in the study were Baptists, Lutheran, Mormon, Methodist, Presbyterian, Catholic, and Episcopal. The findings of the study were that most church leaders did encounter numbers of domestic violence issues, but had not been trained in this area nor did they seek the assistance of outside agencies if an incident was reported.[212] This may have slightly changed in recent years as a result of sexual misconduct lawsuits and the requirements of insurance agencies that provide coverage for clergy. Seminaries have also included training in this area in the curriculum, which unfortunately does not inform the student in responding to domestic violence as much as it does address appropriate and inappropriate relationships between clergy and laity.

Rev. Marie M. Fortune states that "the circle of silence about domestic violence remains tightly closed in the churches."[213] Fortune of the Seattle Center for the Prevention of Sexual and Domestic Violence further states:

> Ministers are often avoided by individuals or families trying to cope with domestic violence. Many clergy say they have never had a parishioner involved in domestic violence come to them for assistance, so they conclude that no one in their church is a victim or offender . . . the victim or offender fears the minister will not understand or know what to do . . . also female victims are reluctant to go to their minister because their minister is usually a man. The long and painful history of the patriarchal oppression of women in the church has contributed to the denial of domestic violence as a problem. The victims of violence in the home are primarily women and girl children. This victimization has been lost in silence, and the silence has helped maintain the status quo of oppression and violence.[214]

The Black church, despite a history of social justice activism, has since the civil rights movement, lost sight of the prophetic mission of the church. The civil rights movement provided the church with the unity of purpose, which resulted in the prophetic ministry of Rev. Dr. Martin Luther King Jr. along with others like Ralph Abernathy, Wyatt Tee Walker, Andrew Young, Hosea Williams, Medgar Evers, Fannie Lou Hamer, Ella Baker, Annie Devine,

---

[212] The study was a part of a seminar which required participants to interview at least three to five ministers or church officers concerning their thoughts on domestic violence.

[213] Adams and Fortune, *Violence Against Women and Children,* 418.

[214] Ibid., 269.

Dorothy Cotton, Mae Bertha Carter, and Winson Hudson, to name a few, who joined in solidarity understanding that Blacks in America were a people in need of deliverance.[215]

Men, women, and children regardless of economic and educational class were a part of the movement as they marched together, prayed together, and even died together. Dwight Hopkins posits that had women been given justice and recognized as equals it would have further strengthened black men and the movement.[216]

Women, children, and poor people continue to be marginalized within the church by male dominance and supremacy, which so much resembles the behavior of the oppressor. They have adopted the behavior of the oppressor using Christianity as the justification. The prophetic vision and voice of the church are lost amidst prosperity preaching, which seems to attract the attention of many Christians. The key to turning this around must be to energize the masses by speaking truth, first to ourselves and then to the power structures, which oppress and marginalize people in the society. The church must serve as liberators as opposed to oppressors.

The silence concerning violence against women must be broken. When one observes the injustices in our society, the question arises—where is the voice of the prophet? Walter Brueggemann states that criticism, a step in dismantling the oppressive empire, is expressed when people grieve openly announcing that things are not right.[217] Brueggemann speaks of the liberation of Israel from Egypt as beginning with Israel grieving and crying out to God. If Israel never complained or cried out against the injustice of their oppression, they may not have been energized to seek freedom or to ask God for deliverance.

The question, which has started to haunt me was, why are not the women, poor, and children in the church crying out? What is wrong with us? Are women openly grieving over the situation? Is there an awareness of the violence and oppression? It is the criticism and ability to grieve that leads to energizing for deliverance. The oppressor does not want the oppressed to be free and the oppressed cannot imagine freedom. Brueggemann urges those would be prophets not to neglect to discern who God is and to express that God is for us.[218] The church must be committed to look for God in the difficult situations and understand that God will be with those who need God most.

---

[215] Jacqueline Anne Rouse, Vicki L. Crawford and Barbara Woods, eds., *Women in the Civil Rights Movement* (Bloomington, IN: Indiana University Press, 1990), 40.
[216] Hopkins, *Shoes That Fit Our Feet*, 191.
[217] Brueggemann, *The Prophetic Imagination*, 11.
[218] Ibid., 16.

The mission of the church must encompass the needs of all the people as it embraces the image of God in all of humanity; the love of a God who has no respect of persons.

Biblical Foundations

This following will focus on the biblical accounts of Tamar and the Samaritan woman both of which address male privilege, violence, and abuse of women as a precursor to structural misogynous practices and oppression.

> Her brother, Absalom said to her, "Has Amnon, your brother been with you? Be quiet for now, my sister, he is your brother, do not take this to heart." So Tamar remained, a desolate woman, in her brother, Absalom's house.[219]

> The woman said to him, "I know that Messiah is coming" (who is called Christ.) "When he comes, he will proclaim all things to us." Jesus said to her, "I am he, the one who is speaking to you." Just then his disciples came. They were astonished that he was speaking with a woman, but no one said, "What do you want?" or "why are you speaking with her?" Then the woman left her water jar and went back to the city. She said to the people, "Come and see a man who told me everything I have ever done! He cannot be the Messiah, can he?" They left the city and were on their way to him.[220]

When scholars address the Fall of humanity, it is often spoken of as disobedience to the instruction given by God to humanity. However, one must not overlook the, not so obvious, immediate result, which was a broken relationship with each other. I consider it likely that the "Fall" changed Adam and Eve's relationship as Adam assumed the role of ruler over his wife. As I compare their lives before the "Fall" to life after the "Fall," it is highly probable that Adam struggled with the appropriate use of the new power, which driven by this sin nature, may have caused him to focus more on his personal concerns than those of Eve. The root of sin is centered in our propensity to focus on ourselves and not others. Reinhold Niebuhr states that the root of sin involves excessive concern for the self.[221]

---

[219] II Sam. 13:20
[220] John 4:25-29
[221] Reinhold Niebuhr, *Faith and History* (Eugene, OR: Reprinted Wipf and Stock Publishers, 2001), 176.

Amnon's rape of his sister, Tamar, was the result of selfish desires, which disregarded her pleas to spare her the humiliation of the act by asking the king for her hand in marriage.

The word force *(innah)* used in the text (v.14) translates as oppress and humiliate.[222] Walter Brueggemann posits that the rape of Tamar represented more than sexual exploitation. Rather, it was an act of power of the "strong against the weak."[223] This is as an act of violence which has nothing to do with love. This is evident by what Brueggemann identifies the "profound emotional reversal" that takes place between verses 14 and 15.[224]

The behavior of Amnon is that of one who is irrational and undisciplined[225]: a potentially dangerous state of being. An individual who is both irrational and undisciplined would not be inclined to hear a voice of reason. Therefore, the words of Tamar "went in one ear and out of the other." Amnon, not only ignored her pleas, but after the rape, dismissed her from his presence as a piece of rubbish. 2 Samuel 13:17 records his words as . . ." Put this woman out of my presence, and bolt the door after her." Tamar's attempts to appeal to his humanity as well as his self-esteem as the crown prince were ignored.[226]

Prior to the rape, Amnon claimed to have loved Tamar, yet immediately following the rape, he despised her. Pamela Cooper-White has an interesting explanation for this behavior as she expresses that Tamar is possibly seen by Amnon as an "It," as opposed to a "Thou."[227]

Cooper-White states that the "It" is also something within us that "cannot respect the selfhood of others."[228] Treating others with respect and dignity will always require that individuals search within themselves to assure that their interaction with others is not motivated by selfish desire.

> Far from ignoring or pretending that we have all risen above our inner It, our inner aggression or even violence, we need to acknowledge that it does, indeed, exist. Repressed into the

---

[222] Walter Brueggmann, *Interpretation A Bible Commentary for Teaching and Preaching, First and Second Samuel* (Louisville, KY: John Knox Press, 1990), 287.

[223] Ibid.

[224] Ibid., 288.

[225] Ibid.

[226] Robert P. Gordon, *1 & 2 Samuel a Commentary* (Grand Rapids, MI: Zondervan Publishing House, 1986), 263.

[227] Pamela Cooper-White, *The Cry of Tamar* (Minneapolis, MN: Fortress Press, 1995), 22.

[228] Ibid.

unconscious, the internal It can wreak havoc unless it is brought into the light of conscious insight.[229]

The relationship with Amnon and Tamar suggests that it is possible for individuals to have less regard for the concerns of people who are not like themselves. Tamar was a woman who was clearly not valued as highly as a man. Apparently, Amnon saw her as an object of his desire and on a subconscious level as an "It." Therefore, he was able to treat her as one who was incapable of suffering.

Amnon's rape of Tamar was clearly rooted in violence and not a loving relationship, because it would have apparently been acceptable for Amnon to marry his half sister (2 Sam. 13:13). This would have been later forbidden by the law given in Leviticus 18:19.[230] Scholarly, sources argue that laws prohibiting marriage between siblings may have been later developed or that the law of consanguinity may have been applied to children of the same mother.[231] Abraham and Sarah were brother and sister, but did not have the same mother—this was apparently acceptable.[232] This does not address that fact that the rape was an act of violence. It is interesting to note that a man who raped an unmarried or unbetrothed woman, was not subject to punishment, but was merely mandated to marry her.[233]

Despite the fact that scripture refers to the love that Amnon had for Tamar, I posit that it was not love, at all. Had Amnon truly loved Tamar, he could have asked the king for her hand in marriage and thus enter into a bond with her that would have been warm and affectionate. The emotion which Amnon described as love was paradoxically expressed as hatred (v. 15), which resulted in the emotional devastation of Tamar, the victim. Susanne Scholz, referencing J. P. Fokkelman, posits that the action was "clearly the sexual act of violence of which Amnon is the subject and Tamar the objectivized, depersonalized victim."[234]

Absalom hated what his brother, Amnon, had done to his sister, but told Tamar to remain silent (2 Sam. 13:20). She initially cried out which Mary

---

[229] Ibid.
[230] Marie M. Fortune, *Sexual Violence the Sin Revisited* (Cleveland, OH: The Pilgrim Press, 2005), 9.
[231] P. Kyle McCarter, *The Anchor Bible 2 Samuel* (Garden City, NY: Doubleday & Company, 1984), 323.
[232] Mary Ann Bader, *Sexual Violation in the Hebrew Bible A Multi-Methodological Study of Genesis 34 and 2 Samuel 13* (New York: Peter Lang, 2006), 71.
[233] Deut. 22:28; McCarter, *The Anchor Bible 2 Samuel,* 324.s
[234] Susanne Scholz, *Rape Plots* (New York: Peter Lang Publishing, Inc., 2000), 137.

Anna Bader states that Phyllis Trible interprets as weeping, but may also be interpreted as a cry for justice.[235]

Her father, King David, was furious, but did nothing. He loved his son, Amnon, because he was his firstborn (2 Sam. 13:21). Scripture is silent concerning any comfort and support that Tamar may have or should have received from others. Her brother told her to remain silent and her father did nothing. Tamar was clearly devastated as a result of the assault by her brother, yet received no comfort, immediate or post care. King David was angry, Absalom plotted murder and revenge, but no one cared for Tamar; the wounded and broken victim.

Who would understand what she felt; traumatized, troubled, humiliated, distressed, distraught, and in a state of shock while those around her appear to be unaffected? The news of engagements, betrothals, weddings, and the birth of children were celebrated year after year. Tamar, no doubt, lived with the disappointing reality that she would never be able to experience this joy nor was she able to speak about how she had been thoughtlessly violated and deprived of the opportunity to know the love of a husband and children. No man would marry her because she was no longer a virgin. There were no support groups or counseling services available. Nor were there law enforcement officials to protect her. I am inclined to believe that she lived a miserable life. Scripture bears witness to the same stating that she remained desolate (2 Sam. 13:20) in the house of her brother, Absalom. Desolate transliterates from Hebrew as *shamem,* which means ruined, devastated, and numb.[236]

When the word *shamem* is used in scripture, it indicated destruction by an enemy (Lam. 1:16) or to be torn in pieces by an animal (Lam. 3:11).[237] Phyllis Trible depicts Tamar as woman of sorrow and grief.

> Raped, despised, and rejected by a man, Tamar is a woman of sorrow and acquainted with grief. She is cut off from the land of the living, stricken for the sins of her brother, yet she herself has done no violence and there is no deceit in her mouth. No matter what Absalom may plan for the future, the narrator understands the endless suffering of her present.[238]

---

[235] Bader, *Sexual Violation in the Hebrew Bible*, 152.
[236] Biblesoft's New Exhaustive Strong's *Numbers and Concordance with Expanded Greek-Hebrew Dictionary,* (Seattle, WA: Biblesoft, 1994).
[237] Phyllis Trible, *Texts of Terror* (Philadelphia, PA: Fortress Press, 1984), 52.
[238] Ibid.

Focusing on the transliterated word for desolate as numb as it applies to the mental state of one who has experienced trauma, it is not to suggest that numbness implies complete absence of feeling. On the contrary, it can produce pain and discomfort. I believe that Tamar lived in this place—the initial shock of the assault had dissipated; she was not totally without feeling, but was unable to function in an emotionally healthy state. Things were not as they were before the violent attack, and it is likely that she experienced clinical depression. It is not uncommon for women who have experienced violence and abuse to also suffer from depression.[239]

Tamar may have suffered from post-traumatic stress disorder (PTSD), a term which describes the long-term effect of trauma.[240] J. Lebron McBride states "many traumatized persons have felt the bonds and connections of life and belief tragically severed. Trauma made them feel cut off from God, from others, and even from themselves. Individuals with chronic PTSD cannot trust; they cannot hope."[241] Tamar, in her desolation, lost her sense of connection, even with herself, because her identity was linked to a relationship with a brother, Amnon, who abused her, a brother, Absalom who asked her to remain silent and a father, David, who failed to comfort her.

Isaiah uses the same word *shamem* (desolate) in his portrayal of Jerusalem as woman who is disgraced.[242]

> Sing, O barren one who did not bear;
> burst into song and shout,
> you who have not been in labor!
> For the children of the desolate woman will be
> more than the children of her that is married, says the Lord.[243]

Alice Ogden Bellis quotes Mary Callaway as she postulates how God uses the lives of those whom society would consider defiled and ruined to accomplish the will of God. Bellis observes that God's works are mysterious as the reproached are instrumental in God's plan.[244]

> The outrageous nature of the situation now becomes clear: Yahweh
> has taken for his wife, a woman whose defilement could never

---

[239] Kroeger and Beck, *Women, Abuse and the Bible*, 131.
[240] J. Lebron McBride, *Spiritual Crisis: Surviving Trauma to the Soul* (New York: The Haworth Pastoral Press, 1998), 12.
[241] Ibid., 13.
[242] Bellis, *Helpmates, Harlots and Heroes*, 186.
[243] Isa. 54:1
[244] Bellis, *Helpmates, Harlots and Heroes*, 187.

be purified to make her marriageable; her position was defined as *smmh* and she was as one who is dead. To hear the words *hps* ["delight in"] and *b'l* ["husband"] replacing *smmh* must have jarred in the ears of Second Isaiah's audience, for she who was untouchable is now called by names of most intimate endearment. Second Isaiah has reminded his community of the old stories of the rivalry between the barren and the fruitful wives and how Yahweh visited the barren one to give her a Son. But he then reinterprets the old story: what he did for Sarah and Rachel who were barren was only done in the days of old; now he is taking to himself Jerusalem, who is *smmh*.[245]

Felder says "In Hebraic or Jewish society of biblical times . . . the human household was male dominated, with women and children regarded as property, much the same as slaves."[246] Tamar, though disregarded by family and a society, which had no regard for her personhood was not one whom God would desert. Scripture provides assurance that God is a very present help in trouble (Ps. 46:1) and of humanity's inability to flee from God's presence (Ps. 139:7). God's presence with Tamar in her time of desolation made her inaudible voice cry until God heard her. She was not alone. Contrarily, it was the presence of God that gave her courage to cry out. Brueggemann posits that the removal of the clothing that identified her as a virgin (v.19) made her pain and humiliation public thus serving as an indictment against Amnon.[247] Tamar carried out four actions that are often identified with bereavement for the dead: she put ashes on her head, rent her long robe, placed her hand on her head and cried loudly. [248]

She screamed until the writer of 2 Samuel heard her and shouted through the annals of time into this present age. She screamed until I heard her voice and have determined and resolved to be an instrument used by God to break the silence of abuse.

The biblical account of maltreatment of women is not limited to the Old Testament. Women of the New Testament also lived in a society where women were not valued the same as men and often suffered from the inequities promulgated by a social construct, which did not believe that women had the same rights as men. However, Jesus' ministry to women and their ministry to

---

[245] Ibid.
[246] Felder, *Troubling Biblical Waters*, 154.
[247] Brueggemann, *First and Second Samuel*, 287.
[248] John E. Ellington and Roger L. Omanson, *A Handbook on the First and Second Books of Samuel*, United Handbook Series (New York: United Bible Societies, 2001), 880.

Him elevated them to a status which encouraged and welcomed women as equal with men in the Body of Christ. The society in which women live is yet to acknowledge the equality of women—the struggle continues!

Two nameless women in the New Testament; one went out of her way to reach Jesus (woman with the issue of blood Matt. 9:20) and the other (the woman at the well, John 4:7-29), whom Jesus went out his way to reach, represent women, who despite their class, race, and gender prejudice, were liberated as a result of an encounter with Jesus.

While the woman with the issue of blood faced double jeopardy, the woman at the well (John 4:4-42) faced triple jeopardy—she was a Samaritan, a woman, and had been married five times (Jewish law allows three marriages) and the man with whom she lived was not her husband.[249] There is no record as to what happened to her husbands, but it is possible that she may have been divorced. When one considers that Samaritans unlike Jews could only divorce for reasons of adultery, this would further add to her being ostracized by her community. One may add a fourth component to her problem; she was poor. One may believe that she was poor because women of social status would not have drawn water as was done in ancient times.[250] This placed her in quadruple jeopardy. Matching her quadruple jeopardy is the four levels of tension that are crossed as a result of her encounter with Jesus: gender, nationality, race, and religion.[251] This was radical, indeed, as Jesus' request for a drink of water from a Samarian transcended and ignored centuries of hostility between Jews and Samarians.[252]

This woman may have been discussed by everyone in the community; men and women alike. Scripture refers to her as the Samaritan woman, but she may have been known as the woman who had five husbands and is living with a man who is not her husband. The Greek pronoun for *her* husband is emphatic, which indicates that she is living out of wedlock.[253]

She traveled to the well alone, which implies that the women in the community have chosen to have no dealing with her—she was an outcast.[254] Unfortunately, this maltreatment of women by other women prevails today. Much too often, even in the church, women ostracize each other based upon

---

[249] Felder, *Troubling Biblical Waters,* 144.

[250] H.D.M. Spence and Joseph S. Excell, ed., *The Pulpit Commentary,* 22 vols., vol. 17 (Peabody, MA: Hendrickson Publishers), 182.

[251] R. Alan Culpepper, *The Gospel and Letters of John* (Nashville, TN: Abingdon Press, 1998), 139.

[252] Ibid., 140.

[253] Ibid., 142.

[254] Wes Howard-Brook, *Becoming Children of God* (Eugene, OR: Wipf and Stock Publishers, 2003), 103.

how many children they have out of wedlock, how many times they have been married, and whether or not they are married to the man with whom they live. The circumstances under which the woman may have come to this state are often ignored and she is characterized as a Jezebel or a Rahab; women whom "respectable" women would not befriend. Misogyny undoubtedly involves women's hatred of each other. A friend and colleague, RoyEtta Quateka-Means, remarked that "the young generation has stated this correctly in the term *hatin'*," which is rooted in jealousy. The initial colloquialism was "player *hatin'*," which implied that "we're in the game and you're winning" or "I want to do what you're doing." "How can she have five husbands and I can't get one?" *Hatin*! Linda H. Hollies refers to the lack of female camaraderie as erecting walls. Hollies says, "we have been kept on the other side of the Old Boys Club walls for so long that now we find ourselves better than they are at erecting them against each other."[255]

There are a few interesting points that are initially visible concerning this passage. Firstly, it is the "longest recorded conversation that Jesus has with anyone"[256] and secondly, this pericope is the only place in scripture where Jesus' ministry to Samaria is mentioned.[257] Additionally, this pericope is the only place in the Gospel of John where Jesus refers to himself as the Messiah.[258] Frances Taylor Gench, writer of *Encounters with Jesus*, points to the historical context of the first century and the prejudice and hostility that divided Jews and Samarians for centuries.[259]

The hostility came about as a result of the division of the United Kingdom. The northern part of the kingdom was conquered by the Assyrians who replaced many of the inhabitants with people from various nations so as to thwart any effort of rebellion. This resulted in different customs and mixing the worship of the God of Israel with the gods of other nations, which includes child sacrifice.[260]

The southern part of the kingdom was conquered by the Babylonians. Cyrus of Persia later allowed the exiles to return to rebuild the temple in Jerusalem at which point the Samarians asked to assist in the process (Ezra 4:2). However, the Judeans rejected the Samarians on the basis that in light of their worship practices their participation would defile the rebuilding of

---

[255] Linda H. Hollies, *Bodacious Womanist Wisdom* (Cleveland, OH: The Pilgrim Press, 2003), 23.
[256] Frances Taylor Gench, *Encounters with Jesus* (Louisville, KY: Westminster John Knox Press, 2007), 30.
[257] Ibid., 31.
[258] Howard-Brook, *Becoming Children of God*, 102.
[259] Gench, *Encounters with Jesus*, 30.
[260] Howard-Brook, *Becoming Children of God*, 102.

the temple.²⁶¹ The angry Samarians wrote a letter to the king asserting that to allow the Judeans to rebuild the temple would result in a rebellion. The letter was initially successful in halting the building process, but the Judeans persisted, holding to the initial consent and approval given by Cyrus. Hence, the temple was rebuilt, but there was "a thick wall of hatred between Jerusalem and Samaria."²⁶²

As a result, Jews and Samarians had no dealings with other. The hostility was so great that Jews traveling to Jerusalem three times per year would go around Samaria, which was a longer route.²⁶³ Therefore, the fact that Jesus is compelled to go to Samaria is significant. The fact that he has a long conversation with a woman who is a Samarian is also significant as men did not speak to women who were not their family members in public.²⁶⁴ The meeting at the well is also significant due to the literary connection. This is how Isaac meets Rebecah, Jacob meets Rachel, and Moses meets Zipporah.²⁶⁵

Gench posits, referencing Sharon Schneiders' *Written That You May Believe* (137), indicates that much attention has been given to the sexual history of the Samarian woman, which contributes to "trivialization, marginalization, and even sexual demonization of biblical women."²⁶⁶

This apparently friendless woman may have experienced trepidation during her encounter with Jesus, which is expressed in her surprise that a Jew is talking to a Samarian, who is also a woman. However, once Jesus told her everything that she had ever done and told her about the living water, as the old preachers used to say "from a well that will never run dry," she was converted. Her conversion caused her to share the story with others, telling them to "Come, see a man . . ." Felder, whose source is R. E. Brown's *The Community of the Beloved Disciple,* calls her the first woman missionary to the Samaritans.²⁶⁷

The text does not tell us that her personal challenges disappeared, that she suddenly had female friends or that she married the man who was not her husband. Yet the strength of her testimony brought others into the presence of the Jesus. Once they encountered Jesus, they also believed. She talked to a man who knew all about her and did not shun her. As a result of having

---

[261] Ibid.
[262] Ibid.
[263] Ibid.
[264] Richard L. Rohrbaugh and Bruce J. Manlina, *Social Science Commentary on the Gospel of John* (Minneapolis, MN: Fortress Press, 1998), 98.
[265] Gench, *Encounters with Jesus,* 32.
[266] Ibid., 30.
[267] Hollies, *Bodacious Womanist Wisdom,* 145.

been in the presence of Jesus, she was compelled to share with others.[268] Gench postulates that it is here that "she embodies one of the primary marks of discipleship in John: bearing witness to Jesus."[269] Belief in Jesus results in the testimony of the newness of life.[270] Gench's interpretation of this passage is interesting as she stresses that there has been emphasis on the details of her marital history despite the fact that much of it is unknown.[271] Gench posits that John points to the nationality of the woman, which may well indicate that Samaritans were accepted by Johannine Christians as brothers and sisters. Thus the woman, in her conversation with Jesus, emerges as a spokesperson for the Samarian people.[272] Gench further postulates, referencing Teresa Okure, that Jesus' necessary journey through Samaria was of a theological necessity as opposed to a geographical necessity—"the divine imperative of Jesus' presence among the Samaritan people."[273] Her questions were theological in nature as she persists in questioning Jesus, not as a shift from discussion of her husbands, but as means to ascertain the location of true worship.[274]

Scholars have interpreted the scene as the woman attempting to seduce Jesus while others such as Gench and Schneiders point to the marital imagery used in the Old Testament. This imagery and prophetic literature is used to "describe the relationship between Yahweh and the covenant people."[275] Gench, referencing Schneiders, refers to Jesus, as the new bridegroom of the New Israel, as one who woos the Samarian woman, she representing the church, into a covenant of fidelity.[276] I am in agreement with Gench and Schneiders. Prior to her encounter with Jesus, it appears that her reputation was without honor. She was ostracized and unacceptable. Jesus knew what she had done, but was also aware of what may have been done to her. The text does not indicate why she had five husbands. Jesus' reason for telling her about her husbands was not to point to her sinfulness, but to show that Jesus had power to know the most intimate secrets of her life.[277]

---

[268] Gench, *Encounters with Jesus,* 36.
[269] Ibid., 31.
[270] Patrick D. Miller, James Luther Mays and Paul J. Achtemeier, ed., *Interpretation a Bible Commentary for Teaching and Preaching* (1988), 54.
[271] Gench, *Encounters with Jesus,* 30.
[272] Ibid., 31.
[273] Ibid., 35.
[274] Ibid.
[275] Ibid., 33.
[276] Ibid.
[277] Francis J. Maloney, *The Gospel of John,* ed. Daniel J. Harrington., Sacra Pagina, vol. 4 (Collegeville, MN: The Liturgical Press, 1988), 127.

Despite her situation, she had a desire to understand the importance of true worship. There was an apparent need to connect with God, which was met when she encountered Jesus. As their conversation closes, she is informed that Jesus is the Messiah. Jesus provides this information using the "I am" words, which connect Jesus with the One who was revealed to Moses in the burning bush.[278] It is through embracing the "I am" that one may connect with the power and provision of God. Gench suggests that revisions of the portrait of the Samaritan woman are in order as one revisits the text.

> In sum, revisions of the Samaritan woman's portrait seem to be in order. In the history of interpretation, much has been made of her irregular marital history, but very little of her witness, her missionary endeavor or Jesus' vindication of her role against the disapproval of male disciples. She is much more than a woman with an interesting love life or a model of sin. She is the first character in John to engage Jesus in a serious theological conversation. Moreover, she is the most effective evangelist in this whole Gospel, hence a model for Christian faith and witness. As Robert Kysar observes, "Because of her, the reader of the Gospel knows that no matter who you are—no matter what your status in society may be—the revelation of God in Christ is for you!"[279]

Jesus came to set the captives free! I posit that women have been oppressed and abused since the beginning of time; Eve, Tamar, Hagar, Dinah, Lot's daughters, the woman with the issue of blood, the woman bent and bowed for eighteen years, and the Samaritan woman, to name a few. Their voices cry out to women of today empowering them to stand up for justice and to fight against injustice. They cry out to the Esthers of today who are positioned as instruments of deliverance; voices for the voiceless! I appreciate the work and ministry of theologians and ministers of the gospel who have embraced the mission of setting the captives free. I am especially encouraged by the work of women, who, through holy boldness, have embraced the words of the Apostle Paul (Eph. 6:13-14) to stand in the midst of adversity. These modern day Esthers will be more empowered by the prayer and fasting of "handmaidens" and men of God who will keep their names before the Lord. Clearly the civil rights movement received the support of Caucasian men and women who knew that Blacks were oppressed and decided to stand for justice at the risk of losing, not only their "white privilege" but their lives. Today, women who suffer physical, psychological, emotional, sexual and

---

[278] Gench, *Encounters with Jesus*, 35.
[279] Ibid., 38.

spiritual abuse need the support of their male counterparts who will stand for justice at the risk of losing their "male privilege".

It is the responsibility of the church to examine, interpret, and present biblical texts in a manner that represents the inclusiveness of the gospel message; a message of hope, healing, and deliverance for all of humanity. This will require careful and ethical reexamination of the texts, which have been used to promote subjugation and marginalization of women.

Theological Foundation

This following will address the theological implications of abuse of women and the silence of the black church concerning the same.

The ministry context of the project is a Black church whose membership is comprised mostly of Black women. Therefore, Black and Womanist theological sources have been engaged, as I explore suffering and lament while observing the response of the church concerning victims of violence and abuse, many of whom are women.

James Cone states that Black theology has roots in the pre-Civil War Black church, which recognized that racism and Christianity were opposites.[280] Nineteenth century Black theological discourse included the belief that the suffering of Blacks in America was ordained by God and redemptive.[281] Maria Stewart, the first to publicly present the argument that women, due to their experiences, played an unique role in this process of redemption.[282]

In *Why Lord?*, the author Anthony Pinn cautions against any hint at positive suffering as it "maintains the possibility of divinely sanctioned oppression."[283]

> . . . any religious explanation for suffering that hints at redemptive suffering should be avoided . . . this position does not move toward the lessening of oppressive circumstances; rather it lessens the accountability and responsibility on the part of oppressors. The possibility of redemption through suffering, although not removing a sense of guilt, significantly, reduces any urgent need to change behavior oppressors might feel. And for the oppressed, it blurs a proper understanding of suffering as demonic, thereby significantly

---

[280] James H. Cone and Gayraud S. Wilmore, ed., *Black Theology a Documentary History Volume One*, 2nd ed. (Maryknoll, NY: Orbis Books, 1993), 106.

[281] Anthony B. Pinn, *Why Lord?* (New York: The Continuum International Publishing Group, Inc., 2006), 47.

[282] Ibid., 45.

[283] Ibid., 89.

softening the perception of suffering as irreducibly and existentially damaging.[284]

Among the significant tenets of Black theology, is the belief that the Christian gospel is a message of liberation.[285] Cone posits that "to speak of the God of Christianity is to speak of him who has defined himself according to the liberation of the oppressed."[286] Cone further asserts that genuine theological speech arises from the community of those who are oppressed.

> If Jesus Christ is in fact the Liberator whose resurrection is the guarantee that he is present with us today . . . This means therefore that authentic theological speech arises only from the community of the oppressed who realize that their humanity is inseparable from their liberation from earthly bondage. All other speech is at best irrelevant and at worst blasphemy.[287]

Womanist theology both affirms and critiques "the liberation theology of Black theologians."[288] Despite the fact that women represent the majority of the populace in the Black community and 75 percent of the membership in the Black church, their experience had "not been visibly present in the development of Black theology."[289] Womanist theology emerging from the "black theology movement during the 1980s and the 1990s"[290] begins with the black woman's struggle and moves to her struggle to survive and be free from oppression.[291]

Jacqueline Grant posits that womanist theology involves the struggle of the black woman who has developed strategies to survive amidst the insurmountable odds of racism and sexism in order to protect the lives of her family and her people.[292] As a Black woman, I identify with the thoughts of

---

[284] Ibid.
[285] Cone and Wilmore, *Black Theology: A Documentary History Volume One*, 109.
[286] Ibid., 257.
[287] Ibid., 112-113.
[288] James H. Cone and Gayraud S. Wilmore, ed., *Black Theology a Documentary History Volume Two* (Maryknoll, NY: Orbis Books, 2003), 257.
[289] Cone and Wilmore, *Black Theology a Documentary History Volume One*, 279.
[290] Cone and Wilmore, *Black Theology a Documentary History Volume Two*, 257.
[291] Ibid., 292.
[292] Ibid., 278.

both Cone and Grant as well as the thought of Dolores Williams who says that womanists cannot limit their concern to the deliverance of women.[293] Black women struggle alongside Black men and children for the liberation of the black community. Thus womanist theology examines the struggle of the Black woman as she relates to God and humanity—she sheds light on the image of God that is found in the Black woman. Challenged by the oppression of her blackness and femaleness, she is presented with obstacles that are different from those of Black men and White women. There is no separation between being Black and being a woman. She is a Black woman.[294]

Kelly Delaine Brown Douglas addresses Alice Walker's description of womanism, as it relates to the commitment "to the survival and wholeness of the entire people."[295] Douglas posits that Black women related to the Black freedom and women's movement based upon how they promoted liberation for Black women and their men.[296]

> Black women were searching for a politics of "wholeness." They needed a political strategy that would insure black people, men and women, rights to live as whole, that is unified, struggling together to survive and be in free relationships of mutuality . . . Unlike Black theology, a womanist theology will not focus on only one aspect of Black oppression . . . it will seek to eliminate anything that prevents Black people from being whole, liberated people, and from living as a whole unified community.[297]

Created in the image of God, who is love, humanity innately expects to be loved. Creation is a reflection of the love and glory of God.[298] Children, from birth, respond to a warm touch, a warm smile, and tender loving care. They are generally happy, cuddly, and only cry when they are uncomfortable, in pain, hungry, or want to be held. Adults cry for the same reasons—they cry out when in both physical and emotional pain, wanting to be comforted. When the physical and emotional needs of an adult are abused or neglected,

---

[293] Emilie M. Townes, ed., *Embracing the Spirit: Womanist Perspectives on Hope, Salvation and Transformation* (Bishop Henry McNeal Turner/Sojourner Truth Series in Black Religion, vol. XIII), (Maryknoll, NY: Orbis, 1997), 97.

[294] Cone and Wilmore, *Black Theology a Documentary History Volume Two*, 257.

[295] Ibid., 295.

[296] Ibid.

[297] Ibid.

[298] Owen C. Thomas and Ellen K. Wondra, *Introduction to Theology* (Harrisburg, PA: Morehouse Publishing, 2002), 118.

it causes that individual to feel pain. Physical, sexual, emotional, verbal, and spiritual abuse tears and wounds both the spirit and soul sometimes to the point of perverting the image of God. This is extremely devastating as being made in God's image lies at the core of what it means to be human.[299] These wounds, produced in the inner part of one's being, can only be healed through a process of love, caring, and nurturing all of which should be found in the church. Since the church is a body of believers; the Body of Christ, the church must represent and live out the love of God as exemplified through the life of Christ. This involves caring for and addressing the social, spiritual, and physical needs of wounded members in the church communities in a manner that reflects the loving image of God.

Steven R. Tracy in *Mending the Soul,* speaks of the three aspects of the image of God; relational, visible, and functional. The relational involves the intimacy between the Father, Son, and Holy Spirit; a relationship of love and unity. The visible involves the "likeness" that we see in each other as a child experiences love and care from a parent. The third aspect, reflected in "and let them rule" speaks to the manner in which humanity will care for creation.[300] Tracy says that when we fail in these areas we "grossly misrepresent who God is."[301] Tracy addresses five kinds of abuses (see appendix B table I), which do not represent every abuse type, and the corresponding perversion of the image of God.[302]

I engage Black and Womanist theological sources, as they are important to gain an understanding of the dynamics between race, gender, and sexual abuse.[303]

Renita Weems speaks to the relationship between husband and wife that is often used metaphorically to describe the sinful, adulterous behavior of the wife (Israel) which results in the wrath of the husband (God). According to Weems, with whom I agree, the marriage metaphor and God's position as the victim would not present God as mean and cruel, but just, in punishing Israel, the unfaithful wife.[304]

Clearly in a place of superiority and ultimate authority, the God of Israel is spoken of as One who loves and provides for humanity, correcting, and restoring those who have gone astray. This is not uncomfortable for me as God is just. Unfortunately, the husband/wife metaphor may well cause men,

---

[299] Steven R. Tracy, *Mending the Soul* (Grand Rapids, MI: Zondervan, 2005), 23.
[300] Ibid., 25.
[301] Ibid.
[302] Ibid., 27.
[303] Adams and Fortune, *Violence Against Women and Children*, 186.
[304] Renita J. Weems, *Battered Love* (Minneapolis, MN: Fortress Press, 1995), 19.

some of whom are often unjust, to pattern their relationships with women based upon a misunderstanding of God.

I have often wrestled with the male image of God and how female victims of male violence relate to this image. Steven Tracy suggests that abuse survivors need to enlarge and expand "their understanding of God."[305] During the early stages of healing from abuse by an earthly father, a distorted image of God may impede the healing process. Therefore, the church must minister through passages that express the loving care provided by a heavenly Father, including images which are feminine or nurturing in nature (see appendix B table II).[306]

Children and adults alike need God's love and protection. Believers need to know that God cares and will provide. Believers enjoy the fellowship with each other and the feeling of love that is often experienced in a healthy familial relationship. One seeks the joy of the Lord and finds peace in God's presence that is not otherwise experienced. This is a wonderful place; utopia! However, life sometimes throws curves in the form of unexpected challenges, illness, financial difficulties, domestic violence, and abuse. What is the response of the Black church and how does the church act an agent of healing?

The church is uncomfortable with talk about suffering as it produces discomfort on many levels. Suffering from abuse may be "hidden from the eyes of the church because of the church's failure to speak about this problem."[307] It is the last thing that one wants to hear about, and it is certainly not something that one wishes to experience. Not only is the church uncomfortable with the discussion of suffering, but is also sometimes insensitive to the suffering of others. Church members become decreasingly sympathetic as time passes, and the victims have not recovered emotionally. Worse yet, if the individual remains in the abusive environment, the thought is that something is wrong with them. The church and humanity, in general, have been conditioned to believe that "they ought to get over it" and frequently ask "why doesn't she/he just leave?" It is not uncommon for friends and family to admonish victims to "get on with their lives."[308] The cliché that "time heals wounds," a statement with which I do not agree, has promulgated a falsehood. On the contrary, time provides the opportunity to seek healing or to cover up the pain. Wounds which are not properly cared for may become infected resulting in prolonged pain and sometimes permanent debilitation.

---

[305] Steven R. Tracy, *Mending the Soul* (Grand Rapids, MI: Zondervan, 2005), 169.

[306] Ibid.

[307] Lisa Barnes Lampman and Michelle D. Shattuck, eds., *God and the Victim: Theological Reflections on Evil, Victimization, Justice and Forgiveness* (Grand Rapids, MI: William B. Eerdmans Publishing Company, 1999), 87.

[308] Ibid., 81.

Clarice J. Martin, quoting William R. Jones, delineates three aspects of African American suffering. First, it is "maldistributed" meaning that suffering is not shared equally with African Americans and the rest of humanity. Secondly, African Americans suffer in "enormity," which is sometimes unto death or oppression that limits longevity and frustrates hope. Thirdly, it is "non-catastrophic" as it does not occur suddenly and dissipates, but afflicts and affects generations; fathers, sons, grandsons, mothers, daughters, and granddaughters.[309] This suffering is sometimes worn as a badge of honor as to complain implies lack of appreciation for God. No matter how bad the situation, we are told that "it could be worse."

The Black church has taught about God as a healer of the brokenhearted, but has acted as physicians who have placed an unrealistic time limit on the process. In addition, the bedside manner is poor due to discomfort with talk about the cause of the wound, lack of sympathy, and/or insensitivity to the intensity of the pain. I recall a conversation with Dr. Daryl Hairston who stated, "As a result of a misrepresentation of who the ecclesiastical church is meant to be, women have been kept out of the mainstream of church life and leadership, which created an unconscious state which allowed the traditional values of the Black church to keep women silent." Thus a collaborative silence continues as women in the church struggle to find their voice, often threatened by institutionalized laryngitis, which is contagious. When one woman is unable to speak, the other is at risk of losing her voice. However, when one woman recovers her voice, there is hope for the other and it is through sharing the stories of pain, suffering, victory, and triumph that one embraces the God-given authority to speak truth to power. The voice becomes an instrument of deliverance. Silent suffering of the abused and violated is not an acceptable way of life for humanity.

It is not uncommon for crime victims to attempt to erase abuse from their memories as a means to handle the pain.[310] Lisa Barnes Lampman postulates that "recognizing the depth of harm provides a vital foundation for healing and complete forgiveness."[311]

Francis E. Wood says that our interpretation of scripture concerning suffering, as set forth by early church fathers, has not been thoroughly examined for centuries. These interpretations include suffering due to sin, suffering to build strength of character, suffering as proof of the favor of God, suffering (particularly for women) as a result of Eve's disobedience.[312]

---

[309] Emilie M. Townes, ed., *A Troubling in My Soul*, (Maryknoll, NY: Orbis Books, 1993), 22.
[310] Lampman and Shattuck, *God and the Victim*, 188.
[311] Ibid.
[312] Townes, *A Troubling In My Soul*, 37.

These interpretations may cause one to accept suffering as a way of life thus having difficulty with rejecting abuse, violence, and oppression as sin against God and humanity. Therefore, many Christians suffer in silence and live their lives in emotional and spiritual bondage perpetuated by a church, which in many instances is unwilling or ill-equipped to the minister to the abused members of the congregation.

How does the church teach that God is One who heals wounds without talking about the wounds, pain, and suffering? The passages found in (Ps. 147:3, RSV) "He heals the brokenhearted, and binds up their wounds" and (Exod. 15:26, RSV) " . . . for I am the *Lord*, your healer," clearly indicate that God is a healer, but there is no reference to the time frame in which the healing will be accomplished. The statement, which is made, is that God is the One who heals. Therefore, it is the responsibility of the church to preach, teach, and live in a manner, which directs the wounded to God so that the healing would take place and to stay with them through the process. Unfortunately, the church has given little care to the victimized members of the congregation.[313]

> Countless women, men, and children have been scarred, injured, and suffered loss of property, and even life with little attention coming from the household of faith.[314]

It is not uncommon for individuals who have life-threatening illnesses to want a loved one to accompany them to the office of their physician. Initially, they may request your presence when they are speaking with the doctor. The next visit may require that you sit in the waiting room while they meet with the doctor. The following visit may be unaccompanied. While we may not have been diagnosed with the illness and do not experience the pain in the manner that the patient does, the love that we have for the individual causes us to partner in hope. Our prayer and desire is the same as the infirmed; that God will heal. Many Black churches have individuals; ministers, deacons, deaconess, missionaries, etc., who are assigned and expected to visit with the "sick and shut-in." However, even when aware of abuse, especially domestic violence, the church has often considered it a private family matter and thus has failed to respond. The church must partner in hope with the abused and brokenhearted just as it would with someone who is physically ill. Violence against women is a social ill, which has plagued the Black community and all too often, the Black church has been silent.

---

[313] Lampman and Shattuck, *God and the Victim*, 72.
[314] Ibid.

The church must fully participate in setting the captives free. The church have become satisfied with what Obery M. Hendricks Jr. calls Church-ianity, and has not embraced the liberating message and mission of Christianity.[315] According to Hendricks, Christianity calls us to work toward the same degree of freedom, justice, health, happiness, and wholeness for others that we would desire for ourselves. Christians come to church to have a good time, sing songs, and feel good, but too often are not concerned with the world. The church may pray for the world, on occasion, feeling that no more is required. Prayers of thanksgiving are offered because one is not suffering; their children are not using drugs, they are not homeless, incarcerated, nor ill. Rarely have I heard prayers for the victims of domestic violence, child or adult sexual abuse in a Sunday morning worship service. All too often, those who come into the church wounded, leave Sunday after Sunday with unanswered questions and without having heard a word of hope for their situation. They ask the question "Where is God in all of this?" "Does God see what is happening to me?"

The Theological Aspect of the Black Church

The Black church undoubtedly needs to gain a better understanding of God in respect to righteousness and justice. J. Deotis Roberts states that "the Black church was born in protest against racism."[316] Black people organized churches and developed their own theology based on a relationship with a God who was with them in the struggle, relating to a God being on the side of the oppressed. Blacks knew that slavery was unjust, that there was a need to be free and must, therefore, know that abuse is unjust and the abused in our society need to be free. As people created by God all of humanity must have the same rights and privileges as others who were created by this same God.

The Black church, in many instances, seems to have forgotten the struggle. Those who are several generations beyond our Egypt/Slavery experience feel that they have arrived, coming to church to thank God for things and to ask God for more. Many mega churches teach prosperity, prosperity, and more prosperity, continuing to accumulate wealth often at the expense of the poor and downtrodden, considering church attendance as faithful service. Jeremiah Wright asserts that this is anti-black theology, further stating that "any people

---

[315] Frederick D. Haynes III, Iva E. Carruthers and Jeremiah Wright Jr. eds., *Blow the Trumpet in Zion* (Minneapolis, MN: Fortress Press, 2005), 77.

[316] Roberts, *The Prophethood of Black Believers,* 25.

who forget their story will die."[317] As a result of prosperity preaching many have become self-serving, idolatrous, and unfaithful.

According to Hosea, Israel had not learned to be faithful. This is referenced in Hosea 6:6. "For I desire steadfast love and not sacrifice, the knowledge of God, rather than burnt offerings." God desires our faithfulness as God is faithful to humanity. This faithfulness of God is defined as "*hesed,*" which is not easily translated into English. The following represents translations of "hesed": "mercy" (KJV), "steadfast love," "goodness" (JPSV) and "loyalty" (REB).[318]

The steadfast love of God is demonstrated by God giving God's only begotten Son to save humanity. It is further demonstrated through Christ in the Garden of Gethsemane. The Bible tells us that the "Word became flesh" (John 1:14, RSV). Jesus experienced pain and suffering, hunger, thirst, grief, disappointment, but was faithful to the assigned mission.

God experiences anger and disappointment as a result of "righteous indignation,"[319] but does not easily retreat from humanity. God keeps asking the question that was asked of Adam in the Garden of Eden; "Adam, where art thou?"

Some would say that this resembles codependency; that humanity needs God and God needs humanity. To the contrary, it is God's relationship with humanity that helps to define God. It is the relationship with God that helps humanity to know God.

It is this loving relationship with One who is faithful that produces faith. Faith is a part of the spiritual fruit spoken of in Galatians 5:22. It seems that it would not be difficult to have *some* faith in One who is *so* faithful. When I look at faith as spiritual fruit, it is seen as a gift from God to humanity, which draws one closer to the Creator. The good thing about this faith is that a small amount can move mountains (Matt. 17:20, RSV).

When one has faith, they will trust God. They will talk to God, believe that God loves them and is willing and able to deliver on promises. According to Major J. Jones, "black theology asks not so much the question of what God has the power to do, but whether black people can get God to use the divine power on their behalf."[320] Black people have faith in a God who is on the side of the oppressed. Faith will help one to embrace the promise

---

[317] Linda E. Thomas, ed., *Living Stones in the Household of God* (Minneapolis, MN: Fortress Press, 2004), 14-15.

[318] Bernhard W. Anderson, *Understanding The Old Testament* (Upper Saddle River, NJ: Prentice Hall, 1998), 277.

[319] David R. Blumenthal, *Facing the Abusing God A Theology of Protest* (Louisville, KY: Westminster/John Knox Press, 1993), 17.

[320] Major J. Jones, *The Color of God* (Macon. GA: Mercer University Press, 1987), 52.

because there is belief that God's thoughts and desires are what is best for humanity (Jer. 29:11-14, KJV).

God reveals God's self as love.[321] God, the Creator, loves humanity, desires and seeks fellowship with humanity, makes agreements to maintain the fellowship, and is eternally faithful. God is One whom humanity must trust. Not only must humanity desire the presence of God, but believe that God's presence will make a difference. When in need of confidence and assurance through every struggle believers must be free to call on God. When assurance is needed one must call on God. In the midst of trials we must call on God. We need to feel the presence of God even when they are unable to hear God's voice. God is always with humanity, unlike friends and loved ones who may grow inpatient and are consumed with their own concerns.

Regardless of how many books one may read about God, it is the relationship, the fellowship, the "koinonia" that helps one to gain a better understanding as to the nature of God. God is love and love does not exist outside of relationship. However, true "koinonia" cannot exist if the needs of the emotionally and spiritually wounded are not addressed.

The failure of the church to minister the victims of violence and abuse, many of whom are women, creates a breach in the fellowship among believers and worse, may interfere with their relationship with God. The church, as previously stated, has a tendency to stifle the cries of the wounded with language that would cause one to feel guilty about crying out to God—a time limit has been placed on pain and suffering.

The Book of Job is often referenced when Christians discuss pain and suffering. Clemens Sedmak discusses Gustavo Guttierez' reappropriation of the Book of Job in his book entitled, *Doing Local Theology*.[322] I find this discussion rather interesting as it relates to suffering, giving a slightly different understanding of suffering and sanctification. Gutierrez asks the question "how are human beings to find a language applicable to God in the midst of innocent suffering?"[323] How does one talk to God in the midst of innocent suffering?

Daniel J. Simundson, author of *Job a Theological Commentary*, postulates that Christian tradition has been to stifle lament as a result of being told to give thanks and praise to God regardless of circumstances.[324]

---

[321] Owen C. Thomas and Ellen K. Wondra, *Introduction to Theology* (Harrisburg, PA: Morehouse Publishing, 2002), 100.

[322] Clemens Sedmak, *Doing Local Theology* (Maryknoll, NY: Orbis Books, 2002), 60.

[323] Ibid.

[324] Daniel J. Simundson, *The Message of Job* (Lima, OH: Academic Renewal Press, 2001), 72.

> Our religious tradition as Christians has often urged us to stifle lament. We have been told to praise and thank God no matter what is happening to us. The strong, silent, stoic, submissive, non-complaining [sic] person has been the model of piety, which we are to emulate.[325]

Simundson further states that lament was a part of the Old Testament often seen in Psalms, which challenged the justice of God.[326] He posits that if relationship with God is important for humanity and humanity is free "to be honest with God, then there must be room for lament."[327]

I have been frustrated, tired, felt like quitting, and sometimes felt physically ill in the place of suffering. There were times when I was angry as a result of undeserved maltreatment by people in the world as well as in the church. There were times of loneliness and feeling that God was not present in the struggle. However, it was not until I began to talk to God as opposed to talking about God that the presence of God in the struggle was apparent.

Patrick L. Miller speaks of lament as the "voice of the human . . . which is not bound to class, race, language, or religious affiliation."[328] How does this connect with Job's suffering? Job believed that he was undeserving of his misfortune, yet he trusted God. His suffering, although not caused by his wife and friends, was certainly increased by their lack of faith and judgmental statements. One must exercise caution in giving meaning to the suffering of another.[329] Simundson posits that it is futile to discuss theological implications of suffering with the sufferer as the sufferer is dealing with feeling and the others are dealing with intellect.[330]

When an individual is in such a state, they really need to talk to someone and Job had no one with whom to speak. His friends either said nothing or when they did speak, said something disheartening. Job became so frustrated by his condition that he lamented and blamed God for what happened to him. It became difficult for Job to pray (chapters sixteen and nineteen) and he began to speak *of* God more than he talked *to* God.[331]

Job had to talk *to* God! Job's suffering caused him to know God in a deeper and different relationship. Job was honest with God, which kept the line of communication open. Simundson posits that God may feel the pain of

---

[325] Ibid.
[326] Ibid.
[327] Ibid., 73.
[328] Brown and Miller, *Lament*, 15.
[329] Simundson, *The Message of Job*, 70.
[330] Ibid.
[331] Ibid., 84.

our lack of trust, but will not desert us in moments of emotional outbursts.[332] Howard Zehr, quoting Walter Brueggemann, says that everything must be "brought to God, even if it is scandalous."[333] As a result of the open line of communication, Job was able to hear when God spoke to him out of the whirlwind (Job 40:6).

There were people around Job who discouraged him and made him feel that the suffering was a result of something that he had done. Yet Job prayed for them and it was at that time that (Job 42:7-10) the Lord restored that which Job had lost.

Likewise, abuse survivors may need to pray for those who do not understand, those who do nothing and those who are judgmental. They too are bound; unaware that they are participants in oppression. God's love has an amazing healing effect on humanity as a whole, which impresses upon us the importance of Jesus' commandment that we should love one another. David R. Blumenthal, a professor of Judaic studies at Emory University, posits that "love is the affirmation of the other, given and received in wholeness."[334]

In recent years, I have had the opportunity to witness love as a part of the healing process in a life skills/job readiness class. There were twenty-five women present and one man. There is an exercise that is done during the class, which requires that the participants share their life experiences as life stages. They are told that they need only to disclose what they are comfortable with sharing. During this process, I stressed that past personal experience often determines our perception of present-day events. One by one, with almost everyone speaking, they began to share their challenges and struggles. Some were abused; some were diagnosed with cancer, lupus, and bone diseases. Others had contemplated suicide, but found the strength to live. One young lady had just buried her son and another had recently miscarried a child. As they shared their stories, both tears and love began to flow. The manner in which they hugged and encouraged each other was powerful! The message that kept coming forth through each survivor is that God is with them in the struggle.

One may trust that God is faithful, but the question is often asked, why does God allow suffering in the Body of Christ? When people accept Christ as their Savior they come to the faith with certain expectations of God. The Apostle Paul may have asked the Lord on the road to Damascus, what he could do for the Lord, but many initially want to know what the Lord can do for them. Those who have suffered the injustice and pain of abuse need and want the Lord to do something for them!

---

[332] Ibid., 73.
[333] Lampman and Shattuck, *God and the Victim*, 151.
[334] David R. Blumenthal, *Facing the Abusing God A Theology of Protest*, 16.

Andrew Sung Park says "Jesus came into the world to set the wronged free from their grief and burden and to forgive the sins of wrongdoers. But between the two—the wronged and the wrongdoers—Jesus was primarily concerned with the former."[335] The gospel must proclaim a message of hope for those who would otherwise be hopeless, but must not end with the preaching, because living the gospel is a viable means to setting the captives free.

The Black church, as a herald for justice, needs to regain the prophetic voice, which has been a source of empowerment through times past that challenged systemic oppression of Black people. If violence against women is not addressed in the church then the gospel message is incomplete.

Karen E. Mosby-Avery posits that the church must reclaim its understanding of Christianity.[336] She states that "the African American church has to reclaim a definition of Christianity and a definition of child of God that includes justice."[337]

I had the privilege of hearing a message delivered by Rev. Dr. Otis Moss Jr. at the Samuel DeWitt Proctor Conference in 2004 during which he shared his thoughts concerning Isaiah 61:1-3. Moss stated that the text opens with theology, addresses social, political, and economic issues and then ends on a theological note. According to Moss, a gospel message that does not deal with the issues between the theological notes is an empty gospel. I posit that the gospel must include a prophetic message that presents a word of hope to the oppressed and a word of correction to the oppressor. The church cannot witness the suffering of others and remain silent nor should the church, experience pain without working to transform the systems and individuals who are responsible. Harold Dean Trulear posits that the church needs to care for victims, breaking the silence of a "seemingly hidden reality of the countless neighbors who are primary victims or secondary victims."[338]

Emilie M. Townes says that Audre Lorde distinguishes a difference between pain and suffering.

> For Lorde, suffering is unscrutinized, unmetabolized pain. Suffering is the inescapable cycle of reliving pain over and again when it is triggered by events or people. It is the static process, which usually ends up in oppression.[339] Pain is an experience that is recognized, named, and then used for transformation. It is a dynamic process pointing toward transformation.[340]

---

[335] Park, *From Hurt to Healing*, 16.
[336] Thomas, *Living Stones in the Household of God*, 35.
[337] Ibid.
[338] Lampman and Shattuck, *God and the Victim*, 74.
[339] Townes, *A Troubling In My Soul*, 84.
[340] Ibid.

Townes addresses suffering and the responsibility of the church in this manner:

> Suffering is sinful, because we do not choose to act through our finite freedom on behalf of our liberation from sin to justice. If, as most African American women in church do, the African American religious community takes the resurrection seriously, true suffering has been removed through the redemptive event of the resurrecting. Through the Suffering Servant, God has spoken against evil and injustice. The empty cross and tomb are symbols of victory. The oppressed are set free to struggle against injustice, not out of suffering, but out of their pain that can be recognized and named as injustice and brokenness. The resurrection moves humanity past suffering to pain and struggle. The resurrection is God's breaking into history to transform suffering into wholeness—to move the person from victim to change agent. The Gospel message calls for transformation.[341]

Yes! Believers are called to work as agents of change—as believers are transformed, they participate in the transformation of others into the image of God. The prophetic voice of the Black church must be revived to speak truth to power and to partner with God in setting the captives free. The church can no longer remain silent concerning violence against women who represent a large part of the congregations, attending church Sunday after Sunday—they suffer in silence. The church must encourage women to speak out concerning their pain, as naming the pain and the source begins the process of the plan to bring about change.

The love of God is made manifest when the church serves as agents of change through caring for the wounded and broken persons in the church, as well as, in the world.

I am reminded of the words of a song written by Charles Albert Tindley in 1905, which is a part of my black Baptist church tradition.

> When the storms of life are raging,
> Stand by me;
> When the storms of life are raging,
> Stand by me.
> When the world is tossing me,
> Like a ship upon the sea
> Thou who rulest wind and water,
> Stand by me.

---

[341] Ibid.

In the midst of tribulation,
Stand by me;
In the midst of tribulation,
Stand by me.
When the hosts of hell assail
And my strength begins to fail
Thou who never lost a battle
Stand by me.

In the midst of faults and failures,
Stand by me;
In the midst of faults and failures,
Stand by me.
When I do the best I can,
And my friends don't understand,
Thou who knowest all about me,
Stand by me.

In the midst of persecution,
Stand by me;
In the midst of persecution,
Stand by me.
When my foes in battle array
Undertake to stop my way
Thou who saved Paul and Silas,
Stand by me.

When I'm growing old and feeble,
Stand by me;
When I'm going old and feeble,
Stand by me.
When my life becomes a burden,
And I'm near the chilly Jordan,
O Thou "Lily of the Valley,"
Stand by me.[342]

---

[342] James Melvin Washington, *Conversations with God* (New York: HarperPerennial, 1994), 100.

Chapter Four

Methodology

Treatment Hypothesis

The hypothesis of this ministry project is that by providing care and services, which will address the physical, spiritual, and emotional needs of female survivors of violence and abuse, will prove instrumental in breaking the silence of victimization and assist victims in the healing process.

The goals were to develop a focus group, which consisted of female victim-survivors of violence and abuse who shared their thoughts, concerns, and ministry requests. This was essential in the collaborative leadership component of the ministry model. While mental health professionals, law enforcement, and clergy bring a level of expertise to the process, emphasis was placed on the active involvement of individuals who have experienced abuse. The goal was to assist them in breaking their own silence and to empower them as leaders who will assist others in doing the same.

Intervention

The context for this ministry project was the Paradise Baptist Church in Newark, New Jersey. The majority of the membership is women, many of whom have experienced domestic violence and abuse. As director of the women's ministry since 1999, I had counseled with several women in the congregation who are victim-survivors of violence and abuse. I discussed the need for a model of care with the pastor, who also acknowledged the necessity of this ministry. Once I received the support needed to move forward, the project was implemented.

Pastor James was supportive of the project and his service to the community has proven vital to my ability to obtain assistance, financial support, and information from law enforcement, elected officials, and community-based organizations.

Research Design

The project was implemented through the collaborative endeavor of the ministry context, Paradise Baptist Church in Newark, New Jersey, social service agencies, mental health professionals, and law enforcement with emphasis upon active involvement of victim-survivor context associates. This project was designed to help victims of domestic abuse and violence to find their voice in order to *break the silence* pertaining to their victimization. The project was implemented with five female context associates who served as the focus group. Four of the women were survivors of child sexual abuse and two of the five were survivors of domestic violence. One of the five women did not indicate having experienced abuse. However, she was specifically requested to become a part of the group. I felt confident that she, as well as the others, would be discreet having respect for confidentiality. The goal in inviting the non-victim into the group was tri-fold: 1) to create sensitivity for survivors, 2) to let survivors know that non-victims care, and 3) determine if the non-victim may have been affected by the abuse of a female family member and/or was in denial concerning her own abuse. The fact that between three and four million women in the United States is battered by an intimate partner[343] suggests that a female who has not been victimized is more the exception than the rule.

The research design involved an alternative hypothesis, which according to Creswell, is based upon predicting an expected outcome.[344] I used a qualitative research design, which requires observation of participant behavior by participating with them in activities, personal narratives, and open-ended interviewing.[345] It was also an action research project of which social research is a component. This involves working with participants for the purpose of education with respect for their opinions, as well.[346] It is a multidirectional educational process where all participants including the researcher are students.

The ministry model included a series of monthly meetings, reading, and discussion with victim-survivor context associates, as well as a three-day women's conference attended by all. The theme of the conference addressed

---

[343] Ruth A. Brandwein, ed., *Battered Women, Children and Welfare Reform*, ed. Claire M. Renzitti and Jeffrey L. Edleson, Sage Series on Violence against Women (Thousand Oaks, CA: Sage Publications, 1999), 18.

[344] John W. Creswell, *Research Design Qualitative, Quantitative, and Mixed Methods Approaches*, 2nd ed. (Thousand Oaks, CA: Sage Publications, 2003), 110.

[345] Ibid., 21.

[346] Pamela Lomax, Jack Whitehead and Jean Mc Niff, *You and Your Action Research Project*, 2nd ed. (New York: Routledge Falmer Taylor & Francis Group, 2003), 40.

spiritual healing. The project also entailed a Women's Fellowship and Summer Bible School; a series of six classes and worship services, which focused on women breaking the silence and healing from the wounds of violence and abuse. The fellowship, which entered its ninth year at the time of the research was attended by 146 participants and was open to women from all churches in the community.

The final activity was a Community Awareness Day during which presentations were made by local law enforcement officials, social service and mental health professionals who provided information concerning services, which are available for victim-survivors of violence and abuse. The workshop was open to both males and females ages twelve years and older.

Measurement

The measurements of the project focused on examining how women break the silence pertaining to violence and abuse. The areas of concentration included the importance of breaking the silence, how victim-survivors feel about telling their story, how they feel children may be better protected, how they define healing, how they define pastoral care/counseling, and how the church can best serve those who have been and/or are in abusive relationships.

Instrumentation

The methodology used to test this hypothesis was qualitative, utilizing a method of triangulation consisting of participant interviews, personal narratives, and pre-test and post-test surveys. All of the data collected was confidential, which was explained to the participants at the onset.

The pre-test and post-test survey questions consisted of twenty questions: five demographic, eight closed-ended, and seven open-ended. All questions, except the demographic, related to their experience and thoughts as victim-survivors of violence as well as identifying female family members who have experienced the same (see appendix C).

The first instrument was the pre-test survey, which collected information concerning their thoughts about abuse of women, what services they felt the ministry context provided, and their suggestions as to what services may best benefit these women.

The second instrument was a narrative, which each participant was asked to prepare. The purpose of the narrative was to gain understanding as to how victim-survivors tell their story. Attention was given to the use of terminology and the amount of details provided (see appendix Q).

The third instrument is the interview, which was comprised of thirteen open-ended questions. The interviews were intentionally conducted at the end of the process as I looked for changes that may have occurred in how the participants expressed their thoughts (see appendix D). Since the project involved breaking the silence, the manner in which the participants communicated and expressed themselves was essential. The post-test survey was also completed at this time as a means to observe changes, which may or may not have occurred as a result of the project (see appendix E).

Chapter Five

The Ministry Model

Designing the Research Project

The hypothesis of the project is, if female victim-survivors of violence and abuse receive care and counseling, it will assist in the healing process of which breaking the silence is a component. Due to prior disclosure by a few women in the ministry context, I asked if they would be interested in collaborating to develop a model of care for victims of violence and abuse. Serving as director of the women's ministry for the context for eight years prior afforded me opportunity to interact with and gain the confidence of many of the women. Realizing that confidentiality would be essential to the effectiveness of the project, I carefully selected context associates who would exercise discretion. I did not assume that every victim-survivor would respect the privacy of others.

The goal of the project was to assist participants in breaking the silence concerning their abuse, which would also serve to empower others. One of the participants was identified as not having experienced abuse, but was asked to participate in the process. The expectation was that it could lead to increased knowledge about the lives of abused women. Considering that non-victims sometimes demonstrate a lack of compassion for victim-survivors, it was an opportunity to promote empathy and unity.

Focus Group

The five context associates; four who experienced abuse and one who did not, were the focus group. I initially met with the four women who were victim-survivors that they would be able to share their stories with each other. Each participant spoke in detail as to how, when, and by whom they were abused. The participants met on two occasions before the fifth person joined the group. I informed them when they were asked to participate that there would be at least one person in the group who did not share their experience; a person who would meet their approval prior to being asked to take part. She was identified to the group, all of whom were comfortable with her presence and participation.

I also met with the non-victim to advise that she would need to be supportive and sensitive to the emotional trauma that is experienced by a person who has been abused. She expressed an interest to participate in a supportive role while gaining increased knowledge about the challenges that victim-survivors face with healing from abuse.

Surveys

Pre-test and Post-test Surveys

The pre-test survey was given in February 2007 and the post-test survey was given in December 2007. The purpose of the pre-test was to obtain information concerning thoughts and perceptions, personal and family experience with violence and abuse. In addition, I wanted to obtain information concerning the participants' thoughts about care provided by the church. The post-test survey was given to find out if there were changes in thoughts and perception as well as the involvement of the church in assisting with breaking the silence of abuse.

Interviews

A private interview was conducted with each participant. They were asked the same questions, all of which were open-ended. During each interview, I was careful to note both verbal and non-verbal response to questions.

Narratives

Each participant was asked to write the story of how they were abused indicating their thoughts concerning the healing process. The purpose of the narrative was to provide an additional instrument to assist in breaking the silence. During this process, I observed whether there would be a marked difference between their oral and written presentation in terms of the details of their story.

Implementing the Research Project

This process began with all five participants meeting to discuss women in the Bible who were abused. None of the participants had read about Tamar or Dinah. They all had some knowledge of Hagar, but had not, prior to our discussions, seen her as a victim.

The next phase moved the group to selecting a book that would be read together. All of the readers would be prepared to discuss their thoughts during subsequent meetings. The meetings took place from February 2007 to April 2007. I presented copies of several books that the group may decide which one would best serve their needs. The book chosen was *Courage to Heal*, written by Ellen Bass and Laura Davis. The researcher supplied all participants with their own copy of the book and designated parts I and II to be read. Among the topics covered were: the effect of abuse, coping, the decision to heal, the emergency stage, remembering, breaking the silence, and forgiveness.

The group met twice monthly; once at the beginning and once at the end. During the meetings, the group discussed how they felt about what they read. One of the participants, (Participant E) stated that she had read both the book and the corresponding workbook, indicated that she "had been through this process already." She seemed disinterested.

I observed the responses of the participants as a means to ascertain the willingness to break the silence of their abuse. Each participant was assured that their identity would not be revealed and that their anonymity would be protected. This was important to all of them. However, I assumed that telling the story would be essential to healing and breaking the silence would have a ripple effect—other victims would find their voice. Despite this assumption, I did not pressure the participants to share their stories publicly.

The next phases of the project were conducted with the context associates as participants, but included individuals who were not a part of the focused group. I felt that the context associates would gain strength from the presence of other women. The thought was triggered by one of the context associates who had attended the fellowship from its inception. She indicated that despite the fact that she never told anyone about her abuse, the women's fellowship had sustained her. It had given her a sense of strength and had been instrumental in her healing. Therefore, as researcher and learner, I used the women's fellowship as a part of the project—it worked.

The next phase of the project was the Women of Divine Destiny Conference, which was done in collaboration with The New Hope Baptist Church in Newark, New Jersey. The theme of the conference was "I am Healed," referencing Isaiah 53:5 (see appendix F). The conference was attended by 150 women from New York, New Jersey, Delaware, and North Carolina. All of the members of the focus group were in attendance.

The two day conference, which was held at a hotel, included two workshops, two worship services, and a concert. The two workshops addressed emotional woundedness and the process of healing. I collaborated with Deaconess Margaret Lewis, women's ministry leader of The New Hope Baptist Church, to select the workshop facilitators. Each facilitator was given an outline and material so that they would have enough information to adequately cover the topic. The workshops were entitled, Sister to Sister, We've All Been Wounded, and From Tragedy to Triumph, the information for which was taken from *The Wounded Woman*, authored by Dr. Steve Stephens and Pam Vredevelt, Chapters one and eleven, respectively.

The next phase of the project involved six lessons, which were taught during the Women's Fellowship and Summer School held on six consecutive Monday nights from June-August. The format of the sessions was the lesson and a worship service, with musicians; four males and one female, in attendance. The registration donation of $25 for all six sessions included dinner every Monday night. I facilitated the lessons. The fellowship was open to women in the church and community with 146 participants registering. The theme for the fellowship was, Jesus: God's Gift to Women. The thought for theme came from a book authored by Dorothy Valcarcel entitled, *Jesus, the Man Who Loved Women*. I contacted the author and explained the project after which she graciously allowed the ministry to purchase the books at a reduced price. The books were offered as optional reading and were purchased by one-third of the fellowship registrants and 80 percent of the context associates. The aforementioned book influenced my selection of topics and lesson titles, as well.

Lesson One, entitled Jesus' Relationships With Women was a brief overview of Jesus' relationships with women in the Bible (see appendix G).

Lesson Two, entitled The Broken and Abused Woman, focused on definitions and abuse, post-traumatic stress disorder. The biblical references were Hagar, Tamar, and the Samaritan woman (see appendix H).

Lesson Three, entitled The Guilty Woman: A Sinner's Response to Forgiveness, focused on forgiving others and forgiving oneself and the forgiveness that is found in Jesus. The woman taken on adultery was discussed. The biblical reference was the woman taken in adultery. The thought for this title was influenced by *The Man Who Loved Women*, page 175 (see appendix I).

Lesson Four, entitled The Labeled and Misunderstood Woman, focused on the challenges that troubled women faced with being misunderstood and labeled by society. The biblical references were the woman bent over for eighteen years and the woman with the alabaster box. The thought for this title was influenced by *The Man Who loved Women,* pages147 and 201, respectively (see appendix J).

Lesson V, entitled The Stressed and Worried Woman, focused on the physical and emotional effects of stress. The biblical reference was Mary and Martha pointing to Martha's stress as a result of Mary's failure to help her. The thought for this title was influenced by *The Man Who Loved Women,* pages 187 and 117, respectively (see appendix K).

Lesson VI was entitled The Transformed and Triumphant Woman: How Do You Spell *Changed?* The thought for part of this title was influenced by *The Man Who loved Women*, page 273. I used the letters in the word changed to teach principles of spiritual transformation. The topics were: commitment, holiness, anointing, nurturing, godliness, empowerment, and determination (see appendix L).

Since the summer months are often the time when persons vacation, not all participants were able to attend all six sessions. Culminating the fellowship was a graduation worship service during which all participants received certificates reflecting the classes which they attended (see appendix M).

The final phase of the project was a Community Awareness Day entitled, *Break the Silence: Stop the Violence* (see appendix N). I solicited the financial support from members of the Newark City Council, the State of New Jersey Senate, and the Newark/North Jersey Committee of Black Churchmen, Inc. for funds to offset the cost of the event. As a result, financial assistance was received from two council members, a State Senator, and the clergy group (see appendix O).

Letters of invitation were sent to the women and churches on our mailing list. There are approximately 288 women and fifty-four churches on our mailing list. The letters to the churches were addressed to the pastor. The free registration included a continental breakfast, three presentations including one designed for clergy persons only. Sixty-five persons attended, which included 100 percent of the context associates. The facilitators were Carmen Diaz Cuevas, a licensed clinical social worker; Pamela McCauley, a representative of the Essex County Prosecutor's Office; Linda Morales Dennis, a context associate who agreed to share her story of surviving violence and abuse. The Essex County Division of Welfare was on-site with a mobile van to take applications for TANF (temporary assistance to needy families), food stamps, and medical assistance. The event was reported by a local newspaper (see appendices N-P).

Evaluating the Research Project

Considering the design of the project, which involved the participation of five women as a focus group who also served as context associates, their cooperation was crucial. I acknowledge that being the wife of the pastor and director of the women's ministry was advantageous. Additionally, the participants were aware that the pastor was in support of the project. When I approached each of the women they seemed interested in working as a part of a team that would develop a model of ministry for abused women.

Pre-test Survey Results

The pre-test survey was given with the following results. Question one asked the age of the participant.

Around 80 percent of the participants were age thirty-six to fifty and 20 percent of the participants were age fifty to sixty-two.

Question two asked the marital status of the participant. Around 60 percent of the participants are married, 20 percent are separated, and 20 percent are single.

Question three asked how many people lived in their household. Around 40 percent live in a household comprised of four persons, 40 percent share a household of three persons, and 20 percent live in a household comprised of two persons.

Question four asked if they owned or rented their homes. Around 80 percent of the participants rent their homes and 20 percent own their homes.

Question five asked their annual family income. Around 40 percent of the participants have an annual household income ranging from $20,000 to $30,000, 20 percent have a household income ranging from $30,000 to $40,000, 20 percent have a household income ranging from $40,000 to $50,000, and 20 percent have a household income over $100,000.

Question six asked if they or any family member had ever been a victim of physical, sexual, or emotional abuse. I included an explanation of emotional abuse for clarity. Around 80 percent reported that either they or a family member has been a victim of abuse. Around 20 percent reported that neither they nor a family member had been a victim of abuse.

Question seven asked if the answer to six was "yes" that the kind of abuse be identified. They were also given the option to add a type of abuse not named. Around 80 percent reported physical, sexual, and emotional abuse and 20 percent reported no abuse.

Question eight asked them to identify their relationship with the abused person(s) in their family. The options were self, mother, grandmother, aunt, sister, cousins, sister-in-law, and daughter-in-law. Around 40 percent identified themselves as the abused person, 20 percent identified themselves and their mother as abused persons, and 20 percent identified themselves, mother, aunt, and cousins. The remaining 20 percent reported no abuse at all.

Question nine asked if they or a family member were currently in an abusive relationship. Around 40 percent answered "yes," 40 percent answered "no," and 20 percent reported no abuse.

Question ten asked if the answer to nine was "yes" that the relationship to that person be identified. The options were self, mother, grandmother, aunt, sister, cousins, sister-in-law, and daughter-in-law. All, 100 percent of those who answered "yes," identified themselves as the person who is currently in an abusive relationship.

Question eleven asked their thought concerning women talking about their abuse.

The following responses were given.

I think by talking about the abuse I will begin the process of healing. Women of color are not open to sharing information about their past, worried [sic] that they will be judged.

My thoughts concerning women talking about their abuse has changed. It used to bother me. It made me very angry. Now I know that women need to talk about their abuse to help them overcome pain.

Needs to be discussed so you can help others in that situation.

Women are afraid to share their thoughts of abuse because of the other person they are confiding in. Talking about the abuse would help if you realize you need help.

I feel that it is necessary for them to talk about their abuse. It will help relieve pressure, inner secrets, and start to feel comfort in knowing someone could listen and not judge.

Question twelve asked what the response of the ministry context has been concerning violence against women. The answers were:

No response.

Meeting together to try to understand silence will help, but the congregation will never really understand it until it has been spelled out.

It is not really talked about, but there are certain people you can speak to.

Paradise Baptist Church will help women in need of help. Their response will make sure that care is provided if the women would talk.

Honestly, I'm not sure. For me, women's Bible study on Monday nights. The retreat has helped me realize that I'm not alone, and I can open up to my sisters in Christ. Maybe help someone along the way.

Question thirteen asked if the ministry context had provided a safe and confidential environment for reporting incidents of violence and abuse. They were asked to explain the answer.

Yes, to Sister James.

As far as my case, I knew I had to tell someone who would listen. When I told Sis. James she made me feel safe and I never heard it from anyone in the church.

Yes (No explanation).

I am not sure because I have not heard of any abuse, but our pastor assures the congregation of confidentiality.

Yes. The only one I see is Rev. James (Kim).

Question fourteen asked if they were victims of violence and abuse if they would tell anyone. They were asked to explain the answer. All, 100 percent, answered "yes," with the following explanations.

Yes. (No explanation)

Yes. (No explanation)

Yes. I feel my silence is not helping me heal. I would rather try to share when necessary to help another individual cope with their problem.

Yes. My story may help someone else to let them know that they are not alone.

Yes. I was and I did after a while receive some treatment. I still find myself needing extended help.

Question fifteen asked if the ministry context has provided information on mental health, legal, and/or social services available to female victims of violence and abuse. They were asked to explain their answer.

Yes. I assume that when and if the time comes the pastor and his wife will do all they could do to help.

No. Not that I am aware of.

No. I have not noticed any literature but know of members within the congregation, if necessary.

No. (No explanation)

No.

Question sixteen asked if they had ever used services available to victims of abuse. They could select more than one of the services. The choices were medical and mental health services, domestic violence agencies, legal or lawyer referral services, other social service agencies, psychological counseling or psychiatric therapy. Around 40 percent indicated no services; 20 percent indicated medical/health services, psychological counseling, and psychiatric therapy; 20 percent indicated psychological counseling; and 20 percent indicated medical/health services.

Question seventeen asked them to express their thoughts concerning sympathy for victims of violence and abuse.

I feel sometimes that I wish I had run from my abuser so that I wouldn't have to feel the pain and sympathy for other victims. I want to help them by listening so I could understand my pain and how I could go on and help myself.

Sympathy is needed. Everyone at some point and time needs a concerned listening ear. But most of all compassion and understanding is needed.

My thoughts concerning sympathy for victims of violence and abuse . . . it can be painful for me to know about the victims' abuse, but I know that the victims can get better with the right steps to healing.

Since being involved, we can help victims by sharing our experience and give suggestions.

As a mother, I worry about my children. You can't always shelter your children. The pain was so intense for me. I wouldn't want my children or someone I love to go through that. After this program, I'm hoping to reach out to my sister and first cousin who also have been abused physically and sexually.

Question eighteen asked how they felt women at the ministry context could help each other as victims of an abusive relationship.

First, have an open mind. Don't judge. Don't get all in the business of why you did that. Listen to the person. Let them talk. Then tell your story. Do not ridicule the person. Always greet your sister with a hug. It goes a long way.

By having a listening ear and concern for another.

By being more sympathetic and listening to each other's pain and making safe for them to share . . . can't tell their business to anyone. Don't point the finger.

We can help victims by sharing our experience and give suggestions.

First being honest and not judge one another. It's hard to help when you don't understand, know, or even see the big picture.

Question nineteen asked how they felt the congregation could help victims of an abusive relationship.

We have members within our congregation that have gone to classes I believe to help with people who need guidance. They can help by counseling.

By having an outreach ministry available to anyone who needs it.

We can be a support system with listening and guidance and praying.

By keeping the victims safe and secure and provide what they need or lead them to where they can get help.

Stand together and pray together. As we stand together the congregation will stay together.

Question twenty asked for additional comments and suggestions.

I'm excited about this process. I'm blessed that Sister James thought it is not robbery to ask me to be a part of this. I'm honored and overwhelmed. I feel in my spirit that now I can reach out to my first cousin and only sister who are crying out to me daily, but don't want to expand [sic] their hand for me to help them. So I can share what God has done for me through this ordeal.

Provide pamphlets for abuse and hotline numbers or safe place for victims to go if needed.

No response.

No response.

Paradise Baptist Church does not need to be spoon-fed information any longer. I feel things need to be said straight out so that they know this abuse is serious (see appendix C).

Post-test Survey Results

The post-test survey was given with the following results. The purpose of the post-test was to observe and evaluate changes that may or may not have occurred as a result of the implementation of the project.

Question one asked the age of the participants. The age ranges remained the same.

Question two asked the marital status of the participants. The data remained the same.

Question three asked how many people lived in their household.

Participant B increased household size from three to four. Participant D increased household size from four to five. The other participants remained the same.

Question four asked if they owned, rented, or lived with a family member. The information remained the same.

Question five asked their annual family income. This data remained the same with the exception of the 20 percent, which had an income in the range of $20,000 to $30,000 decreased to $10,000 to $20,000.

Question six asked if they or any family member had ever been a victim of physical, sexual, or emotional abuse. The writer included an explanation of emotional abuse for clarity. This is increased by 20 percent with 100 percent indicating that they or a family member had experienced abuse.

Question seven asked if the answer to six was "yes" that the kind of abuse be identified. They were also given the option to add a type of abuse not named.

Around 80 percent reported physical, sexual, and emotional abuse and 20 percent reported physical and emotional abuse. The physical, sexual, and emotional abuse category remained the same. The category of no abuse indicated physical and emotional abuse in the post-test.

Question eight asked them to identify their relationship with the abused person(s) in their family. The options were self, mother, grandmother, aunt, sister, cousins, sister-in-law, and daughter-in-law. Around 40 percent identified themselves as the abused person, 20 percent identified themselves and their mother as abused persons, and 20 percent identified themselves, mother, aunt, and cousins. The 20 percent that reported no abuse in the post-test changed to self, mother, sister, and sister-in-law.

Question nine asked if they or a family member were currently in an abusive relationship. Around 80 percent answered "no" and 20 percent answered "yes." Those who answered "no" increased by 40 percent from the pretest results.

Question ten asked if the answer to nine was "yes" that the relationship to that person be identified. The options were self, mother, grandmother, aunt, sister, cousins, sister-in-law, and daughter-in-law. The 20 percent who answered "yes" indicated cousins as victims of abuse.

Question eleven asked their thought concerning women talking about their abuse.

I think that it helps to discuss, it helps to vent out so that the process of healing is successful.

It is not really talked about, but it is getting better.

My thoughts today are the pain women go through when sharing about their abuse.

Women who talk about their abuse would be able to heal. Talking to another person who has been through an abusive relationship could help them heal or move on to getting help that is needed. Talking or speaking out today about abuse is key to getting women to talk about abuse that they may not even be aware of is happening to them.

Talking about abuse will start the healing, but it would have to be someone who can help not someone who is nosy and like to run their mouth.

Question twelve asked what the response of the ministry context has been concerning violence against women.

In the beginning of the project response was not well, but because of it women and men are starting to be more open and understanding.

Paradise Baptist Church has and will extend their self to any woman who is willing to ask for help and support. They will also help in spiritual counseling.

They had a workshop open to women at our church giving positive outlooks on things that can be helpful if you are in an abusive relationship.

Our Pastor and First Lady, Rev. James, have shown concern to women in our church by openly having a team of counselors come to our church to discuss violence and how to get help. They have also said they are available when needed.

An overwhelming response.

Question thirteen asked if the ministry context had provided a safe and confidential environment for reporting incidents of violence and abuse. They were asked to explain the answer.

No. Somewhat, we don't really have the space.

Yes, Rev. Kim James has been very supportive in the confidentiality of our discussions.

I'm not sure if there is a specific place at the church where you can go.

Yes (No explanation). Yes. People are feeling more comfortable to say something.

Question fourteen asked if they were victims of violence and abuse if they would tell anyone. They were asked to explain the answer.

Yes. (No explanation)

Yes. Today, I would be able to share my experience of abuse.

Yes. Now I will 'cause I realize there is help out there. I didn't know that before.

Yes. I would openly explain my abuse when necessary for example, to a victim to help them with their silence.

No. (No explanation)

Question fifteen asked if the ministry context has provided information on mental health, legal, and/or social services available to female victims of violence and abuse. They were asked to explain their answer.

Yes. Through a workshop that Rev. Kim James developed.

Yes. (No explanation)

Yes. (No explanation)

Yes. (No explanation)

Yes. With the workshop that was given.

Question sixteen asked if they had ever used services available to victims of abuse. They could select more than one of the services. The choices were medical and mental health services, domestic violence agencies, legal or lawyer referral services, other social service agencies, psychological counseling or psychiatric therapy.

Around 60 percent indicated psychological counseling, which was a 20 percent increase from the pretest; 20 percent indicated medical/health services, other social service agencies, and psychological counseling; and 20 percent indicated no services.

Question seventeen asked them to express their thoughts concerning sympathy for victims of violence and abuse.

I was once a victim so I have sympathy for all people who are abused. I think it's a shame that you have to carry around such pain on your heart like that.

I would like to encourage them of the help that is available to them. It's hard to open up to anybody at first telling about your abuse. Victims would have to try trusting that one friend to confide into help break their silence. Telling someone you can trust is always the hardest.

Some women have a tendency to look down on other women. I think it is very important to be concerned about each other and have a heart to care.

I think now since the congregation has been informed more people have gotten an understanding of how domestic violence affects a person and attitudes have changed so people tend to be more sympathetic.

My thoughts today concerning sympathy for victims of violence and their pain and brokenness and discomfort for any woman who has been where I was and need healing.

Question eighteen asked how they felt women at the ministry context could help each other as victims of an abusive relationship.

Women at Paradise Baptist Church should have more empathy and compassion concerning an abused woman, but I realize if you never experienced it yourself you wouldn't understand, and also anonymity is very helpful until a person is ready to be exposed.

Women at Paradise can help by sharing their love for their sister. A "good morning" would do. An acknowledgment of how good it is to see ya[sic] or just "I love you and there is absolutely nothing you can do about it." Women at Paradise don't need to get in a private discussion, but if I see someone who needs help I would inform them to seek help.

Providing private workshops, counseling, and reading the Bible. You'd be surprised that there are a lot of women in the Bible that have been abused. This is not something that happened overnight. It's been going on for decades.

Women are starting to open up and the shame is starting to be lifted so they can feel more comfortable sharing what has happened or is happening to them. They don't feel so alone anymore.

By showing real love and concern about one another and stop dealing with petty things that take up valuable time. Get rid of our self-centered motives and sometimes just think about helping another sister.

Question nineteen asked how they felt the congregation could help victims of an abusive relationship.

By having a ministry or support group that would be able to assist in any way they can. They must be trained for it. Not a group that just wants to be in the know of everything.

By being supportive, not judgmental.

Talking to other couples who may or may not have been in abusive relationships and survived after all this time.

Provide services that can assist victims when necessary. Literature, counseling, support groups, or even just a special prayer request.

The congregation can help by anonymity and by being supportive, provide the information they need.

Question twenty asked for additional comments and suggestions.

No response.

No response.

I'm glad, I opened up. I'm a mother of a little girl. I'm very cautious about who I leave her with at any given time. I even talk to my boys too . . . talking to them, telling them to come and talk to me. Observe your children, if they start acting strange, check things out!

No response.

Flyers, posters, or anything that could direct victims of abuse to get help should be posted at all times (see appendix E).

Interviews and Narratives

For the purpose of clarity and continuity, I placed the narrative and interview of each participant together; the interview preceding the narrative (see appendix Q). This allowed me to more readily evaluate the results. The analysis involved the observation of language and behavior during the process of telling. After examining pre and post-test survey, interviews, and narratives of each participant, I looked for threads in use of language that may be common or uncommon among the participants. Chapter six indicates how 80 percent of the women who participated in the research broke their silence concerning abuse.

Chapter Six

Reflection, Summary, and Conclusions

Summary of Research Project

The results of the project were both educational and transformational. The context associates through sharing their experiences provided valuable information, which was instrumental in learning how female victim-survivors of abuse break their silence.

The Collaborative

The participants, social service professionals, and law enforcement were cooperative in sharing information essential to the process. Aside from the pastor of the ministry context, I was unable to engage pastors in the community. Of the fifty-four male pastors of churches who were invited to attend the clergy workshop none of the pastors responded or participated in the Community Awareness Day.

The Interviews and Narratives

Each context associate was interviewed privately. The twelfth of the thirteen interview questions asked why they agreed to participate in the project. Approximately 50 percent of those who were abused indicated that they needed to be healed or helped. Approximately 50 percent stated that they felt abuse of women needed to be exposed. My analysis of these responses is that the participants associate talking about their abuse with healing and feel that exposing the problem will be beneficial. Participant D (see appendix), who said she needed help indicated that healing takes time and that it is a process. Participant C (see appendix), who said she needed healing, defined it as being able to speak freely and that telling the story is a part of the healing.

How the Silence was Broken

The initial breaking of silence began with my open discussion of the project during Sunday morning worship. Upon receiving both the approval and support of the pastor, I was able to make announcements concerning the themes of both the Women of Divine Destiny Conference and the Women's Fellowship and Summer Bible School which were, "I am Healed" and "Jesus: God's Gift to Women," respectively. I used my voice as a female leader in the church to stress the importance of ministry to the female victim-survivor of abuse.

The meetings with the focus group resulted in a climate of trust, but did not, initially appear to lead to any of them speaking publicly about their abuse. The focus was on their healing. Serving as a vehicle to open the door for dialogue in the ministry context concerning abuse of women, I allowed the process to determine how and if the silence would be broken by the participants.

The silence was initially broken during Lesson II of the Women's Fellowship and Summer Bible School (see appendix). As the evening ended, I asked if there was anyone present who needed to tell their story of abuse. They were asked if anyone as a result of the night's ministry felt free of the shame associated with their victimization. Participant C was the first to stand and take the microphone. She was followed by twenty women, each sharing stories of sexual, emotional, physical, and psychological abuse. Many had never publicly shared this information. The atmosphere in the sanctuary was emotionally overwhelming for all who were present. Yet, there was a sense of freedom and liberation. There were three male musicians present during this presentation who were visibly shaken by what they were hearing. There were a lot of tears, prayers, and hugging among all of the women.

I sensed that it was not an accident that the young men were present and used this as an opportunity to speak to them. They were advised to pay close attention to what they heard on that evening and to understand that their words and actions, if abusive, could potentially devastate the lives of women with whom they have relationships.

Four of the five context associates were present on this night and three spoke about their abuse. Participant B, one who indicated that she had not been abused, did not speak. The context associate who was not present on this evening was later asked to speak during the Community Awareness Day, which was held on October 27, 2007. She admitted that she was nervous, but agreed to do so. I felt she would be willing to do so due to her training as an addiction counselor and also felt that it was important for the workshop participants to hear from a victim-survivor. She indicated that she had told her story many times, but never in a church setting. She was concerned about using inappropriate language.

Her presentation held everyone's attention. The Awareness Day was open to both males and females ages twelve and older. She shared her life of abuse from early childhood to present. At the end of her presentation, a twelve-year-old girl, who is a member of the ministry context, walked up to her and gave her a long hug. It was a "picture that spoke a thousand words."

The day ended with questions and answers for the presenters who were a part of a panel. There was an eleven-year-old boy who was present and asked what he should do if he were physically abused. He was given information by the three panelists. Many of the women, who are members of the ministry context, were also present. Many asked questions to the panelists. The result of this was that several weeks later a member of the context congregation asked for an appointment to speak with me concerning her abuse. In addition, as a result of the project the ministry context has been asked by a representative of the Essex County Prosecutor's Office Victim Witness Unit, to consider how the context may become as an outreach site. The purpose of the site would be to provide a safe space for victims to obtain information and referrals for services.

How the Participants Inform and Protect Their Children

All of the participants indicated the importance of educating and protecting their children from abuse. Each participant, with the exception of Participant B, has told their children about their abuse. Participant B only recently understood that she has been affected by the abuse of her mother, sister, and sister-in-law.

Healing and Pastoral Care and Counseling

All of the participants stress the importance of healing using the words and terms; "it's a process," "stronger," "better," "coming to grips," "rising above it," and talking freely. They each indicate pastoral care and counseling involves speaking freely with assurance that someone cares, that discussions will be confidential and direction will be received.

Education and Transformation

I gained a considerable amount of knowledge as I reviewed literature concerning the phenomenon of silence among women as well as the importance of women mentoring women. The historical, biblical, and theological aspects of violence against women provided insight as to the roots of violence against women and the foresight concerning the need for women to break the silence.

The result of this model is that it began with one person who was willing to speak. I feel that the project presented the church community with the opportunity to dialogue. I participated as an educator and a learner; an educator by providing information and a learner by hearing the voices of the experts in the field and abused women in the context.

In order for one to be heard there must be someone who is willing to listen. I positioned myself as a listener and as a result have been transformed. I have become more sensitive to the challenges that abused women face as well as the lack of services that are provided by the Black church.

The focus group was also educated and transformed. Four of the five context associates; those who indicated that they were abused at the beginning of the process describe their feelings at the end as "freer", "sense of kinship", "feels good not to be judged," "peace," "it wasn't my fault," "stronger," "I'm gonna be all right," "my story is out there," "I told it and I can move on" (see appendix Q).

Participant A agreed to participate in the project, but doubted how she would be able to contribute to the group. She did not have difficulty speaking about her abuse with me but was challenged by writing her narrative. Despite her having left the ministry context to join another church, she committed herself to complete the interview, narrative, post-test survey, and to attend the Violence Against Women Community Awareness Day. She continues to visit the church on occasion. When questioned as to why she chose to leave she stated that she needed to learn how to engage in spiritual warfare. The data presented in Participant A's interview, narrative and post-test survey suggests that she feels a sense of freedom as a result of sharing her story. Her transformation as a result of breaking the silence indicates moving from bondage to freedom.

One of the more poignant transformational experiences was that of Participant B, who, at the beginning of the process, stated that neither she nor any female member of her family had been abused. However, her post test survey indicated that she, her mother, sister, and sister-in-law had been victimized. I spoke with her by telephone during which time she expressed that she didn't realize that her mother was a victim of abuse because her mother physically defended herself when hit by her father. However, the teaching and ministry caused her to focus on all that her mother endured at which point she understood her mother's experience to be both physically and emotionally abusive. She spoke freely about her father's womanizing and that he had abandoned the family. He became ill in later years and her mother allowed him to come back to the home where she cared for him until his death. She never spoke of her sister's physical abuse, because she felt that since it didn't happen to her that it did not or should not affect her. My analysis is that the participant may have decided not to acknowledge this abuse due to the phenomenon of silence. It is a part of the culture of African American people to teach children not to discuss what happens in the home. Her sister's abuse occurred when the Participant B was very young and she was still maintaining the family silence. The participant indicates that her sister has never discussed being assaulted with a knife by her ex-husband.

Her response to the question asking if she were a victim of abuse if she would tell anyone was "no." That was unchanged from the beginning of the project to the end. Ironically, when asked what she gained from participation, she acknowledged that it helped her to "go deeper."

However, Participant B was so shaken by the thought of writing her story that she could not do it and had difficulty speaking with me. She spoke in code language and only opened up after it was brought to her attention. As I began to share the story of the abused women in my family Participant B spoke more freely. She expressed that they appeared to be a "good family," but no one knew what was going on behind the closed doors.

She expressed over and over again that what she was feeling was "so crazy" because it didn't happen to her. She kept asking, "Why do I feel like this? It didn't happen to me?" I explained the she had been victimized by her mother's abuse.

In essence, one woman's abuse is every woman's abuse. Women who have not been victims of abuse may very well be traumatized by the abuse of a loved one. Witnessing the abuse of another can be a form of victimization.

Participant C, despite her willingness to participate, was somewhat sketchy with the details of her abuse. However, as the project progressed she emerged as a leader. She volunteered to obtain information, pamphlets, and booklets to be included in the folders for the Violence Against Women Community Awareness Day. She has also been vocal in her workplace concerning violence against women and has assisted a coworker with obtaining a temporary restraining order against her abuser. Participant C states that she feels a sense of peace after having broken her silence. The data presented in Participant C's interview, narrative, post-test survey as well as my observations suggest that she has moved from silence to advocacy.

Participant D expressed eagerness to participate in the project. She initially told of being raped as a young child, but did not tell about being abused by her step-grandfather until she wrote her personal narrative. The narrative was instrumental in breaking her silence. When interviewed, she described herself as feeling broken up, dirty, and disgusted about what happened to her. However, at the end of the project, she says that she realizes that she was a victim, it wasn't her fault and she feels stronger. The data suggest that Participant D, as a result of breaking her silence has gained strength and hope.

Participant E, having completed alcohol and drug rehabilitation as well as having been trained as an addictions counselor, describers herself in the personal interview as "still nuts." She agreed to participate in the project but often exhibited the "been there, done that" attitude. She was present at meetings but sometimes seemed disinterested or bored. During the course of the implementation of the project, Participant E shared fears and present circumstances that challenged her. She realized that she had not "been there and done that."

Participant E was asked to participate as a facilitator at the Violence Against Women Community Awareness Day. She agreed to do so and was well received. She acknowledged her personal challenges and has taken the necessary measure to confront the issues. Participant E came into the process feeling that she had done all of the work needed for healing. However, after the implementation of the project, she realized that healing is a continual process. The data presented in Participant E's post-test survey and personal narrative indicates that continued care is needed. As a result of sharing her story, which included information about present day challenges, Participant E has moved from denial to realistic optimism.

There was a noticeable reticence to write the personal narratives. However, the writing was a significant tool in breaking her silence as the participants wrote in language that was not easily spoken.

The overall result is that, based upon the responses of the participants, they have been empowered by their participation in the project. They indicate, in their responses that they have gained strength and are interested in reaching out to other women. They were asked if they would consider further study that would equip and train them as Christian counselors. One of the participants is no longer a member of the congregation. Therefore, I have not had the opportunity to speak with her. The remaining four participants expressed interest in further training.

Suggested Changes

It is suggested that clergy be contacted earlier in the process. This may provide the researcher with a larger time frame within which to work toward gaining their support. Additionally, the researcher may ask to present a workshop at a clergy group event or regularly scheduled meeting. It may also be beneficial to speak with pastors and/or their staff directly in addition to sending letters of invitation for a workshop.

Modified Research Project

I would include journaling as a part of the process, which may be easier for participants than writing narratives. Most of the participants seemed challenged with the narrative. Journaling may indicate more of an expression of feeling, which is not focused on accuracy.

Recommendations for Further Research

I recommend the following:

- Examination of the effect that abuse of women has on lives of all women whether or not they see themselves as victims or victim-survivors. Considering that Participant B did not initially identify herself as a victim but may have ended the process feeling less than whole, presents the need for further work in this area.
- Research that examines how abuse effect the lives of children of victims.
- Examination as to how male and female members of the church define abuse. This may open dialogue between men and women in the congregation concerning abuse. These conversations may explore how the church, which is comprised of men, women, and children, can collaborate to eliminate victimization.
- Research that addresses methods that will engage pastors and clergy persons in this area of ministry.

Appendix A

Power and Control Wheel

Developed By and used by Permission of the Domestic Violence Intervention Project

202 E. Superior Street

Duluth, MN 55802

218-722-2781—*www.duluth-model.org*

Appendix B

Five Kinds of Abuse

Table I

Sexual Abuse	A perversion of "one flesh"	Genesis 2:24
Physical Abuse	A perversion of "let them rule"	Genesis 1:26
Neglect abuse	A perversion of "cultivate the ground"	Genesis 2:5
Spiritual Abuse	A perversion of "image"	Genesis 1:26
Verbal Abuse	A perversion of "be fruitful"	Genesis 1:28[347]

Table II

Image	Scripture Reading
A Mother who gave birth to the world	Psalm 90:2
The one who bore and nursed Israel	Numbers 11:12, Deuteronomy 32:18
A Mother comforts her child	Psalm 131:2
A nursing Mother who has compassion	Isaiah 49:15
A Mother who tenderly feeds her child	1 Peter 2:2-3
A Mother who protects her cubs	Hosea 13:8
A hen that shields her chicks under her wings	Luke 13:34[348]

---

[347] Stephen R. Tracy, *Mending the Soul* (Grand Rapids, MI: Zondervan, 2005), 27.
[348] Ibid., 169.

Appendix C

Paradise Baptist Church
Newark, New Jersey
March 2007
Pre-test Survey Questions
Confidential Survey—Female Participants

Please be advised, this survey is completely confidential. All data collected will be used anonymously. In order to preserve your anonymity, do not place your name anywhere on this survey. **Instructions**: Please answer each question. Place a check in the answer that applies to you. Explain your answer where applicable. Please *print* or write *clearly*. Thank you for taking the time to complete this survey that may serve as a model for congregations nationwide.

1. What is your age?

    a. Fourteen-eighteen years old ☐
    b. Nineteen-twenty-five years old ☐
    c. Twenty-six-thirty-five years old ☐
    d. Thirty-six-fifty years old ☐
    e. Fifty-sixty-two years old ☐
    f. Over sixty-two years old ☐

2. What is your marital status?

    a. Single ☐
    b. Married ☐
    c. Separated ☐
    d. Divorced ☐
    e. Widowed ☐

3. How many people currently live in your household?

    a. One (you live alone) ☐
    b. Two ☐
    c. Three ☐
    d. Four ☐

e. Five ☐
f. Six ☐
g. Seven ☐
h. Eight ☐
i. Nine ☐
j. Ten or more ☐

4. Do you own your own house or rent?

   a. Own ☐
   b. Rent ☐
   c. Live with a family member ☐

5. Annual Family Income

   a. Under $10,000 ☐
   b. $10,000 to $20,000 ☐
   c. $20,000 to $30,000 ☐
   d. $30,000 to $40,000 ☐
   e. $40,000 to $50,000 ☐
   f. $50,000 to $75,000 ☐
   g. $75,000 to $100,000 ☐
   h. Above $100,000 ☐
   i. No income ☐

6. Have you or any female member of your family ever been a victim of physical, sexual, or emotional abuse (i.e., verbal or psychological abuse)? "Emotional abuse may be defined as a controlling or abusive act that leaves an emotional scar."

   a. Yes ☐
   b. No ☐

7. If the answer to Question #6 was yes, what type of abuse?

   a. Physical abuse ☐
   b. Sexual abuse ☐
   c. Emotional abuse ☐
   d. Other type of abuse ☐

   _____
   Explain other type of abuse

8. If the answer to #6 was yes, identify the relationship of the abused person to yourself by checking the box below. You may check off all that apply.

   a. Self ☐
   b. Mother ☐
   c. Grandmother ☐
   d. Aunt ☐
   e. Sister ☐
   f. Cousins ☐
   g. Sister-in-law ☐
   h. Daughter-in-law ☐

9. Are you or a family member currently in an abusive relationship?

   a. Yes ☐
   b. No ☐

10. If the answer to #9 was yes, identify the person's relationship to you by checking the box below. You may check off all that apply.

    a. Self ☐
    b. Mother ☐
    c. Grandmother ☐
    d. Aunt ☐
    e. Sister ☐
    f. Cousins ☐
    g. Sister-in-law ☐
    h. Daughter-in-law ☐

11. What are your thoughts concerning women talking about their abuse?

12. What has been the response of Paradise Baptist Church to violence against women?

13. Has Paradise Baptist Church provided a safe and confidential environment for reporting incidents of violence and abuse? Explain your answer.

    a. Yes ☐
    b. No ☐

14. If you were a victim of violence and abuse would you tell anyone? Explain your answer.

   a. Yes   ☐
   b. No   ☐

15. Has Paradise Baptist Church provided adequate information on mental health, legal, and/or social services available to female victims of violence and abuse? Explain your answer.

   a. Yes   ☐
   b. No   ☐

16. Have you ever used any of the following services as a victim of abuse?
    Yes _____ No _____ Please check all that apply.

   a. Medical and/or health services   ☐
   b. Domestic Violence agency   ☐
   c. Legal or lawyer referral services   ☐
   d. Other social services agency   ☐
   e. Psychological Counseling   ☐
   f. Psychiatric Therapy (Medical Doctor)   ☐

17. What are your thoughts concerning sympathy for victims of violence and abuse?

18. How do you feel women at Paradise Baptist Church can help each other as victims of violence and abuse?

19. How do you feel the congregation at Paradise Baptist Church can help victims of violence and abuse?

20. Additional Comments. If you have any additional comments or suggestions, please feel free to write them below.

Pre-Test Survey Responses

Question	Participant A	Participant B	Participant C	Participant D	Participant E
1. What is your age?	36-50	50-62	36-50	36-50	36-50
2. What is your marital status?	Separated.	Married.	Married.	Single.	Married.
3. How many people currently live in your household?	2	3	4	4	3
4. Do you own your own house or rent?	Rent.	Own.	Rent.	Rent.	Rent.
5. What is the annual family income?	$20,000-$30,000	$30,000-$40,000	Above $100,000	$40,000-$50,000	$20,000-$30,000
6. Have you or any female member of your family ever been a victim of physical, sexual, or emotional abuse?	Yes.	No.	Yes.	Yes.	Yes.
7. If the answer to question #6 was yes, what type of abuse?	Physical Abuse, Sexual Abuse, Emotional Abuse.	N/A	Physical Abuse, Sexual Abuse, Emotional Abuse, Psychological Abuse.	Physical Abuse, Sexual Abuse, Emotional Abuse.	Physical Abuse, Sexual Abuse, Emotional Abuse.
8. If abuse was indicated in #7, identify the relationship of the abused person to yourself.	Self.	N/A	Self, Mother, Aunt, and cousins.	Self.	Self and Mother

Question	Participant A	Participant B	Participant C	Participant D	Participant E
9. Are you or a family member currently in an abusive relationship?	No.	N/A	No.	Yes.	Yes.
10. If the answer to #9 was yes, identify the person's relationship to you.	N/A	N/A	N/A	Self.	Self.
11. What are your thoughts concerning women talking about their abuse?	My thoughts concerning women talking about their abuse has changed. It used to bother me and made me angry. Now I know that women need to talk about their abuse to help them overcome pain.	I feel that it is necessary for them to talk about their abuse. It will relieve pressure, inner secrets, and start to feel comfort in knowing someone could listen and not judge.	Women are afraid to share their thoughts of abuse because of the other person . . . confidentiality. Talking about the abuse would help if you realize you need help.	I think by talking about the abuse will begin the process of healing. Women of color are not open to sharing information about their past, worried they will be judged.	Needs to be discussed so you can help others in that situation.
12. What has been the response of the Paradise Baptist Church to violence against women?	Paradise Baptist Church will help women in need of help. Their response will make sure there is care if women will talk.	No response.	The congregation will never really understand until it has been spelled out.	Honestly I'm not sure. For me Women's Bible Study on Monday Nights and the Retreat (2006) have helped me realize that I'm not alone and I can open up to my sisters in Christ and maybe help someone along the way.	It's not really talked about, but there are certain people you can speak to.

Question	Participant A	Participant B	Participant C	Participant D	Participant E
13. Has Paradise Baptist Church provided safe and confidential environment for reporting incidents of violence and abuse? Explain your answer.	Yes. As far as my case I knew I had to tell someone who would listen. When I told Sis. James she made me feel safe and I never heard it from anyone in the church.	Yes. The only one I see is Rev. James (Kim).	Yes. I am not sure because I have not heard of any abuse, but our pastor assures the congregation of confidentiality.	Yes. Through Sis. James.	Yes.
14. If you were a victim of violence and abuse would you tell anyone? Explain your answer.	Yes. My story may help someone else to let them know that they are not alone.	Yes.	Yes. I feel my silence is not helping me heal. I would rather try to share when necessary to help another individual cope with their problem.	Yes. I was and I did after a while and I did receive some treatment but still find myself needing extended help.	Yes.
15. Has Paradise Baptist Church provided adequate information on mental health, legal, and/or social services available to female victims of violence and abuse? Explain your answer.	No. Not that I am aware of.	No.	No. I have not noticed any literature but know of members within the congregation, if necessary.	Yes. I will assume that if the time came the pastor and his wife will do all they can do to help.	No.

Question	Participant A	Participant B	Participant C	Participant D	Participant E
16. Have you ever used any of the following services as a victim of abuse? Medical and/or health services, Domestic Violence Agency, Legal or lawyer referral services, other social service agency, Psychological Counseling, Psychiatric Therapy (Medical Doctor).	Psychological Counseling.	N/A	No.	Medical and/or health services.	Yes. Medical and/or health services, Psychological Counseling, and Psychiatric Therapy.
17. What are your thoughts concerning sympathy for victims of violence and abuse?	My thoughts concerning sympathy for victims of violence and abuse is it can be painful for me to know about the victims of abuse, but I know that the victims can get better with the right steps for healing.	Sympathy is needed. Everyone at some point and time needs a concerned listening ear. But most of all, compassion and understanding is needed.	I feel sometimes that I wish I had run from my abuser so that I wouldn't have to feel the pain and sympathy for other victims. I want to help them by listening so I could understand my pain and how I could go on and help myself.	As a mother I worry about my children. You can't always shelter your children. The pain was so intense for me. I wouldn't want my children or someone I love to go through that. After this program I'm hoping to reach out to my sister and first cousin who also have been abused physically and sexually.	Not that great. People just feel you should be able to stop and get out of the situation.

Question	Participant A	Participant B	Participant C	Participant D	Participant E
18. How do you feel women at Paradise Baptist Church can help each other as victims of an abusive relationship?	We can help individuals by sharing our experience and give suggestions.	By having a listening ear and concern for one another.	First, have an open mind. Don't judge. Don't get all in the business of why you did that. Listen to the person. Let them talk. Then tell your story. Do not ridicule the person. Always greet your sister with a hug. It goes a long way.	First, being honest and not judge one another. It's hard to help when you don't understand, know or even see the big picture!	Since being involved we can help victims by sharing our experience and give suggestions.
19. How do you feel the congregation at Paradise Baptist Church can help victims of an abusive relationship?	By keeping the victims safe and secure and provide what they need or lead them to where they can get help.	By having an outreach ministry available to anyone who needs it.	We have members within our congregation who have gone to classes. I believe to help with people who need guidance. They can help by counseling.	Stand together and pray together. As we stand together the congregation will stay together.	We can be a support system with listening and guidance, also praying.

Question	Participant A	Participant B	Participant C	Participant D	Participant E
20. Additional Comments. If you have any additional comments or suggestions, please feel free to write below.	Provide pamphlets for abuse and hotline numbers of safe place for victims to go, if needed.	No Comments.	Paradise Baptist Church does not need to spoon-feed information any longer. I feel things need to be said straight out so that they know this abuse is serious.	I'm excited about this process. I'm blessed that Sis. James thought it not robbery to ask me to be a part of this. I'm honored and overwhelmed. I feel in my spirit that now I can reach out	No comments.

Appendix D

Interview Questions

1. Prior to this interview have you ever discussed the detail of your abuse with others? If yes, why? If no, why not?

2. Why did you choose to tell your story?

4. How did you feel about telling or not telling your story?

5. When you read literature about violence against women how do you feel?

6. What do you think about sharing the story of your abuse with your children?

7. How do you feel children can be better protected from abuse?

8. How can the church serve as an instrument of healing for victim-survivors of abuse?

8. How do you define pastoral care and counseling?

9. If you had the opportunity to speak to your abuser(s) today what would you say?

10. How do you define healing?

11. How would you help to prevent other women and children from being abused?

12. Why did you agree to be a part of this project?

13. What, if anything, have you gained from your participation in this project?

Appendix E

Post-test Responses

Question	Participant A	Participant B	Participant C	Participant D	Participant E
1. What is your age?	36-50	50-62	36-50	36-50	36-50
2. What is your marital status?	Separated.	Married.	Married.	Single.	Married.
3. How many people currently live in your household?	2	4	3	5	3
4. Do you own your house or rent?	Rent.	Own.	Rent.	Rent.	Rent.
5. Annual Family Income?	$20,000-$30,000	$50,000-$75,000	Above $100,000	$40,000-$50,000	$10,000-$20,000
6. Have you or any female member of your family ever been a victim of physical, sexual, or emotional abuse?	Yes.	Yes.	Yes.	Yes.	Yes.
7. If the answer to #6 was yes, what type of abuse?	Physical abuse, sexual abuse, emotional abuse	Physical abuse, emotional abuse.	Physical abuse, sexual abuse, emotional abuse.	Physical abuse, sexual abuse, emotional abuse.	Physical abuse, sexual abuse, emotional abuse.
8. If the answer to #6 is yes, identify the person's relationship to you.	Self.	Self, Mother, Sister, Sister-in-law.	Self, Mother.	Self, Sister, cousins.	Self.
9. Are you or a family member currently in an abusive relationship?	No.	No.	No.	No.	No.
10. If the answer to #9 was yes, identify the person's relationship to you.	N/A	N/A	N/A	Cousins.	N/A

Question	Participant A	Participant B	Participant C	Participant D	Participant E
11. What are your thoughts concerning women talking about their abuse?	My thoughts today are the pain that women go through when sharing about their abuse.	Talking about the abuse will start the healing, but it would have to be someone who can help, not someone who is nosy and likes to run their mouth.	Women who talk about their abuse would be able to heal. Talking to another person who has been through an abusive relationship could help them heal or move on to getting help that is needed. Talking or speaking out today about abuse is key to getting women to talk about abuse that they may not even be aware of is happening to them.	I think it should be discussed. It helps to vent out so that the process of healing is successful.	It is not really talked about but it is getting better.

Question	Participant A	Participant B	Participant C	Participant D	Participant E
12. What has been the response of Paradise Baptist Church to violence against women?	Paradise Baptist Church has and will extend themselves to any woman who is willing to ask for the help and support. They will also help in spiritual counseling.	An overwhelming response.	Our pastor and first lady, Rev. James has shown concern to women in our church by openly having a team of counselors come to the church to discuss violence and how to get help. They have also said they are available for help when needed.	They had a workshop open to women in and out of our church giving positive outlooks on things that can be helpful if you are in an abusive relationship.	In the beginning, the project response was not well, but because of it women and men are starting to be more open and understanding.

Question	Participant A	Participant B	Participant C	Participant D	Participant E
13. Has Paradise Baptist Church provided a safe and confidential environment for reporting incidents of violence and abuse? Explain your answer.	Yes. Rev. Kim James has been very supportive in the confidentiality of our discussions.	No. Somewhat, we don't really have the space.	Yes.	I'm not sure if there is specific place in the church where you can go.	Yes. People are feeling more comfortable to say something.
14. If you were a victim of violence and abuse would you tell anyone? Explain your answer.	Yes. Today, I would be able to share my experience of abuse.	No.	Yes. I would openly explain my abuse when necessary, for example, to a victim to help with their silence.	Yes. Now I will 'cause I realize there is help out there. I didn't know that before.	Yes.
15. Has Paradise Baptist Church provided adequate information on mental health, legal, and/or social services available to female victims of violence and abuse? Explain your answer.	Yes.	Yes. Through a workshop that Rev. Kim James developed.	Yes.	Yes.	Yes. Through a work shop that was given, all information was given.
16. Have you ever used any of the following services as a victim of abuse? Medical and/or health services, domestic violence agency, legal or lawyer referral services, other social service agency, psychological counseling, psychiatric therapy.	Psychological counseling.	No.	Psychological counseling.	Psychological counseling.	Medical and/or health services, other social service agency, psychological counseling.

Question	Participant A	Participant B	Participant C	Participant D	Participant E
17. What are your thoughts concerning sympathy for victims of violence and abuse?	My thoughts today concerning sympathy for victims of violence and abuse is their pain and brokenness and discomfort for any woman who has been where I was and need healing.	Some women have tendency to look down on other women. I think it is very important to be concerned about each other and have a heart to care.	I would like to encourage them of the help that is available to them. It's hard to open up to anybody at first, telling them about your abuse. Victims would have to try trusting that one friend to confide in to help break their silence. Telling someone you can trust is always the hardest.	I was once a victim so I have sympathy for all people who are abused. I think that it's a shame that people have to carry around such pain on your heart like that.	I think now since the congregation, has been informed more people have gotten an understanding and how domestic violence affects a person and attitudes have changed. So people tend to be more sympathetic.
18. How do you feel women at Paradise Baptist Church can help each other as victims of an abusive relationship?	Women at Paradise should have more empathy and compassion concerning an abused woman. But I realize that if you never experienced it yourself you wouldn't understand and also anonymity is very helpful until the person is ready to be exposed.	By showing real love and concern about one another and stop dealing with petty things that take up valuable time. Get rid of our self-centered motives and sometimes just think about helping a Sister.	Women at Paradise can help by showing their love for their sister. A "good morning" would do. An acknowledgment of how good it is to see you or just "I love you and there is absolutely nothing you can do about it." Women at Paradise don't need to get in a private discussion, but if I see someone who needs help I would inform them to seek help.	Providing private workshops, counseling, and reading the Bible. You'd be surprised that there are a lot of women in the Bible that have been abused. This is not something that has happened overnight. It has been going on for decades.	Women are starting to open up and the shame is starting to be lifted, so they feel more comfortable sharing what has happened or is happening to them. They don't feel so alone anymore.

Question	Participant A	Participant B	Participant C	Participant D	Participant E
19. How do you feel the congregation at Paradise Baptist Church can help victims of an abusive relationship?	The congregation can help by anonymity and by being supportive. Provide information that they need.	By having a ministry or support group that would be able to assist in any way they can. They must be trained for it. Not a group that just wants to be in the know of everything.	Provide services that can assist victims when necessary. Literature, counseling, support groups, or even just a special prayer request.	Talking to other couples who may or may not have been in abusive relationships and survived after all this time.	By being supportive, not judgmental.
20. Additional Comments.	No Comments.	Flyers, posters, or anything that could direct a victim of abuse to get help should be posted at all times.	No Comments.	I'm glad I opened up. I'm a Mother of a little girl and I'm very cautious about who I leave her with at any given time. I even talk to my boys too, telling them to come and talk to me. Observe your children. If they start acting strange check things out!	No Comments.

Appendix F

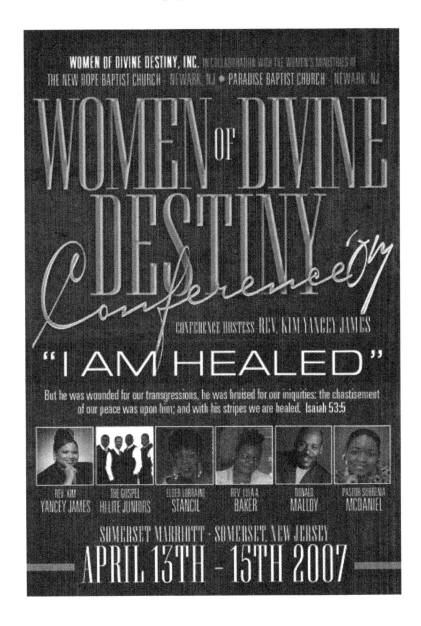

Appendix G

Women's Fellowship and Summer Bible School

Paradise Baptist Church
348-352 Fifteenth Avenue
Newark, New Jersey 07103
Rev. Dr. Jethro C. James Jr., Pastor
(973) 624-6614

Please Join Us For Our
Ninth Annual Women's Fellowship
and
Summer Bible School

Classes will be held on Monday nights from 7:00 p.m.-9:00 p.m.
June 18, 2007-July 23, 2007

Registration night service will be held on Monday, June 11 at 7:00 p.m.

Theme: "Jesus: God's Gift to Women."
This year's donation will be $25 per person, which covers all six classes,
Materials and a light snack every night!

Our graduation service will be held on Friday, August 3 at 7:30 p.m. at the
Paradise Baptist Church.

We will end the summer with a graduation celebration aboard the Spirit of
New Jersey Cruise for a Gospel Cruise Luncheon!

Facilitator: Rev. Kim Yancey James—Executive Minister/Director of
Women's Ministries

Appendix G

Women's Fellowship and Summer Bible School @Paradise Baptist Church, Newark, NJ—Rev. Dr. Jethro C. James Jr., Pastor

Monday, July 18, 2007

Jesus' Relationships with Women
A Brief Overview of Jesus' Relationships with Women in the Bible

Rev. Kim Yancey James, M. Div. Facilitator

As we approach the study of the encounters and relationships that Jesus had with women it is important that we examine the historical and social setting, which serves as a backdrop for these life changing experiences. An understanding of the times in which these women lived will help in our appreciation of the positive, radical, and even revolutionary attitude that Jesus had toward women.[349]

Most modern day women would find the life of the ancient Hebrew woman to be totally unacceptable. The structure of the family was based upon the total and unquestionable authority of the father who ruled his wives and his children as his property.[350] He had the authority to sell his daughters as slaves, have disobedient children killed, divorce his wife at will and was not required to support her. The wife, on the other hand, could not leave her husband because she was his property as were the sheep and the goats. Women were not able to inherit property and thus the widow was often also poor.[351]

So as not to paint a picture that is totally bleak, it is important to note that both mother and father were honored and respected by their children. Women also participated in the feasts and celebrations.[352] They were leaders (Deborah) and prophetesses (Miriam, Isaiah's wife, Huldah, Anna) who, created in the image of God, were anointed and empowered to serve. Esther Fuchs argues that the "subservience of women to men is a social construct. It neither reflects historical reality, nor is it an immutable law of human

---

[349] Esther Fuchs, "Moses /Jesus/ Women: Does the New Testament Offer a Feminist Message," *Cross Currents*, Winter 1999, 463 [database on-line]; available from Questia, http://www.questia.com/PM.qst?a=o&d=5001865837; Internet; accessed 24 November 2007.

[350] E. W. Heaton, *Everyday Life in Old Testament Times* (New York: Charles Scribner's Sons, 1956), 69.

[351] Ibid.

[352] Ibid.

nature."³⁵³ In essence, the subordination of women to men has been socially constructed and maintained as means to under gird systems of oppression, which promote the power of one group over another. Where there is power there is always the potential to abuse the same, which is often tantamount to abuse of persons. Thus, the women that Jesus encountered were likely to have experienced verbal, physical, emotional, and spiritual abuse as victims of a society, which denied the equality of women.

This may appear, on the surface, an excellent reason for women to be attracted to the Jesus movement. However, the only legal statement that Jesus makes, which is specific to women's issues, is that He speaks to banning divorce (Mark 10:2-12). Tal Ilan implies that one should not assume that Jesus' message would have appealed to women because of their state of oppression.³⁵⁴ I assert that Jesus' message to the downtrodden, hurting, and abused members of society, many of whom were women, serves as a word of hope for those who would have otherwise been hopeless.

Let us consider the following:

Matthew 5:3
Blessed are the poor in spirit: for theirs is the kingdom of heaven.³⁵⁵

> In His beatitudes, in His extraordinary concern for the outcasts and marginalized, in His wholly unconventional treatment of women (speaking to them in public, touching them, eating with them, even with harlots, above all, teaching them), in the seriousness with which He took children, in His rejection of the dogma that high-ranking men are the favorites of God, in His subversive proclamation of a new order in which domination would give way to compassion and communion, Jesus overturned the most rigidly upheld mores of His time.³⁵⁶

---

[353] Esther Fuchs, "Moses/Jesus/Women: Does the New Testament Offer a Feminist Message," *The Cross Currents*, Winter 1999. 463

[354] Ingrid Rosa Kitzberger, ed., *Transformative Encounters Jesus & Women Re-Viewed* (Boston, MA: Brill, 2000), 128.

[355] Unless otherwise noted all scripture from the New *Oxford Annotated Bible, New Revised Standard Version, Third Edition* (New York: Oxford University Press, 2001).

[356] Walter Wink, *Engaging the Powers* (Minneapolis, MN: Fortress Press, 1992), 45.

Matthew 11:28-30

> "Come to me, all you that are weary and are carrying heavy burdens and I will give you rest. Take my yoke upon you, and learn from me, for I am gentle and humble in heart, and you will find rest for your souls. For my yoke is easy, and my burden is light."

The message of hope and the power that is in the Word of God, spoken by One who is the embodiment of the Word has the authority to reach those who are in need. God's word does not return to its source without having accomplished God's will. (Isa. 55:11) Furthermore, Jesus states the purpose of His ministry and the source of His power for the mission as He quotes Isaiah 61 saying:

> "The Spirit of the Lord is upon me, because he has anointed me to bring good news to the poor. He has sent me to proclaim release to the captives and recovery of sight to the blind, to let the oppressed go free," *Luke 4:18*

In light of this passage, one cannot deny his appeal to women, who would have been among the captives and the oppressed. Certainly, Jesus' ministry was not exclusive to women, but it was undoubtedly inclusive of women. This writer agrees with Tal Ilan that there were additional issues and circumstances, which would have drawn women to Jesus.[357] Therefore, as we approach a study of Jesus' encounters and relationships with women, we will examine some of the things that Jesus may have had in common with women.

We understand Jesus as gift from God as found in the words of John 3:16. God loved the world so much that God gave us Jesus who clearly represents the love of God. We are told that if we believe in Him that we may not perish, but may have eternal life. Jesus, who is the love of God, exemplified the same through loving even His enemies and praying for those who persecuted Him. Jesus ministry may be further identified by two related activities; prophecy and healing.[358]

The Role of the Prophet

History teaches us that in many cultures power is usually found in the hands of older males with the most obvious examples located in patriarchal

---

[357] Kitzberger, *Transformative Encounters Jesus & Women Re-Viewed*, 128.
[358] Ibid.

or male-dominated religion. Women and younger men generally had little access to the power structure, which may indicate why the prophetic voice has come from this segment of society.[359] Let us bear in mind that prophets are seers who speak forth the Word of God. Men and women, alike have been identified as prophets in both the Old and New Testaments with both having been accused of false prophecy.[360]

The scriptures are full of accounts of persecuted prophets. Matthew speaks to the reward of those who are falsely accused.

> "Blessed are you when people revile you and persecute you and utter all kinds of evil against you falsely on my account. Rejoice and be glad, for your reward is great in heaven, for in the same way they persecuted the prophets who were before you." Matthew 5-11-12

Prophets were even less honored in Jesus times due to the destruction of the temple. Prior to the Jewish exile, the prophets were seen as holy men. When their place of worship was destroyed, a new religious order; the scribes became more prominent. The temple priest was born into (Levites) and raised up in a tradition of service. The prophet was trained charismatic and had a relationship with God. On the other hand, the authority of the scribes came from their sophistication, knowledge, and intellect.[361]

Jesus was not honored among the religious leaders of the day and received even less honor among His own people. Much too often, it is the people who know us best who fail to recognize that change that has taken place in our lives since we came to know Jesus. Some folks really do prefer to remember "the way we were." For some reason seem to have difficulty in giving honor to whom honor is due. When you don't do what you used to do people will try to make you feel guilty about your transformation. They will accuse you of being uppity or acting like you are better than they are. Well, the response to that ought to be "No, I'm not better than you are, I'm just better than I was!" I know, I look familiar to you, but you really don't know me because I am a new creature. Yes, I am new. The person that you used to know no longer exists. The one who used to get high with you—gone! The person who used to talk about everybody—gone! The person who used to come to church out of habit—gone! The one who was looking for love in all the wrong places—gone! Now, let me tell you about the new me! When the Lord changes our lives we really do want the folks who we know are lost,

---

[359] Ibid., 132.
[360] Ibid., 133.
[361] Ibid., 131.

to know that there is healing in the name of Jesus. Yet it can be extremely frustrating because they are the most difficult to reach!

> Then Jesus said to them, "Prophets are not without honor, except in their hometown, and among their own kin, and in their own house." And he could do no deed of power there, except that he laid his hands on a few sick people and cured them. And he was amazed at their unbelief. **Mark 6:4-5**

Considering that Jesus was identified as the prophet from Nazareth (Matt. 21:11), a place from which nothing good was expected to emerge (John 1:46), He was not sophisticated enough to be accepted by the Jewish rulers. This is a point of identification with female prophets and healers who also lived on the margins of society.

Let's Look at Jesus' Identification with Women as Healers

The Gospel is full of accounts of the healing ministry of Jesus Christ. The healing took place by his touching the sick and at times by the sick touching Him. Demons were cast out with the spoken word releasing those who were bound from the hold of Satan. Historical data also reveals that large numbers of women were involved in practicing healing. The story is told of a female physician named, Bat-Dominiatus, who treats Rabbi Yohanan with an ointment. It seems that the secret formula for the ointment was known only to members of a guild, which may have been made up exclusively of women. The Palestinian Talmud also records a story of how Rabbi Meir complained that his eye was sore and asked that a woman come to heal him. Saliva was a necessary ingredient for healing the sore eye and it is said that the woman spits into the sick person's eye. It is interesting to note that when Jesus heals the blind man He spits on his eye (Mark 8:23) and in John 9:6, He mixes saliva with the dust. It is quite possible that Jesus may have learned physical application from these women while the spiritual application was the power of the Holy Ghost.[362]

Women, as healers, were more than likely, very popular and sought after providing that their cures worked. However, if they did not work they were characterized as witches, an accusation that was applied to most women. Healing and sorcery were often connected, which helps to explain why Jesus was often accused of using evil, magic powers to cure.[363]

Jesus was victim of countless lies and false accusations being called a magician and a false prophet. However, there is no record that there was

---

[362] Kitzberger, *Transformative Encounters Jesus*, 129.
[363] Ibid., 130.

ever a failed attempt at healing or prophetic word that did not come to pass. Many who were in need of healing believed that if they could just get to Jesus they could be cured of their infirmities.

The Canaanite Woman Seeks Healing For Her Daughter

There are many instances in which Jesus healed and spoke healing words to women. Tonight, we will focus on the encounter that Jesus had with the Canaanite woman (Matt. 15:21-28).

21 Jesus left that place and went away to the district of Tyre and Sidon.
22 Just then a Canaanite woman from that region came out and started shouting, "Have mercy on me, Lord, Son of David, my daughter is tormented by a demon."
23 But He did not answer her at all. And His disciples came and urged Him, saying, "Send her away, for she keeps shouting after us."
24 He answered, "I was sent only to the lost sheep of the house of Israel."
25 But she came and knelt before Him, saying, "Lord, help me."
26 He answered, "It is not fair to take the children's food and throw it to the dogs."
27 She said, "Yes, Lord, yet even the dogs eat the crumbs that fall from their masters' table."
28 Then Jesus answered her, "Woman, great is your faith! Let it be done for you as you wish." And her daughter was healed instantly.

Here we find a Gentile woman coming to Jesus asking that He heal her demon-possessed daughter. It is important to note that the text uses the word *healed* concerning her daughter's condition as opposed to *deliverance, which* is the commonly used term in both the Old and New Testaments. One of the Greek words used for deliver is *rhoumai*, which means to rescue. The verb represents a continual process because God constantly rescues us from danger. However, the Greek word for healed in this text is *iaomai* (ee-ah'-om-ahee); middle voice of apparently a primary verb; to cure (literally or figuratively): KJV—heal, make whole.[364] So the healing makes us whole and complete. The healing cures us of sickness, both physical and mental. God's delivering power continually rescues us when the enemy would try to counteract the healing.

Let's look at the encounter and conversation between Jesus and the Canaanite woman. This woman is said to suffer from triple jeopardy; she is a woman, the mother of possessed daughter, and a Canaanite, whose ancestors were the enemies of Israel.[365] However, she did not allow this to get in the way of her asking Jesus to heal her daughter. This is a serious Sister! She is so serious that she made Jesus change His program!

Daniel Patte argues that there are several instances of transformation (the demon-possessed daughter, the Canaanite, woman, Jesus) change and which take place in this text, all of which help to define a model of discipleship.[366] Disciples are followers of Christ who learn from Christ how to live their lives according to the will of God. Disciples follow the Jesus example of ministry and service as the One who came for no other purpose other than to do the will of the Father. Well, what does a woman asking that her child be healed have to do with discipleship? The things that take place between Jesus and this persistent, yet humble woman helped *Him to model a ministry that we will follow!* Jesus initially told her that He was sent for the lost sheep of Israel. He then proceeded to tell her that it was unfair to give the children's food to the dogs. Jesus is calling this woman a dog! Now, I really had to look at this!

Historically, the Jews considered all Gentiles as dogs and the term was actually an ethnic slur. Well, how does Jesus, the Savior, insult this woman? Remember, Jesus was both human and divine and it is in His humanity that He speaks from background as a Jew. Jesus himself was constantly undergoing change, from His birth, continuing in His ministry

---

[364] "Biblesoft's New Exhaustive Strong's Numbers and Concordance with Expanded Greek-Hebrew Dictionary," (Biblesoft and International Bible Translators, Inc., 1994).

[365] Kitzberger, *Transformative Encounters Jesus*, 41.

[366] Ibid., 40.

and in His passion until He receives His ultimate authority as a resurrected Savior, who has all power in His hands.[367] So despite the insult she was determined to get Jesus to do what she needed Him to do. She needed a miracle and she knew that He had miracle-working power. Let's look at her actions.

1. She is a Gentile, but she acknowledges that Jesus is the Son of David and calls Him Lord, which according to Matthew is a title used by true believers.[368] This statement, in itself, indicates a level of faith on her part. One cannot be a disciple unless they believe.
2. She acknowledged that she was a dog. However, the word that Jesus used was not a "street dog" but that of a household pet.[369] This explains why she responds that even dogs eat crumbs from their master's table. In other words, I cannot believe that my daughter will be denied healing just because she is not a Jew! She put Jesus on the spot! In essence, she is saying, I may not be a Jew, but I'm in the house. Rahab, a Canaanite, is mentioned by Matthew in the genealogy of Jesus as the grandmother of King David (1:5)[370] Remember, she refers to Jesus as the Son of David. Therefore, she claims, as a Canaanite to be a part of the house of Israel.
3. Through this dialogue she also brings out some very important aspects about discipleship. Discipleship is not just about meekness and submission, but it is also about faith and relationship.[371] A true disciple is one who talks to Jesus and Jesus talks to them. A true disciple must be in conversation with the Lord and is always looking to better understand the will of God. How better to understand than to ask the Lord what you need to know? Daniel Migliore's, *Faith Seeking Understanding, an Introduction to Christian Theology,* is an example of how we have faith but continue to *seek* understanding.
4. When the story ends, Jesus' perception of the woman has changed and she is now viewed as a woman of great faith. This actually opens the door to the relationship that Jesus has with other Gentiles in the scripture, whose faith is greater that the scribes and Pharisees.

---

[367] Ibid., 43.
[368] Ibid., 41.
[369] Kitzberger, *Transformative Encounters Jesus,* 70.
[370] Ibid., 69.
[371] Ibid., 34.

As a result of this woman's faith, her daughter is healed and Jesus mission, which was intended for all who would believe, expands to include the "whosoever will." Now some of us can identify with the Canaanite woman. The church has ignored you. Your cries have gone unheard because you don't look like church folks. You don't have the church hats and the Sunday suit. You come directly from the street with all of your issues—still drugging, still lying, still sleeping around, mind still messed-up, still cussing folks out—still calling your kids names, still crazy and Sunday after Sunday your cries are silent—your pain can be seen in a look, in a gesture, in a glance—but nobody is looking at you and if they're looking they see what you don't have. They see what you do wrong. They look at you through eyes of judgment. They forgot about how many kids they had before they got married. They forgot about the pregnancies that nobody knows about. Some can identify with the church—we're so busy dealing with who we *think* needs help—we're so busy dealing with the ones who make the most noise—we're so busy dealing with the front of the church, that we have dealt with the back of the church. What about the demon-possessed daughters? Demon-possessed folk come to church Sunday after Sunday and leave the same way they came. When they don't get healed in one church they go to another one. Demon-possessed people are church hoppers! They want to be free, but church folks don't want to be bothered.

> Who's crying out for them?
> What about the ones who can't get to the pastor?
> What about the ones who can't get to the first lady?
> What about the ones who can't get to the deacon?
> What about the ones who can't get to the deaconess?
> What about the ones who think they can't get to Jesus?
> Who's crying out for the demon-possessed daughter?
> Why aren't we on the altar for their healing?
> Where are the praying Mothers?
> Why aren't we calling on Jesus for a breakthrough?

God is calling us tonight to pray for every troubled woman,

- to pray for the depressed woman, to pray for the sexually abused,
- to pray for the physically abused,
- to pray for the emotionally abused,
- to pray for the verbally abused, to pray for the spiritually abused,
- to pray for the healing of every hurt,
- to pray for the binding up of every wound,
- to dry every tear,

- to lift up every head,
- to restore joy, to restore peace,
- to restore love,
- to restore power!

Appendix H

Women's Fellowship and Summer Bible School

@ Paradise Baptist Church, Newark, NJ-Rev. Dr. Jethro C. James Jr., Pastor

Lesson II

Monday, June 25, 2007

The Broken and Abused Woman

Healing the Broken and Releasing the Captives

Rev. Kim Yancey James, Facilitator

The reading and interpretation of both Old and New Testament scriptures has profoundly influenced the women's understanding of themselves as well as how they are perceived by men.[372] As late as the nineteenth century, women who spoke in public were called "disobedient Eves" or "Jezebels."[373] Unfortunately, even into the twentieth and twenty-first centuries, misinterpreted biblical stories still impact the way that women are seen by themselves and others.[374]

Women and men, alike are liberated as we explore new readings of the ancient texts and are disturbed by the stories of violence against women. Certainly biblical stories have been used against women. However, the same may prove to be instruments for healing and wholeness.[375]

I have engaged both a feminist and womanist hermeneutic in the study of scripture; feminist as a woman and womanist as an African American woman.

---

[372] Agnes Ogden Bellis, *Helpmates, Harlots and Heroes* (Louisville: Westminster/John Knox Press, 1994). 3.
[373] Ibid.
[374] Ibid.
[375] Ibid. 4

Feminist interpretation of biblical texts has its roots in the nineteenth century women's rights movement.[376] Those who were against the movement used the Bible to express their opposition by asserting that Eve's creation from Adam's rib means that woman is subordinate to man.[377] Today, we hear the text interpreted in a manner that expresses man's love for woman as she was created from the rib that was close to his heart. These reviews of the text may have been influenced by white women of the feminist movement as well as African American women such as Jarena Lee, an African Methodist Episcopal preacher from New Jersey.[378] They were vocal concerning their belief, which is represented by Elizabeth Cady Stanton organizing a committee to write *The Woman's Bible*.[379]

Let's define feminism:

> Feminism is broadly defined as a point of view in which women are understood to be fully human and thus entitled to equal rights and privileges. In no way can they be considered subordinate or inferior . . . Feminism includes an awareness that society's norms are masculine and that to be a woman in that society involves marginality.[380]

Let's define womanism:

> Womanism as defined by Alice Walker, in preface *In Search of Our Mothers' Gardens,* has four parts. The term derives from the adjective "womanish" as opposed to "girlish." A Mother says to her daughter, "You are acting womanish," meaning that she is acting grown up, but in a way that is willful, courageous, audacious, even outrageous. This does not mean that acting womanish is bad; nor is the woman who describes her daughter a bad Mother.[381]

Womanism differs from feminism in that womanists are troubled by sexist behavior in African American men, particularly, and in men, generally. However, unlike the relationship between white women and white men, there is a strong connection between African American men and women.

---

[376] Ibid.
[377] Ibid.
[378] Ibid. 4
[379] Ibid.
[380] Ibid. 6
[381] Ibid. 9

This unity is related to their common history of oppression, suffering, and exploitation. This experience undoubtedly creates tension between fighting against sexism and affirming African American men.382 Nevertheless, it is important that we do not compromise the truth, as to do so results in failure to educate, liberate, and promote the justice/love that is found in relationship with God and others.

As we approach the following texts we will do so engaging a womanist hermeneutic, rereading the text from the woman's point of view, without regard to the expectations of the society in which they lived. We will view these women through they eyes of women and not through the eyes of a culture, which defines what a woman is or is not. As women, we define who we are, which as Christian women must be linked to the God whom we serve. God is a God of love and justice.

> But let justice roll down like waters,
> and righteousness like an ever-flowing stream.[383]
>   Amos 5:24

Tonight's lesson will focus on the lives of three women; Hagar, Tamar, and the Samarian woman. We may feel that we've heard a lot *about* these women, but tonight, with the help of the Holy Spirit, we will hear them speak for themselves. These are women who have suffered various levels of abuse, a state with which many women of twenty-first century can identify. Prior to hearing their stories it is appropriate to define the types of abuse that has been experienced by women as a result of misogynist (hatred of women) practices, which have been prevalent in both ancient history and modern day times.

Definitions of Abuse/Violence Against Women

Physical Violence—Beatings, slapping, threatening with weapons, forced pregnancies, the motive of which is to keep women needy and submissive.[384]

Non Physical Violence—sudden outbursts of anger and rage, behaving in an overprotective manner, become jealous without reason, preventing

---

[382] Ibid.

[383] Unless otherwise noted all scripture from the New *Oxford Annotated Bible, New Revised Standard Version, Third Edition* (New York: Oxford University Press, 2001).

[384] Eastern and Central Africa Women in Development Network, ed., *Violence against Women Trainers Manual* (Kenya: Paulines Publications Africa, 1997). 15

from seeing family or friend, going to school, working, destroying personal property, denying access to family assets such as bank accounts, credit cards, or the car, control of finances forcing you to account for what you spend, insult you or calling derogatory names, turning minor incidents into major arguments.[385]

Sexual Violence—it is an "act of violence, hatred, and aggression," which usually results is both physical and psychological injuries.[386] This involves any act that is sexual in nature that is done by one individual to another without consent. Child sexual abuse is in this category, because children are not able to give consent. For this reason, a sexual act with a child is called statutory rape. The age of consent varies from according to the state law. Rape is an act that is sexual in nature but is considered violent and not sexual. Thus "rape is not sex."[387]

Spiritual Abuse—This involves denial of equality in religious settings, demeaning, and openly giving less respect/opportunity; "the stained glass ceiling." Scriptures are often misinterpreted in a way that will give one group power over another. It is an abuse of power in which persons are brainwashed and alienated from family and friends.

Let us focus on a few women in the Bible in light of the previous definitions and determine the kind of abuse they may have experienced. Again, they will, with the help of the Holy Ghost, speak for themselves.

Hagar
"The woman who lost a bottle, but found a well."[388]

Genesis 16; 21-9-17; 25; 12; Galatians 4:24, 25

I am the Egyptian slave of Sarai, the wife of Abram. I loved Sarai and was devoted to her as a servant. Sarai always wanted a child, but was unable to conceive. God promised both she and Abram that they would have a child, but apparently they couldn't wait. So Sarai hatched a scheme to give her husband a child. She gave me to her husband and told him to lie with me so that I would become pregnant with his child.

---

[385] Mary Susan Miller, *No Visible Wounds* (New York: The Random House Publishing Group, 1995). 9-10

[386] Marie M. Fortune, *Sexual Violence the Sin Revisited* (Cleveland: The Pilgrim Press, 2005). 4

[387] Ibid. 51

[388] Herbert Lockyer, *All the Women of the Bible* (Grand Rapids: Zondervan Publishing House; reprint, 1998). 61

The moment that I realized that I was pregnant with Abram's child I could not stand Sarai. You may look at me as if I am a slave and according to the culture and social structure of the time, it was expected that I would do what my mistress told me to do. Well, that does not mean that I had to be happy about it. Your ancestors were slaves too. Do you think they were happy about it? I wanted a husband to love me just like Sarai. I wanted to be somebody's wife too. I wanted a family too, but I was a slave. So yes I did what I was supposed to do. I had sex with an eighty-six-year-old man—there wasn't even any love between us because he loved Sarai. I conceived his child. Well, you know the story. Sarai and I really didn't get along too well after that. I was bitter. I was angry, and to be honest with you, I felt used. I mocked her because she was old—seventy-six to be exact—and couldn't have a child. I admit I was wrong. I shouldn't have done that. But what about what she made me do? Did anyone think about how I felt or was I just the means to get what they wanted and couldn't wait for God to provide? God promised them a Son, but they couldn't wait on God so I became their instrument—Sarah and Abraham! He didn't have to listen to her.

He should've been a man and stood up saying—"I'm gonna wait on God." Things got so bad between Sarai and I and she complained to Abram and can you believe that he had the nerve to tell her to do whatever she wanted to do to me! She treated me so badly that I ran away. I had no family. I had no friends. I had no husband and I was pregnant by a man who was married to somebody else. I was in distress, but the Angel of the Lord found me in the wilderness on my way to Shur and asked me where are you going and where are you coming from? The Lord is asking some of you the same thing—where are you going and where are you coming from? The angel told me that I had to go back and submit to my mistress. I really didn't want to hear that so I began to call on the Lord for myself and the Lord heard my cry! I knew that the Lord saw and I also saw the Lord. He is El Roi—the God who sees. I went back and it didn't get much better, but this was all apart of the process. I had a child and God also blessed Sarah, at ninety to have a child, which turned into the family feud. The mothers didn't like each other and my son didn't get along with her son. Abraham was sad about this because he loved both of his sons. Sarah wanted Abraham to send us away and he did because God promised to provide for us. So early one morning, he got up, gave us some bread and water and sent us on our way. We wandered into the wilderness of Beersheba and the water ran out. I knew that without water we were going to die and couldn't stand the thought of seeing the death of my son, Ishmael. So I sat him under a tree and I went off in the distance across from him. I cried and I cried and I cried out to the *Lord* and God heard my son's voice—He must've been crying too. The Angel of the *Lord* spoke to me again and said, "Fear not, for God had heard the voice of the lad . . . I will make him a great nation (Gen. 21:17, NKJV)." Then God opened my eyes and I saw a well of water. When God opens your eyes you can see the blessings that are before you and not focus on the pain of your past. When God opens your eyes you can see the glory of the Lord and not worry about what was done to you. When God opens your eyes you can move forward and stop looking back. I'm standing tonight as a witness to tell somebody to move forward and stop looking back!

Tamar, the Daughter of King David
The woman who was raped by her brother

2 Samuel 13; 1 Chronicles 3:9

My brother raped me! Yes, you heard it right. My brother raped me! I am Tamar, the daughter of King David. My brother, the one who raped me, his name is Amnon. He is actually my half brother. King David is our father, but we have different mothers, but he's still my brother! I am the daughter of Maacah and he is the Son of Ahinoam. Amnon claimed to have had such great love for me that he was overcome with desire. So he pretended to be sick and asked my father if I could come to his dwelling to bring him something to eat. My father told me to go and care for my brother, which is what I planned to do. Well, when I arrived, he asked me to have sex with him, but I said no! He began to force himself on me, and I begged him to stop. I begged and I pleaded with him not to dishonor me by doing such a horrible thing. If he did this I would no longer be a virgin and no one would marry me. I even reminded him that if he asked, our father would allow him to marry me—it was legal. But no matter how much I cried nor how much I pleaded with him he would not listen—he raped me!

Then, as if I were a piece of rubbish, he called his servant and told him to put me out and close the door behind me! Then this man who claimed to have loved me so much treated me worse than dirt. I felt vile, humiliated, and dirty and I wanted to die. My life was ruined. I put ashes on my head.

Virgins wore robes of many colors—I ripped mine up because I no longer needed it! My brother, Absalom saw me crying and asked if my brother had "been with me." When I told him yes, he told me to hold my peace and not to take it to heart because he is my brother. What! I was numb. I couldn't speak, but my spirit was saying, do you have any idea how I feel? Do you understand that my life will never be the same? Do you know that I will never be married? I will never know the love of a man. There will never be a wedding celebration for me. I will never have children or grandchildren. Do any of you know how I feel or are you saying that I need to get over it? Well, let me tell you, you don't know how it feels unless you have been there. I had no one to talk to because I was told to be silent. My father, the great king was angry, but he did nothing! He loved Amnon because he was his first born Son, but what about me? Absalom killed Amnon a couple of years later, but to be honest with you, I don't know if it was about me or because he wanted make sure that Amnon wasn't the next king. If you read about me in the Bible it will tell you that I lived the rest of my life as a desolate woman in the house of my brother. Do you know what desolate means? Desolate transliterates from Hebrew as *shamem,* which means ruined, devastated, and numb.[389] I may have suffered from what is known as post-traumatic stress disorder (PTSD), a term which describes the long-term effect of trauma.[390] A writer, J. Lebron McBride states "many traumatized persons have felt the bonds and connections of life and belief tragically severed. Trauma made them feel cut off from God, from others, and even from themselves.

Individuals with chronic PTSD cannot trust, they cannot hope."[391] So in my desolation, I lost my sense of connection, even with myself, because my identity was linked to a relationship with a Brother, Amnon, who abused me and a father, David, who failed to comfort me.

Allow me to switch persons and to the voice of Kim Yancey James.

Isaiah uses the same word (*desolate*) in his portrayal of Jerusalem as a woman who is disgraced.[392]

> Sing, O barren one who did not bear;
> burst into song and shout, you who have not been in labor!

---

[389] "Biblesoft's New Exhaustive Strong's Numbers and Concordance with Expanded Greek-Hebrew Dictionary," (Biblesoft and International Bible Translators, Inc., 1994).

[390] J. Lebron McBride, *Spiritual Crisis: Surviving Trauma to the Soul* (New York: The Haworth Pastoral Press, 1998). 12

[391] Ibid., 13

[392] Agnes Ogden Bellis, *Helpmates, Harlots and Heroes* (Louisville: Westminster/John Knox Press, 1994). 186

> For the children of the desolate woman will be more
> than the children of her that is married, says the *Lord*.
>
> (Isa. 54:1)

Alice Ogden Bellis quotes Mary Callaway as she postulates as to how God uses the lives of those whom society would consider defiled and ruined to accomplish his will. Bellis observes that God's works are mysterious. There are times when the reproached and defiled are used as instruments to accomplish God's divine will.[393]

> The outrageous nature of the situation now becomes clear: Yahweh has taken for his wife a woman whose defilement could never be purified to make her marriageable; her position was defined as *smmh* and she was as one who is dead. To hear the words *hps* ["delight in"] and *b'l* ["husband"] replacing *smmh* must have jarred in the ears of Second Isaiah's audience, for she who was untouchable is now called by names of most intimate endearment. Second Isaiah has reminded his community of the old stories of the rivalry between the barren and the fruitful wives and how Yahweh visited the barren one to give her a Son. But he then reinterprets the old story: what he did for Sarah and Rachel who were barren was only done in the days of old; now he is taking to himself Jerusalem, who is *smmh*.[394]

Cain Hope elder says "In Hebraic or Jewish society of biblical times . . . the human household was male dominated, with women and children regarded as property, much the same as slaves."[395] Tamar, though disregarded by family and a society, which had no regard for her personhood, was not one whom God would desert. Scripture assures us that God is very present in trouble (Ps. 46:1) and of our inability to flee from God's presence (Ps. 139:7). God's presence with Tamar in her time of desolation made her inaudible voice cry until God heard her. She was not alone. She screamed until the writer of 2 Samuel heard her and shouted through the annals of time into this present age until this we hear her voice and become determined and resolved to be instruments used by God to break the silence of abuse.

The Samarian Woman

---

[393] Ibid. 187
[394] Ibid.
[395] Felder, *Troubling Biblical Waters*, 154.

The Woman Who Left Her Water Pot.[396]

John 4

I promise not to take too much of your time because many of you already know a great deal about me and those who don't may read the fourth chapter of John. The Bible will tell you that I went to the well for some water in the middle of the day. The reason that I was there by myself was because I had no friends. You see, I had been with too many men so the "ladies" did not want to be seen with me. I really didn't want to see them either, because I was tired of them looking down their noses at me. Who did they think they were? They only know what they heard about me. They don't know me! If I had five husbands do they think that I had five happy marriages? I could have very well been an abused woman. But no one was concerned about me until I met this man at the well. Initially, I thought something was up. I could tell from his accent that he was a Jew and Jews and Samarians don't get along. Also, I was a woman and men did not speak to women in public.

While the woman with the issue of blood faced double jeopardy, the woman at the well (John 4:4-42) I face triple jeopardy—I am a Samaritan, a woman, and have been married five times (Jewish law allows three marriages) and the man with whom she lived was not her husband.[397] There is no record as to what happened to my husbands, but it is possible that I may have been divorced. You never heard anything about my children, so you don't even know if I could have children. If I couldn't have children that would have been just cause for my husbands to kick me to the curb. When one considers that Samaritans unlike Jews could only divorce for reasons of adultery, this would further add to my being ostracized by my community. One may add a fourth component to my problem; I am poor, which places me in quadruple jeopardy. Women of social status would not have drawn water as was done in ancient times.[398]

Think about it—I was probably talked about by everyone in the community; men and women alike. Scripture refers to me as the Samaritan woman, but I was probably known in the community as slut; the woman who had five husbands and is living with Henry.

---

[396] Herbert Lockyer, *All the Women of the Bible* (Grand Rapids: Zondervan Publishing House; reprint, 1998). 236

[397] Ibid., 144.

[398] H.D.M. Spence and Joseph S. Excell, ed., *The Pulpit Commentary*, 22 vols., vol. 17 (Peabody: Hendrickson Publishers), 182.

I traveled to the well alone, which implies that the women in the community have chosen to have no dealing with me. Unfortunately, this maltreatment of women by other women prevails today. Much too often, even in the church, women ostracize each other based upon how many children they have out of wedlock, how many times they have been married, and whether or not they are married to the man with whom they live.

The circumstances under which the woman may have come to this state are often ignored and she is characterized as a Jezebel or Rahab whom respectable women will not befriend. Misogyny undoubtedly involves women's hatred of each other. The young generation has stated this correctly in the term hatin'," which is rooted in jealousy. The initial colloquialism was "player hatin'," implied that "we're in the game and you're winning, "I want to do what you're doing." "How can she have five husbands and I can't get one?" Hatin! Linda H. Hollies refers to the lack of female camaraderie as erecting walls. Hollies says, "We have been kept on the other side of the Old Boys Club walls for so long that now we find ourselves better than they are at erecting them against each other."[399]

Allow me to switch voices—

This apparently friendless woman may have experienced trepidation during her encounter with Jesus, which is expressed in her surprise that a Jew is talking to a Samarian, who is also a woman. However, once Jesus told her everything that she had ever done and told her about the living water, as the old preachers used to say "from a well that will never run dry," she was converted.

Jesus reveals to her that He is the Messiah and the woman whom no one wanted to talk to, now has a voice to tell the men to "Come, see a man." She becomes the first woman evangelist in Samaria and she has a voice now. She had a conversation with Jesus and it changed her life. She had a talk with Jesus and the shame that she felt disappeared. She had a talk with Jesus and now she could tell her story. She had a talk with Jesus and she didn't have to be silent about her life. She had a talk with Jesus and she became a voice for the voiceless. She had a talk with Jesus and represents the Hagars, the Tamars, the Jephthah's daughters, my mother, your mother, my aunt, your aunt, my sister, your sister, my grandmother, your grandmother—every ostracized woman, every criticized, every abused woman, every abandoned woman, every wounded, every hurting woman. I stopped by to tell somebody tonight that Jesus already knows all about your trouble. Jesus already knows all

---

[399] Linda H. Hollies, *Bodacious Womanist Wisdom* (Cleveland: The Pilgrim Press, 2003), 23.

about your struggles. He already knows all about your burdens. Jesus already knows about every heartache. Jesus knows about every disappointment. Jesus came to set the captives free. If you're held captive by a bad relationship—If you're held captive by the memory of a bad relationship—Tonight, you can be released from the bondage. Tonight, you can be free from the shackles. Tonight, you can be separated from your past. Tonight, you can walk out of your past and into your destiny. Tonight, you can take hold of the promise. Tonight, you can receive your power. Tonight, you can walk in your anointing. Tonight, you can get your voice. Tonight, you can break the silence.

Tonight, you can be a sanctified witness that God is able. Tonight, somebody has got to tell the story. Tonight, somebody has a testimony. Tonight, somebody has a word from the Lord. Tonight, somebody is going to lead another Sister out of bondage. If you've been healed you have a voice. If you've been made free you have a voice. If the Lord has brought you out you have a voice! Your healing gave you your voice. They know what they did to you, but you're still here! The enemy knows that he tried to kill you, but you survived. I need the saints, who have been delivered, to shout out right now "Lord, I thank you." Tonight, God is going to get the glory. Not by power, nor by might, but by my Spirit, saith the Lord of hosts.

Appendix I

Women's Fellowship and Summer Bible School

@ Paradise Baptist Church—Rev. Dr. Jethro C. James Jr., Pastor

Lesson III

Monday, July 2, 2007

The Guilty Woman

A Sinner's Response to Forgiveness

Forgiveness though taught and mandated by Jesus Christ, is a concept that the modern day church struggles with as we have difficulty forgiving others as well as ourselves. Christians must always bear in mind that we are all sinners saved by grace. Therefore, at any given time we may be subject to act in a manner that is offensive to others and displeasing to God. Let's face it—We are far from perfect! During tonight's lesson, we will focus on some of the teachings of the early church concerning forgiveness and how the application of these principles to our every day life serves to grow the church. When the church is able to forgive and receive forgiveness it helps to preserve the health and unity of the Body.

The early church was apparently concerned with maintaining healthy relationships between members and the church community.[400] The writer of Matthew gives instruction as to how we should resolve conflict (Matt. 18:15-18), which delineates three steps.[401] This will be discussed tonight. Andrew Sung Park, in *From Hurt to Healing,* states that the church often has a message of forgiveness and salvation for sinners, but often leaves the

---

[400] Andrew Sung Park, *From Hurt to Healing a Theology of the Wounded* (Nashville: Abingdon Press, 2004), 70.

[401] Ibid.

sinned against with unanswered questions.[402] I have embraced Park's thoughts concerning the same and will therefore discuss forgiveness as it applies to both the sinned against and the sinner.

It is important to acknowledge that we fit both categories. There have been occasions when the actions of others have resulted in our pain and there have been occasions when our actions have caused the pain of others.

Using the three-step model that is found in Matthew, let us look at the Christian response of the sinned against as it applies to the resolution of conflict. We must bear in mind that conflict is a part of every relationship and when managed appropriately has the ability to enhance and strengthen the bond of unity.

1. If your brother or sister offends you discuss it between the two of you alone. "The private encounter without a witness is designed to preserve the full honor of the straying person."[403] Why would you want to preserve the honor of a person who offended you? Remember, the goal is to restore the fellowship not to punish them. We are our brother's or sister's keeper. Be on your guard! If another disciple sins, you must rebuke the offender, and if there is repentance, you must forgive. And if the same person sins against you seven times a day, and turns back to you seven times and says, "I repent," you must forgive.[404] Luke 17 3-4

> Therefore encourage one another and build up each other, as indeed you are doing. (1 Thess. 5:11)

> See that none of you repays evil for evil, but always seek to do good to one another and to all. (1 Thess. 5:15)

2. If step one doesn't work, it is at this time that we take a witness, but the goal is the same; restoration.

3. If step two doesn't work then the individual was brought before the church, which was expected to resolve the conflict. If the person failed to repent, then they were treated as a tax collector or a Gentile (the first Christians were Jews). This did not mean that they were excommunicated from the church, but that the believers were waiting for them to repent and

---

[402] Ibid., 9.

[403] Ibid., 71.

[404] Unless otherwise noted all scripture from the New *Oxford Annotated Bible, New Revised Standard Version, Third Edition* (New York: Oxford University Press, 2001).

return.⁴⁰⁵ The Gentiles and tax collectors were not thought of as enemies but as targets of evangelism.⁴⁰⁶

Park offers a modern day application of this in terms of the structure of the church today. Pastors, ministers, deacons, other leaders, and even friends of the parties may serve as the intermediary between Christians who have a conflict.⁴⁰⁷ However, they should only be asked to intercede after the offended has spoken with the offender. More often than not, persons who have a conflict will not talk to each other before they have told several people. This usually results in hard feelings, people taking sides, and yeast being added to the story.

It is also important to note that in certain instances legal action may be appropriate. In the case of domestic violence, sexual abuse, and child abuse, the incident may have to be reported to the police. This is not intended to destroy the offender, but to correct the behavior and protect the offended. Forgiveness must involve repentance and a change in the behavior of the forgiven. The church cannot remain silent concerning abuse as to do so will condone and excuse the victimizer giving them a false sense of forgiveness.

The long-term effect of silence of the church concerning abuse has been brought to light in recent years. The Catholic Church, in particular, and the church at large, generally has been the object of numerous lawsuits concerning the clergy sexual abuse and misconduct. It is for this reason that many churches must have insurance to cover these areas and the companies are requiring screening of employees, especially those who come in contact with children.

What does this have to do with forgiveness? The church must teach and practice forgiveness, but not at the expense of the physical and emotional well-being its members. The sinner must be corrected and encouraged to repent of his or her actions. The sinned against must be first nurtured to healing and not just told that they must forgive the offender. Forgiveness is a part of the healing process, but it can be lengthy depending upon the severity of the offense. The Korean language has a word that describes the deep wounds of these victims. It is called *han*. It is a tear in the soul that is caused by "abuse, exploitation, injustice, and violence."⁴⁰⁸ Continued abuse produces a deeper pain or *han* in the "depths of the soul."⁴⁰⁹ Dr. Gerald Kay, who chairs the Department of Psychiatry at Wright State University's

---

⁴⁰⁵ Park, *From Hurt to Healing*, 71.
⁴⁰⁶ Ibid., 72.
⁴⁰⁷ Ibid.
⁴⁰⁸ Ibid., 12.
⁴⁰⁹ Ibid.

School of Medicine say that when children are injured or frightened, "that it not only produces a traumatic memory, it also changes the developing brain."[410] According to Kay, who employs the research of Paul Plotsky of Emory University, "people who have been abused have parts of their brains that are different sizes than others. And those different parts of their brains function in different ways."[411] Scientists have found that individuals who are victims of child abuse have an active "fear center" and a "smaller connection between the right and left brain hemispheres, which enables the more rational right brain to better control feelings or anger."[412] Therefore, a person, who is deeply wounded, does not respond in the same manner as those who have not had the same experience. The deeply wounded person may have learned to live in a shell; their comfort zone. There are also behaviors that are a result of fear but are interpreted by others as irresponsible, shady, and unstable. In all honesty, rational thinkers are uncomfortable with those who have an active fear center and it is only with the help of the Holy Spirit that one is able to identify the fear and respond in a godly manner. This writer has intuitively known that the relationships between female members in the church are often affected by emotions and irrational behavior, which is a result of *han*. This study is helping my understanding and developing the level of patience that is required to minister to wounded and broken persons. It troubles this writer deeply when the church fails to love one another. This doesn't mean that we excuse bizarre behavior. We must address it if we really love each other with healing, reconciliation, and restoration as the desired outcome.

As you can see, physical, sexual, and psychological abuses are not at the same level as a verbal disagreement or misunderstanding between members. These kinds of conflicts ought to be handled immediately using the Matthean model and if the church is really the church. When we live according to the Word of God it works!

The church is community of believers who love God, follow the teachings of Christ, living not as the world, but loving and forgiving one another. God is able to forgive in an instant. The deeply wounded person needs more time.[413] Park speaks of conscious and unconscious forgiving in which he expresses that one should not attack the personalities of offenders but focus on the issues. The conscious mind is able to handle this, but the unconscious mind has images of the offense. In essence, the unconscious mind deals with

---

[410] Ibid.
[411] Ibid.
[412] Ibid.
[413] Ibid., 87.

feelings much longer. This explains that while it may be difficult to recall the exact details of some offenses, the memory of the pain associated with it is still vivid. It is for this reason that the negative images of the person needs to be replaced with positive ones.[414] As Christians, we are mandated to forgive, but forgiveness and repentance ought to accompany one another. This is why Park talks about internal and external forgiveness. We must forgive unconditionally whether or not there is repentance.

Then Peter came up and said to him, "Lord, how often shall my brother sin against me, and I forgive him? As many as seven times?" Jesus said to him, "I do not say to you seven times, but seventy times seven." *Matthew 18:21-22, RSV*

The Jewish tradition was that offenders be forgiven three times. Therefore, Peter may have thought himself generous for considering seven.[415] Time and space does not permit a detailed study of forgiveness. This may be undertaken at a later time in a workshop setting.

Let us look at forgiveness as it relates to the offender. When we are forgiven, the response should be repentance. There are three words used in the New Testament, which describe repentance: *epistrepho, metanoeo, and metamelomai*. The first two words indicate a "turning around" and "turning oneself around," which is indicative of change a devotion to God. The third term involves a feeling of regret and failure but does not involve "turning toward God."[416]

The guilty woman whom we will discuss in this lesson was forgiven but was also given an instruction to sin no more. This indicates that repentance was to accompany her forgiveness. Let's look at this woman.

The Woman Taken In Adultery
The Woman Christ Saved From Death by Stoning[417]
John 8:1-11, Deuteronomy 17:5, 6

While Jesus went to the Mount of Olives, early in the morning he came again to the temple. All the people came to him and he sat down and began to teach them. The scribes and the Pharisees brought a woman who had been caught in adultery; and making her stand before all of them, they said to him, "Teacher, this woman was caught in the very act of committing adultery. Now in the law Moses commanded us to stone such women. Now what do

---

[414] Ibid., 88.
[415] Ibid., 89.
[416] Ibid., 73.
[417] Herbert Lockyer, *All the Women of the Bible*, reprint 1998 ed. (Grand Rapids, MI: Zondervan Publishing House), 239.

you say?" They said this to test him, so that they might have some charge to bring against him. Jesus bent down and wrote with his finger on the ground. When they kept on questioning him, he straightened up and said to them, "Let anyone among you who is without sin be the first to throw a stone at her." And once again, he bent down and wrote on the ground. When they heard it, they went away, one by one, beginning with the elders; and Jesus was left alone with the woman standing before him. Jesus straightened up and said to her, "Woman, where are they? Has no one condemned you?" he said, "No one, sir." And Jesus said, "Neither do I condemn you. Go your way, and from now on do not sin again."

It is clear from looking at the text that this woman was somehow caught in the act of adultery. However, it is not possible for her to have committed adultery by herself. So there are a few things going on here. According to Jewish law, both the man and the woman be put to death by stoning (Lev. 20:10), but the woman was dealt with more harshly than the man.[418] Unfortunately, the same hold true for today. A man and a woman can be guilty of the same sin and we excuse the behavior of the man and the woman becomes the lowest thing imaginable! Women, we are very unforgiving and judgmental concerning each other failing to hold men accountable for their actions. We even make excuses for our sons and allow them to disrespect women. Gone are the days when we, as a people, continue to make statements that "he's grown" and "she's grown." "I can't make him stop beating her." I can't tell him what to do." "I don't believe in interfering." "That's between her and her husband." "That's between him and his wife." The devil is a liar! No, we can't make our grown children do anything (unless they live in our house), but they need to know that if we find out that their messing up we do have something to say! I have a problem with parents who don't correct their children. I don't care how old they are!!!

So this woman was clearly wrong and she was brought into temple to be judged by Jesus. Here, this woman is publicly exposed as having done wrong. She is probably embarrassed and humiliated by having her business and her faults paraded before everybody. Now check this out—the Bible says, she was caught, which indicates that she was trying to hide. If you're not sneaking around, you be *caught* because it's out in the open. The fact that she was *caught* may indicate that she knew that what she was doing was wrong. There's no record that anyone tried to talk to her or the man. They were a group of self-righteous, heartless folks. We don't know if she was physically or verbally abused. We don't know if the man was extremely charming and manipulative or if she was just a loose woman. There was no excuse for what she did because sin is sin. However, life can you throw

---

[418] Ibid., 240.

some curves that put you a place that you expected. These people acted like some church folks. Their goal is not restoration. They just wanted to kill somebody. The other thing is when folks tell on others they don't always want to correct the behavior; they want to see how the leader is going to handle it. Bringing her to Jesus was not just about punishing her. They wanted to see how Jesus was going to handle it. They were testing Him to see if He really came to fulfill the law.

1. If Jesus failed to say she was a sinner He would have broken the Jewish law.
2. If He said she was a sinner and must be killed He would have broken the Roman law, which didn't see adultery as an offense punishable by death.[419]

The Pharisees and Scribes really thought they had Jesus between a rock and a hard place. This was just as much a set up for Him as it was the woman. But look at how Jesus handles this—He never says that she's not a sinner. He begins to write with his hand on the ground. We don't know if He wrote the Ten Commandments, which all of them had broken. We don't know if He was writing the details of all of their sins. Whatever, He was writing when He said "He who is without sin, cast the first stone," not one stone was thrown. The Bible tells us that Jesus started writing again and while He was writing they all began to walk away, one by one beginning with the elders. I stopped by to tell somebody tonight that when you put your trust in Jesus not only will He make your enemies your footstool, but He will make them shut their mouths! They thought they were gonna kill you, but they brought her into the presence of the Lord. Folk don't understand—when they talk about you—when they put you down—when they make a mockery of you—when they put your business on the six o'clock news—you have no place to go but to the Lord. Somebody tried drugs. Somebody tried alcohol. Somebody tried men, but once you got to Jesus—the Man who loves you—the Man who promised never to leave—the Man who promised never to forsake you got power to overcome. This woman could've left the presence of the Lord when her accusers left, but I stopped by to tell somebody tonight you gotta stay with the Lord. The troublemakers left but she stayed with Jesus. I want you to know tonight that your biggest accusers are not where you are in the Lord. Your staunchest critics are not where you are in the Lord. Your greatest fault finders are not where you are in the Lord. The ones who said you would be nothing are not where you are in the Lord. Just like this woman, yes, you were

---

[419] Zondervan Publishing, ed., *The Preacher's Outline & Sermon Bible* (Grand Rapids, MI: Zondervan Publishing), 158.

guilty. You did everything they said you did and some stuff they don't even know about, but you came to Jesus just as you were—messed up—crossed up and mixed up. One day, you heard the voice of the Lord telling you your sins are forgiven—go and sin no more! God made you the head and not the tail. Old things are passed away and all things have become new. The first shall be last and the last shall be first. You're more than a conqueror through Him that loved you. He picked you up, turned you around, and placed your feet on solid ground.

Appendix J

Women's Fellowship and Summer Bible School

@ Paradise Baptist Church—Rev. Dr. Jethro C. James Jr., Pastor

Lesson IV

Monday, July 9, 2007

The Labeled and Misunderstood Woman

The Bent-Over Woman and The Sinner From The City

Bishop T. D. Jakes, in his "Woman Thou Art Loosed" conferences and productions has called much attention to the woman spoken of in Luke 13:10-17. Women from all over the United States and perhaps other countries, as well, have flocked to these meetings looking for a miracle.

Tonight we will look the interaction between Jesus, the woman, and the leader of the synagogue, who represents the religious authorities of that day. Hermeneutical and exegetical methods are always crucial as we seek to interpret the text in a manner that is applicable to the lives of all of humanity.

As we approach this text, it is important to note that this story is only recorded in the gospel as reported by Luke. Luke's writings indicate that he had concern for the poor and outcast[420], many of whom would have been women.

> Luke, the beloved physician and Demas greet you.
> ***Col 4:14, NKJV***[421]

---

[420] Thomas Nelson, *Nelson's Bible Dictionary* (Seattle, WA: Biblesoft, 1998).

[421] Unless otherwise noted all scripture from the New *Oxford Annotated Bible, New Revised Standard Version, Third Edition* (New York: Oxford University Press, 2001).

> Since many have undertaken to set down an orderly account of the events that have been fulfilled among us, just as they were handed on to us by those who from the beginning were eyewitnesses and servants of the word, I too decided, after investigating everything carefully from the very first, to write an orderly account for you, most excellent Theophilus, so that you may know the truth concerning the things about which you have been instructed.
> **Luke 1:1-4**

So in light of the extent, to which Luke went in order to investigate and report these events, let us examine the details of the story. It is clear that Jesus is teaching in the synagogue, which is the last time that He will do so. It is also second among the three instances of healing, which take place on the Sabbath.[422] It may be important to note the struggle between Jesus and the religious leaders and to explore the reasons why Luke was the only one of the four Gospel writers to record this story. However, our point of focus for this study will be this woman, who was nameless and obviously insignificant until she met Jesus.

Let's look at the text

> Now he was teaching in one of the synagogues on the Sabbath. And just then there appeared a woman with a spirit that had crippled her for eighteen years. She was bent over and was quite unable to stand up straight. When Jesus saw her, he called her over and said, "Woman, you are set free from your ailment." When he laid his hands on her, immediately she stood up straight and began praising God. But the leader of the synagogue, indignant because Jesus had cured on the Sabbath, kept saying to the crowd, "There are six days on which work ought to be done, come on those days and be cured, and not on the Sabbath day." But the Lord answered him and said, "You hypocrites! Does not each of you on the Sabbath untie his ox or his donkey from the manger, and lead it away to give it water? And ought not this woman, a daughter of Abraham whom Satan bound for eighteen long years, be set free from this bondage on the Sabbath day?" When he said this, all his opponents were put to shame; and the entire crowd was rejoicing at all the wonderful things that he was doing. **Luke 13:10-17**

---

[422] Ingrid Rosa Kitzberger, ed., *Transformative Encounters With Jesus & Women Re-Viewed* (Boston: Brill, 2000), 5.

The King James version uses the terms *"And behold a woman . . ."* According to Hisako Kinukawa, a Japanese feminist theologian, the word *behold* placed before *woman* implies that she would have been ignored as one of the *"others"* in society.[423] These are the people who are deemed not important and therefore do not have access to the benefits and services that are common place to some.

There is no reason to believe that this is the first time that she appeared in the synagogue because there is no indication that anyone was surprised. There is no record that she, unlike the woman with the issue of blood, had even sought medical treatment for her condition. She may have attended the synagogue on a regular basis unnoticed. Now, it was impossible for the natural eye to dismiss a person who is physically bent over from the waist down. However, the spiritual eyes of the religious leaders were apparently dimmed and indifferent because there is no record that anyone prayed for her healing. She lived in pain and in silence concerning her infirmity for eighteen years. She was so insignificant that she was anonymous![424]

She didn't try to touch Jesus' garment. She wasn't like Jairus' daughter who had a father like Jairus to appeal to Jesus on her behalf.[425] She wasn't even like the daughter of the Canaanite woman who had a mother who made a plea to the Lord on her behalf. She was probably known in the community as the bent-over woman. She was labeled by society based upon her condition without regard for how she came to such a state—and worse yet without concern. Her condition was even ignored. They didn't even know her name. Unfortunately, the church of today is guilty of the same. We label people without even realizing that we're doing it.

1. The one with all the children
2. The one whose son was in trouble
3. The one whose husband left her
4. The one whose mother died
5. The one who wears the short dresses
6. The one who wears the tight dresses
7. The one who used to go with _____
8. The one walks with a limp
9. The heavy-set lady
10. The skinny woman

---

[423] Ibid., 297.
[424] Ibid., 297.
[425] Ibid.

If we must describe people because we can't remember their names at least let the description be something that is kind and positive!

Let's look further—

The scripture does not say that she is infirmed, but that she has a spirit of infirmity. This means that her physical illness was likely to have been caused by her spiritual condition.[426] In other words, she became physically ill because she was spiritually ill. These are psychosomatic illnesses.

How often have we seen the physical and even spiritual condition of people in the church and fail to minister to their needs? I don't know how the exact number of people who attended the synagogue, but scripture often used the word *many* in reference to those who heard Jesus' teachings. So it is safe to assume that *many* were present and *many* had seen her. Yet, no one did anything.

There is nothing to indicate that she was even trying to get Jesus' attention, but Jesus saw her.

Now, let's look at this bent-over condition. In the Japanese language, the character, which is actually from the Chinese language, which is used for the lower back, waist, or hip area, identifies the linchpin of the entire body. This means that if the linchpin is broken an individual is not able to support their body.[427] One may imagine that as a result of being bent over, she was also unable to breathe properly, her vision was limited, her mobility was restricted[428], and she was in constant pain.

King James version uses *bowed together*—The Greek word for this is *Sugkupto*, to stoop altogether, i.e., be completely overcome by:[429]

Can you imagine being bent over and unable to straighten yourself up, no matter how hard you try? Just imagine going through life always looking down and never being able to look up. Your body is close to the ground so even when the wind blows the dirt and dust hits you in the face. If you try to look up it hurts your neck so badly that you decide that it's better to keep looking down. This is what happens to women who are abused, persecuted, and humiliated. They are bent over by the persecution, oppression, shame, and disgrace. Trying to look up, trying to get out is such a struggle that it seems less painful to keep looking down. Someone may ask the question—"why is she still there?" or "why is she putting up with that mess?" Well, if you've

---

[426] W. Marshall Davis, *Twisted Sister*; available from home.comcast.net/~wmarshalldavisjr/03-04-07.html/ (Accessed July 6, 2007).

[427] Kitzberger, *Transformative Encounters With Jesus*, 297.

[428] Ibid., 298.

[429] "Biblesoft's New Exhaustive Strong's Numbers and Concordance with Expanded Greek-Hebrew Dictionary," (Biblesoft and International Bible Translators, Inc., 1994).

always been able to stand up straight you can't see life from a bent-over position. If you've always been able to look up you can't imagine what life is like when you've only been able to look down. But if you've ever been bent over, if you've been in a place where you could only see the ground, but the Lord loosed you from that bondage, you know that if it had not been the Lord who was on your side you would still be bent over, you can give God the glory!

One thing that I like about this Sister is that she came to the house of worship. She didn't let her condition get in the way of her worship. She could have made all kinds of excuses. I'm too tired. It's too hot. It's too cold. It's too early. It's too late. The music is too loud. The choir is singing the same songs. The preacher is preaching too long. The deacon is praying too long. The members are shouting too long. My mother used to say, "Any excuse is better than none." In other words, that is a sorry excuse, but I guess you had to come up with something. Likewise, church folks can come up with the craziest excuses as to why they cannot worship. However, the real reason that they let anything get in the way of their worship is because they don't understand that it's not all about them. This woman did not let her condition, which was real and painful, get in the way of her worship. Well, there are some folks who come to church Sunday after Sunday while they may appear to be physically well, they may be bent over in spirit. They're broken by problems, worried about finances, worried about children, worried about husbands, but a true worshiper will worship the Lord anyhow. This woman was a true worshiper!

The other thing is that when Jesus called her, she came to Him. I stopped by to tell somebody tonight that when deliverance is in the house don't let what people think about get in the way of your release. You know when the Lord is calling your name. You know when the word is just for you. You know when the ministry of song is just for you. You know when the prayer is just for you. Don't let the enemy rob you of your release. Don't let the enemy rob you of your healing. Don't let the enemy rob you of your breakthrough!

The Sinner from the City
The Alabaster Box; Useless Unless Broken

Luke 7:37-50

And behold, a woman of the city, who was a sinner, when she learned that he was at table in the Pharisee's house, brought an alabaster flask of ointment, and standing behind him at his feet, weeping, she began to wet his feet with her tears, and wiped them with the hair of her head, and kissed his feet, and anointed them with the ointment. Now when the Pharisee who had invited him saw it, he said to himself, "If this man was a prophet, he would have known who and what sort of woman this is who is touching him, for she is a sinner." And Jesus answering said to him, "Simon, I have something to say to you." And he answered, "What is it, Teacher?" "A certain creditor had two debtors, one owed five hundred denarii, and the other fifty. When they could not pay, he forgave them both. Now which of them will love him more?" Simon answered, "The one, I suppose, to whom he forgave more." And he said to him, "You have judged rightly." Then turning toward the woman he said to Simon, "Do you see this woman? I entered your house, you gave me no water for my feet, but she has wet my feet with her tears and wiped them with her hair. You gave me no kiss, but from the time I came in she has not ceased to kiss my feet. You did not anoint my head with oil, but she has anointed my feet with ointment. Therefore, I tell you, her sins, which are many, are forgiven, for she loved much, but he who is forgiven little, loves little." And he said to her, "Your sins are forgiven." Then those who were at table with him began to say among themselves, "Who is this, who even forgives sins?" And he said to the woman, "Your faith has saved you, go in peace." **RSV**

The story in the Bible of the sinner woman from the city with the alabaster box who anointed Jesus (Matt. 26: 7-13, Mark 14: 3-9, Luke 7:36-50) speaks of her "extravagant worship born out of deep gratitude to God."[430] Some of the people with Jesus were angry that such a lavish gift would be "wasted" in this manner. Jesus responded that "The poor you will always have with you," but she had chosen the better thing to do. Jesus wasn't suggesting that the poor and needy be neglected but was establishing priority for worship.

People do come to church for things other than worship. Let's look at some of the reasons:

> This is what I do on Sunday.
> My choir is singing.
> It's my Sunday to usher.
> This is my family church.
> It's the church anniversary.
> It's Christmas, Easter, Mother's Day, Father's Day, etc.

---

[430] Bobb Fitts, *Alabaster Ministries*; available from www.bobfitts.com/alabaster.html/ (Accessed July 8, 2007).

Sometimes church attendance is really not about worship and trust me, you can tell! How can you tell? When folks don't come to worship they do everything but worship! No prayer—No amen—No singing! Unless you come to worship, it's just like being a member of a social club, a sorority, or fraternity. You may gather for a good cause. You may do wonderful things for the community, but this is not church. The purpose of the believers gathering is to worship; to bow down in humble submission before the Lord as we honor God for being God.

There are similarities between the bent-over woman and the sinner from the city. They were both misfits. They were both rejected. The church leaders created a controversy around the fact that Jesus healed the bent-over woman on the Sabbath and had a problem with Jesus dealing with the sinner woman, at all. The bent-over woman came when Jesus called her, despite the fact that the people in the synagogue may have looked down on her. The sinner from the city came to Jesus knowing that she wasn't welcomed in Simon's house. The bent-over woman was broken in body and spirit having a spirit of infirmity. Likewise, the sinner from the city had been broken by life ups and downs. This explains why she wept when she came into the presence of the Lord.

So she approaches Jesus for the purpose of anointing his feet, but as she comes near Him she begins to weep. When I looked at the word weep—the Greek word is *klaio* (klah'-yo); of uncertain affinity; to sob, i.e., wail aloud. Being in the presence of the Lord will do something to you. She couldn't even express what she was feeling; all she could do was cry.

This was a loud, wailing cry for help from a sinner who needed a touch from the Lord. She cried because she was sick and tired of being sick and tired. She cried because she was tired of being hopeless. She cried because what used to be fun was making her miserable. She cried because she was looking for a way out. You see, when folks come out of the world into the house of the Lord, it's usually their last resort. They've tried all the drugs they can, their hands on. They have smoked and drank everything under the sun. They have walked the floor all night. They've walked the streets day and night. Their bank accounts couldn't help them. They were educated and still miserable—good jobs—still miserable—married and miserable—unmarried and miserable. Political connections but still miserable. Every now and then you need to think about the day the Lord changed your life. Think about how you were losing your mind and the Lord you kept you. Think about how you were about to give up, but the Lord didn't give up on you.

The Bible doesn't give us great detail as to what happened when the bent-over woman and the sinner from the city got their breakthrough. We don't have too much information as to what they did beyond the moment of deliverance, but there are two things that happened at the point of release. The bent-over woman stood up! She was no longer walking with a bowed-down head. She wasn't living in the past. She didn't see herself has she was. She had a new view of life. She had a different perspective of her surroundings. The movement that used to cause pain can now be done with ease. She's free now to walk upright before the Lord. She's free now to look to the hills from whence cometh her help. Then after she stood up she began praising God. Praise is the appropriate response to deliverance. Praise is the appropriate response to healing. Praise is the appropriate response of the redeemed. The redeemed of the Lord just ought to say so!

Let's look at the sinner from the city. She came, she gave, she was forgiven, and she had peace. Let's look at what she gave. The cost of ointment that she used would have equaled a year's wages, yet she gave it all. This woman gave her all from the start. She didn't have to hear thirty-five sermons on tithing or see a print out of the church financial report, she just gave. She was not stingy with what she had. This anointing was precious. It was costly and it was everything that she had. Yet because she was willing to pour it out, the Lord poured into her. She touched Him and He touched her.

Hal Steenson says that if there were instructions on the bottom of the alabaster box they should have read "useless unless broken."[431] The anointing doesn't belong to you. You can't earn it. You can't buy it. You can't make it. The only thing that you can do is open the alabaster box and use it! Look at your neighbor right and ask them—what are you waiting for? open the box!

The anointing is useless unless you are willing to pour it all out for the Lord. The anointing is useless if you do it to yourself. The anointing is useless unless to break open the box. I stopped by with an encouraging word tonight for any woman who has ever been humiliated and broken, ever been distressed and cast down, ever been looked down on, put down, told that you would be nothing, told that you could be nothing, told that you're not good enough—the devil is a liar! You are somebody. If the Lord saved you, holding back is not an option because we could not save ourselves. *Break open the box!* Look at somebody and say—Break open the box! When you begin to pour out what God has given you it frees you from the bondage of old wounds, old hurts, old pain, old scars, old disappointments. Listen, I'm

---

[431] Hal Steenson, *Useless Unless Broken*; available from www.3abn.org/devotional.cfm?id+1671/ (Accessed July 8, 2007).

not trying to have a conversation with the devil tonight, but if I did would I have to tell him—You can't take advantage of me.

> You can't use me.
> Don't think you can make me quit.
> You can't make me hold back my anointing.
> You can't make me sit down on God.
> You can't make me give up on God.
> I'm holding on to my faith.
> I'm pressing toward the mark.
> I'm standing on the promise.
> I can't wait 'til the battle is over.
> I've got to shout now.
> Look at your neighbor and tell them—
> *Break open the box!*
> Because He's worthy—*Break open the box!*
> Because He loves you—*Break open the box!*
> Because He saved you—*Break open the box!*
> Because He healed you—*Break open the box!*
> Because you're no longer bent over—*Break open the box!*
> Because you can lift your head up now—*Break open the box!*
> Because He gave you peace in the midst of the storm—*Break open the box!*
> Because He turned midnight your into day—*Break open the box!*
> Because the joy of the Lord is your strength—*Break open the box!*
> Because no weapon formed against you prospered—*Break open the box!*
> Because He made your enemy your footstool—*Break open the box!*
> Because the Lord is Your Light—*Break open the box!*
> Because the Lord is a strong tower—*Break open the box!*
> Because the Lord is a mighty fortress—Give Him All You Got!
> Because the Lord is a very present help in the time of trouble—*Break open the box!*
> Because the Lord is a way maker—*Break open the box!*

Appendix K

Women's Fellowship and Summer Bible School

@ Paradise Baptist Church—Rev. Dr. Jethro C. James Jr., Pastor

Lesson V

Monday, July 16, 2007

The Stressed and Worried Woman

Words of Comfort from the Prince of Peace

Rev. Kim Yancey James, M. Div., Facilitator

As Christian women, our quest is to arise every day with the mind-set that "This is the day that the Lord hath made and we will rejoice and be glad in it." However, despite the fact that Lord is good, we are faced with the possibility of dealing with incidents and events that are stressful. Stressful situations seem to be unavoidable as they may present themselves in our homes, in the supermarket, on the job and even in the church. Medical science has revealed that stress affects both the physical and emotional health. Stress factors are indicated as the cause of irregular menstrual periods and difficulties in child bearing.[432]

Modern day society, understanding the reality that stress is a part of life continues to study the cause and effect. The American Institute of Stress, established in 1978, functions as a clearinghouse to gather information concerning issues related to stress. The AIS (American Institute of Stress) published a *Time* magazine article, which identified stress as America's No.

---

[432] TJ Laatikainen, "Corticotropin-Releasing Hormone and Opioid Peptides in Reproduction and Stress," (PubMed, 1991).

1 health problem.[433] The following chart and corresponding information was obtained from their website.

1. Frequent headaches, jaw clenching or pain
2. Gritting, grinding teeth
3. Stuttering or stammering
4. Tremors, trembling of lips, hands
5. Neck ache, back pain, muscle spasms
6. Light headedness, faintness, dizziness
7. Ringing, buzzing or "popping sounds
8. Frequent blushing, sweating
9. Cold or sweaty hands, feet
10. Dry mouth, problems swallowing
11. Frequent colds, infections, herpes sores
12. Rashes, itching, hives, "goose bumps"
13. Unexplained or frequent "allergy" attacks
14. Heartburn, stomach pain, nausea
15. Excess belching, flatulence
16. Constipation, diarrhea
17. Difficulty breathing, sighing
18. Sudden attacks of panic
19. Chest pain, palpitations
20. Frequent urination
21. Poor sexual desire or performance
22. Excess anxiety, worry, guilt, nervousness
23. Increased anger, frustration, hostility
24. Depression, frequent or wild mood swings
25. Increased or decreased appetite
26. Insomnia, nightmares, disturbing dreams
27. Difficulty concentrating, racing thoughts
28. Trouble learning new information
29. Forgetfulness, disorganization, confusion
30. Difficulty in making decisions.
31. Feeling overloaded or overwhelmed.
32. Frequent crying spells or suicidal thoughts
33. Feelings of loneliness or worthlessness
34. Little interest in appearance, punctuality
35. Nervous habits, fidgeting, feet tapping
36. Increased frustration, irritability, edginess
37. Overreaction to petty annoyances
38. Increased number of minor accidents
39. Obsessive or compulsive behavior
40. Reduced work efficiency or productivity
41. Lies or excuses to cover up poor work
42. Rapid or mumbled speech
43. Excessive defensiveness or suspiciousness
44. Problems in communication, sharing
45. Social withdrawal and isolation
46. Constant tiredness, weakness, fatigue
47. Frequent use of over-the-counter drugs
48. Weight gain or loss without diet
49. Increased smoking, alcohol or drug use
50. Excessive gambling or impulse buying

---

[433] American Institute of Stress, *America's No. 1 Health Problem*(accessed July 15 2007); available from www.stress.org/about.htm?AIS=6dd.

It is interesting to note that stress has a definite impact on overall health and well-being and thus should be avoided whenever possible. Certainly, we are aware that life will present challenges and that stress in inevitable. However, we must use godly wisdom in our response to the same. When we are able to cast our cares on Him we will spend less time in the doctor's office. Let's look at some of the effects of stress.

Effects of Stress

Stress is not easily defined because it is a "highly subjective phenomenon"[434] that differs with each individual. Things that are stressful for some individuals may be enjoyable for others. We also respond differently to stress. Some individuals blush, some are pale, some eat more while others eat less. As demonstrated in the list above, stress can have extensive ranging effects on emotion, temperament, and behavior.

There are numerous emotional and physical disorders that have been linked to stress including depression, anxiety, heart attacks, stroke, hypertension, immune system disturbances that increase susceptibility to infections, a host of viral linked disorders ranging from the common cold and herpes to AIDS, and certain cancers, as well as autoimmune diseases like rheumatoid arthritis and multiple sclerosis. In addition, stress can have direct effects on the skin (rashes, hives, atopic dermatitis,) the gastrointestinal system (GERD, peptic ulcer, irritable bowel syndrome, ulcerative colitis) and can contribute to insomnia and degenerative neurological disorders like Parkinson's disease. In fact, it's hard to think of any disease in which stress cannot play an aggravating role or any part of the body that is not affected (see stress effects on the body stress diagram) or, this list will undoubtedly grow as the extensive ramifications of stress are increasingly being appreciated. Additional information is available at ***Current and Past Stress Scoops***, ***Current and Past Newsletters,*** and elsewhere on ***www.stress.org***[435]

As one ponders this information, it is evident that stress is hazardous to one's health and should be minimized. Abusive relationships are undoubtedly stressful and should be avoided. As Christian women, we are responsible for raising our children to become godly men and women. We must also educate them concerning abuse that they will recognize the patterns in themselves as well as in others. Abuse comes in many forms and often people are not aware of the patterns until after they are deeply involved with an abusive partner. Abuse is always about power and control. The feeling of being overpowered

---

[434] American Institute of Stress, *Effects of Stress* (2007, accessed July 16 2007); available from www.stress.org/topic-effects./(Accessed July 16, 2007).

[435] Ibid.

and controlled produces stress and anxiety for the victim and the need for more power and control on the part of the victimizer. The abuse doesn't subside. It escalates! Abusers do not change unless they acknowledge that they have a problem and seek professional help.

Power and Control Wheel[436]

The Power and Control Wheel is used by permission of
The Domestic Violence Intervention Project

---

[436] Domestic Violence Project *www.turnungpointservices.org/domesticviolence%20violence%-%power%20andcontrol%wheel.htm/* (Accessed July 16, 2007).

We must also be mindful that stress when not properly addressed has long-term effects on the mind that is revealed in behavior patterns of the victim. The church needs to be educated as to the signs and symptoms that we may become active participants in nurturing victim-survivors as opposed to judging them.

Let's take a brief look at post-traumatic stress disorder (PSTD)

> Post-traumatic stress disorder is an anxiety disorder that can develop after exposure to a terrifying event or ordeal in which grave physical harm occurred or was threatened. Traumatic events that may trigger PTSD include violent personal assaults, natural or human-caused disasters, accidents, or military combat.
>
> Signs and Symptoms
> People with PTSD have persistent frightening thoughts and memories of their ordeal and feel emotionally numb, especially with people they were once close to. They may experience sleep problems, feel detached or numb, or be easily startled.
>
> Treatment
> Treatments for post-traumatic stress disorder are available, and research is yielding new, improved therapies that can help most people with PTSD and other anxiety disorders lead productive, fulfilling lives.[437]

How do Christians deal with stress? First, we have to put our trust in Jesus knowing that He came that we might have life more abundantly. Abundant life includes good physical and mental health. Just as we seek the help of medical professionals, we should not be afraid to seek mental health counseling. We should not allow the enemy to steal our joy.

> The thief comes only to steal, kill, and destroy. I came that they may have life, and have it abundantly. **John 10:10**[438]

If we believe God's word then we understand that much of the stress that we are faced with is not of God, but a trick of the enemy. When we focus

---

[437] National Institute of Mental Health; available from www.nimh.hih.gov/healthinformation/ptsdmenu/cfm./ (Accessed July 16, 2007).

[438] Unless otherwise noted all scripture from the New *Oxford Annotated Bible, New Revised Standard Version, Third Edition* (New York: Oxford University Press, 2001).

on the situation and not on God, who is in control of the situation, we get stressed out. When we focus on what folks are *doing or not* doing and not on what the Word of God *says*, it will literally make you sick. Listen, let's be honest. If you let them, people will give you a headache, stomach ache, and hypertension. I'm not just talking about strangers and coworkers. I'm talking about family, so-called friends, and church folks. Family, you can't get rid of and so-called friends seem to stick to you like glue. They leave for a season and before you know it, they're back again. Some folks need to be delivered from so-called friends. They are taking up your time with nonsense; whining, and moaning about a problem they've had for the past ten years that could have been solved ten years ago! Now, church folks are another story. They will do you in, in the name of Jesus, grin in your face, never apologize, and then ask you for a favor. If you try to figure them out, you will be stressed out and crazy! Church people will stress you out!!!

Let's look at what the Word of God says about stress—

> Now as they went on their way, he entered a certain village, where a woman named Martha welcomed him into her home. She had a Sister named Mary, who sat at the Lord's feet and listened to what he was saying. But Martha was distracted by her many tasks; so she came to him and asked, "Lord, do you not care that my sister has left me to do all the work by myself? Tell her then to help me." But the Lord answered her, "Martha, Martha, you are worried and distracted by many things, there is need of only one thing. Mary has chosen the better part, which will not be taken away from her." **Luke 10:38-42**

Martha's problem was that she was distracted. The KJV uses the word "cumbered" (*periespato*) which means to draw around, to twist, to be drawn here and there and to be distracted. The thought is that Martha was drawn around and twisted with stress and worry.[439]

Martha was the kind of person who was busy working in the church. You could count on Martha because she had a big heart and apparently loved to entertain. It was not uncommon for Jesus and the disciples to visit Martha's house. She was hospitable and was apparently a great cook! There was no doubt that Martha loved Jesus because she did so much for Him. However, Martha had a problem. She was so busy working that she didn't take time

---

[439] Alpha-Omega Ministries, Inc., *The Preacher's Outline & Sermon Bible*, Wordsearch 7.0 [Software Program] (Leadership Ministries Worldwide, 2007 1992, accessed July 16 2007).

to be spiritually nurtured. She was so busy serving others that she didn't get what she needed. So when she was faced with all of the things that she had to do and realized that her sister wasn't helping her, she flipped! Now, if we would be honest tonight, it is frustrating to work in a ministry and the folks who are supposed to help you are doing something else. It's extremely frustrating when you're trying to build and you feel like you're on the wall by yourself. It's discouraging when you put all you have into what you do and other folks are half stepping. Martha must have had experience with some folks in the ministry who promised one thing and did another. Martha was so aggravated and distracted that she could not appreciate that Mary wasn't slacking on the job. Mary was at the feet of Jesus where she could get the spiritual food that would sustain and empower her for the work of kingdom building. Mary was receiving the Word of God that would be a lamp unto her feet and a light unto her path.

- Prayer time should be a part of every ministry
- A scripture should be read at every meeting
- There ought to be a testimony at every gathering
- The Lord ought to present whenever the saints of God gather
- When the Lord is there the enemy may show up, but he will have to leave!

> Submit yourselves therefore to God. Resist the devil, and he will flee from you. James 4:7, KJV

Unfortunately, we cannot go through life without a struggle. We cannot live this life problem free. Job 14:1 tells us that man that is born of a woman is of a few days and full of trouble, but John tells us that in Christ there is peace.

> These things I have spoken unto you, that in me ye might have peace. In the world ye shall have tribulation: but be of good cheer; I have overcome the world. John 16:33, *KJV*

Tribulation is (thlip'-sis);[440] which means pressure, affliction, mental anguish, burdens, and trouble. At any given time you can expect to run into trouble and if you don't run into trouble—trouble will run into you. But I stopped by to tell somebody tonight that you may have trouble, but trouble

---

[440] "Biblesoft's New Exhaustive Strong's Numbers and Concordance with Expanded Greek-Hebrew Dictionary," (Biblesoft and International Bible Translators, Inc., 1994).

doesn't have you. The Lord is bigger than tribulation. The Lord is mightier than every struggle. The Lord is more powerful than any enemy. He can take the heaviness out of pressure, the torture out of anguish, the pain out of affliction, the load from a burden, and the snare out of trouble. If God be for us who can be against us?

Who shall separate us from the love of Christ? shall tribulation, or distress, or persecution, or famine, or nakedness, or peril, or sword? "*Yes*"

As it is written, For thy sake we are killed all the day long; we are accounted as sheep for the slaughter.

Nay, in all these things we are more than conquerors through him that loved us.

For I am persuaded, that neither death, nor life, nor angels, nor principalities, nor powers, nor things present, nor things to come.

Nor height, nor depth, nor any other creature, shall be able to separate us from the love of God, which is in Christ Jesus, our Lord.

Because you're in Christ and Christ is in you—you can have peace and not stress. I'm so glad that Jesus overcame the troubles of the world. Because He overcame—We're more than conquerors through him that loved us. Because He overcame—Greater is He that is in us than he that is in the world. Jesus, Mary's Baby, Lily of the Valley, the bright and morning star—

- He overcame being lied on
- He overcame being talked about
- He overcame being despised and rejected
- He overcame being a man of sorrow, acquainted with grief
- He overcame being marched from judgment hall to judgment hall
- He overcame being whipped all night
- He overcame being nailed to a cross
- He overcame the nails in his hands
- He overcame the nails in his feet
- He overcame the sting of death
- Can I get a witness in here?
- Death where is thy sting?
- Grave where is your victory?
- They hung him high—they stretched him wide
- Peace hung on the cross all day Friday
- Peace hung on the cross all day Saturday
- Peace went down in the grave
- But early that Sunday morning—he got up with all power in his hands
- the Prince of Peace,
- the King of Kings,

- the Lord of Lords, Wonderful Counselor,
- Everlasting Father
- My wheel in the middle of a wheel
- A bridge over trouble water
- Bread in a starving land
- Water when I'm thirsty
- He walks with me
- He talks with me
- One of these old days trouble will be over
- There'll be peace in the valley for me someday
- If you the love the Lord—say yes!

Appendix L

Women's Fellowship and Summer Bible School

@ Paradise Baptist Church—Rev. Dr. Jethro C. James Jr., Pastor

Lesson VI

Monday, July 23, 2007

The Transformed and Triumphant Woman

How do you spell Changed?

Committed, Holy, Anointed, Nurtured, Godly, Empowered, and Determined

Rev. Kim Yancey James, M. Div., Facilitator

Encounters between Jesus and women have been life changing and transformational from the conception in Mary's womb (Luke 1:26-38) until Jesus' final encounter with Mary Magdalene in the garden following his own final transformation (John 20:11-18).[441]

Jesus' life and ministry as recorded in the Gospels involves meetings and conversations with women whom he meets publicly and privately (Luke 10-38-42; John 11:1-46; 12:1-8). Some even came to meet Him in the streets (Mark 5:24-35) and in the homes of others (Mark 14:3-9; Luke 7:36-50).[442] All of these encounters result in transformation as women are healed and delivered from diseases both physical and spiritual.

During the past few weeks we have focused on many of these life changing encounters that Jesus had with women in the Bible. However, no study of scripture is complete unless it is inclusive of present day life application.

---

[441] Ingrid Rosa Kitzberger, ed., *Transformative Encounters Jesus & Women Re-Viewed* (Boston: Brill, 2000), 1.

[442] Ibid.

Tonight, we will focus on what is involved in transformation by using the word *Changed*. We will look at each letter in the word in terms of transformation trusting that, with the help of the Holy Ghost, this will come to life.

C—Committed

Psalms 37:5
Commit thy way unto the *Lord*; trust also in him; and he shall bring it to pass.
Proverbs 16:3, KJV

Commit thy works unto the *Lord*, and thy thoughts shall be established. KJV

The Hebrew word for commit is *galal* (gaw-lal'); a primitive root; to roll (literally or figuratively): *KJV*—commit, remove, roll (away, down, together,) run down, seek occasion, trust, wallow.[443]

- When we commit our ways to the Lord it involves a decision to do what is right according to the Word of God
- It has nothing to do with what we feel like doing
- It has nothing to do with what other folks are doing
- It is an act of courage; doing the right thing when everybody else in doing wrong.
- We can't be committed when we can't finish anything that we start
- We can't be committed when we quit every ministry that we join
- We can't be committed when we don't serve in any capacity in the ministry
- Commitment is not easy, but the more you do it the easier it gets.
- Commitment is habit-forming just like quitting is habit-forming
- The difference between success and failure is not giving up
- We need to stop living like losers!
- We're always talking about victory, but we live like losers!

H—Holy

1 Peter 1:15-16
But as he which hath called you is holy, so be ye holy in all manner of conversation; 16 Because it is written, Be ye holy; for I am holy. KJV

---

[443] Biblesoft's New Exhaustive Strong's Numbers and Concordance with Expanded Greek-Hebrew Dictionary, (Biblesoft and International Bible Translators, Inc., 1994).

The Greek word for holy is *hagios* (hag'-ee-os); sacred (physically, pure, morally blameless or religious, ceremonially, consecrated): KJV—(most) holy (one, thing), saint.[444]

- Holiness involves the act of consecration; to be set aside for a particular purpose by and for God.
- To be holy is be morally blameless.
- To holy is to embrace honesty and integrity.
- There ought to be some things that we just will not do under any circumstances—we are holy.
- Holiness is not homeliness!
- Holiness is not the elimination of cosmetics, white doilies, and long dresses!
- However, we are not free to dress like we're going to the club or to show everything!
- The outward appearance will reflect the inward change.
- God calls us to be Holy because God is Holy.
- We are made in the image of God; therefore we must strive to live up to that image.
- When Christians fail to live according to standards of holiness and Christian integrity we participate in distorting the image of God.

A—Anointed

2 Corinthians 1:21-22

> 21 Now he, which stablisheth us with you in Christ, and hath anointed us, is God;
> 22 Who hath also sealed us, and given the earnest of the Spirit in our hearts. KJV

NT: 5548 chrio (khree'-o); probably akin to NT: 5530 through the idea of contact; to smear or rub with oil, i.e., (by implication) to consecrate to an office or religious service:

NT: 5530 The primary Greek word for anoint is *chraomai* (khrah'-om-ahee); middle voice of a primary verb; to furnish what is needed; (give an oracle, "graze" [touch slightly], light upon, etc.), i.e., (by implication) to employ or (by extension) to act toward one in a given manner: KJV—entreat, use.[445]

---

[444] Ibid.
[445] Ibid.

- We are anointed and given power for the assignments that God has given us.
- The anointing supplies us with everything that we need to get the job done.
- The anointed have been touched by God through the power of the Holy Spirit.
- The anointing will destroy the yoke of bondage.
- However, we cannot accomplish anything until we recognize the power of the anointing.
- Christians suffer from paralysis by analysis—we analyze everything.

N—Nurtured

Ephesians 6:4
And ye fathers, provoke not your children to wrath: but bring them up in the nurture and admonition of the Lord. KJV

The Greek word for nurture is *paideia* (pahee-di'-ah); from NT: 3811; tutorage, i.e., education or training; by implication, disciplinary correction: KJV—chastening, chastisement, instruction, nurture.[446]

- Transformation involves a willingness to be taught, corrected, instructed, chastised, disciplined, educated without which there can be no growth.
- Many Christians make the mistake of self-proclaimed maturity. Chronological age and spiritual maturity are not always synchronized. It is possible to grow into adulthood as a member of the church, without growing up in Christ.
- Every Christian should desire to grow closer to the Lord, nurtured with spiritual food. We like to share chicken, collard greens, potato salad, and cake; things that will make us fat. However, it's time for us to fatten up through the Word of God.
- As transformed women, we need to spend time at the feet of Jesus.

G—Godly

2 Corinthians 1:12
For our rejoicing is this, the testimony of our conscience, that in simplicity and godly sincerity, not with fleshly wisdom, but by the grace

---

[446] Ibid.

of God, we have had our conversation in the world, and more abundantly to you—ward. KJV

2 Corinthians 7:9-10

Now I rejoice, not that ye were made sorry, but that ye sorrowed to repentance: for ye were made sorry after a godly manner, that ye might receive damage by us in nothing. 10 For godly sorrow worketh repentance to salvation not to be repented of: but the sorrow of the world worketh death. KJV

Titus 2:12-14

Teaching us that, denying ungodliness and worldly lusts, we should live soberly, righteously, and godly, in this present world; 13 Looking for that blessed hope, and the glorious appearing of the great God and our Savior Jesus Christ; 14 Who gave himself for us, that he might redeem us from all iniquity, and purify unto himself a peculiar people, zealous of good works. KJV

The Greek word for godly is *eusebos* (yoo-seb-oce'); adverb from NT: 2152; piously: KJV—godly. The root word is *eu* (yoo); neuter of a primary eus (good); (adverbially) well: KJV—good, well (done).[447]

- Godliness is not self-righteousness, but deep-rooted desire to do good, to sacrifice our personal will to do God's will.
- Christ is our example of what is good in the sight of God.

We are saved because we accept Christ as Lord, believe in our hearts, and confess with our mouths that Jesus died for our sins. We believe that he rose and the third day, ascended to heaven, is making intercession for our sins and one day, is coming back again. Salvation causes us to want to be more like Christ. The Spirit, who lives inside, causes us to have a desire to do what is pleasing to God becoming more and more like Christ. We have not yet reached this goal. We may still sin, but we are not slaves to sin nor are we subject to the penalty of sin. We are not condemned. We may sometimes miss the mark, but we continue to "press toward the mark for the prize of the high calling of God in Christ Jesus."

Our salvation gives us the desire to live in fellowship with God and humanity. Following the example of Christ, our goal is to love our neighbors as ourselves and to show the love of God. Our desire should be to let out lights shine that those who don't know Christ may see Christ in us. The result of salvation is that the believer will turn away from his or her own interests and become concerned with others. As we become more Christ-like, we

---

[447] Ibid.

bless those who curse us, and we sacrifice our personal desire for the greater good—"not my will but thine will be done."

Salvation results in humanity becoming more Christ-like through the witness and actions of those who have been saved. When one receives the gift of salvation and embraces the love of Christ, they begin to share this love with others through ministry and caring for the needs of all humanity. Salvation is not only concerned with the restored relationship with God and the gift of eternal life. Salvation is not just a position of blessing, but a gift that keeps giving. As a result of the indwelling of the Holy Spirit, those who are saved will be moved and compelled to serve God through serving humanity.

E—Empowered

Luke 10:19-20

19 Behold, I give unto you power to tread on serpents and scorpions, and over all the power of the enemy: and nothing shall by any means hurt you. 20 Notwithstanding in this rejoice, not that the spirits are subject unto you; but rather rejoice, because your names are written in heaven. KJV

> *[To tread on serpents]* Preservation from danger. If you tread on a poisonous reptile that would otherwise injure you, I will keep you from danger. If you go among bitter and malignant enemies that would seek your life, I will preserve you.
>
> *[Scorpions]* The scorpion is an animal with eight feet, eight eyes, and a long jointed tail, ending in a pointed weapon or sting. It is found in tropical climates, and seldom exceeds four inches in length. Its sting is extremely poisonous, and it is sometimes fatal to life. It is in Scripture the emblem of malicious and crafty men. When rolled up, it has some resemblance to an egg, Luke 11:12; Ezekiel 2:6. The annexed cut will give an idea of its usual form and appearance.
>
> *[The enemy]* Satan. The meaning of this verse is that Jesus would preserve them from the power of Satan and all his emissaries—from all wicked and crafty men; and this shows that he had divine power. He that can control Satan and his hosts that can be present to guard from all their machinations, see all their plans, and destroy all their designs, must be clothed with no less than almighty power.[448]

- We must realize the power and authority that God has given us.

---

[448] Albert Barnes, *Barnes' Notes on the Old and New Testament* (Seattle, WA: Biblesoft, 2001).

- We must not live in fear of the attacks of the enemy.
- God has not given us a spirit of fear, but of love, power, and a sound mind.

Acts 1:8

But ye shall receive power, after that the Holy Ghost is come upon you: and ye shall be witnesses unto me both in Jerusalem, and in all Judaea, and in Samaria, and unto the uttermost part of the earth. **KJV**

NT: 1411

dunamis (doo'-nam-is); from NT: 1410; force (literally or figuratively); specially, miraculous power (usually by implication, a miracle itself):

KJV—ability, abundance, meaning, might (-ily, -y, -y deed,) (worker of) miracle (-s,) power, strength, violence, mighty (wonderful) work.[449]

D—Determined

- We have to be determined to stay the course.
- We have to be determined to hold on to our faith.
- We have to be determined live for Jesus.
- We have to be determined to walk with Jesus.
- We have to be determined to know Jesus.
- Education is wonderful, but we need to know Jesus.
- Political connections are wonderful, but we need to know Jesus.
- Money in the bank is wonderful, but we need to know Jesus.

1 Corinthians 2:2

For I determined not to know anything among you, save Jesus Christ, and him crucified. **KJV**

NT: 2919

krino (kree'-no); properly, to distinguish, i.e., decide (mentally or judicially); by implication, to try, condemn, punish: KJV—avenge, conclude, condemn, damn, decree, determine, esteem, judge, go to (sue at the) law, ordain, call in question, sentence to, think.[450]

The Apostle Paul, in this text makes a conscious decision, not to know anything, not to try to impress anybody. He determined not to talk about his

---

[449] Biblesoft's New Exhaustive Strong's Numbers and Concordance with Expanded Greek-Hebrew Dictionary. (Seattle, WA: Biblesoft, 2001).
[450] Ibid.

education. He determined not to talk about his connections. He determined not to talk about his expertise. He determined to talk about power that is in the name of Jesus. He determined to tell a dying world, He Jesus hung, bled, and died that we might have a right to the tree of life. He's determined the troubled in spirit.

> We are troubled on every side, yet not distressed; we are perplexed, but not in despair;
>
> Persecuted, but not forsaken; cast down, but not destroyed;
>
> He determined to tell a Christian soldier to Eph 6:11-17
> Put on the whole armor of God that ye may be able to stand against the wiles of the devil.
>
> For we wrestle not against flesh and blood, but against principalities, against powers, against the rulers of the darkness of this world, against spiritual wickedness in high places.
>
> Wherefore take unto you the whole armor of God that ye may be able to withstand in the evil day, and having done all, to stand.
>
> Stand therefore, having your loins girt about with truth, and having on the breastplate of righteousness;
>
> And your feet shod with the preparation of the Gospel of peace;
>
> Above all, taking the shield of faith, wherewith ye shall be able to quench all the fiery darts of the wicked.
>
> And take the helmet of salvation, and the sword of the Spirit, which is the Word of God:
>
> He determined to tell a weary saint of God—
> And let us not be weary in well doing: for in due season we shall reap, if we faint not.
>
> If God be for us who can be against us?
>
> And we know all things work together for good to them that love God to those who are the called according to his purpose.
> I can do all things through Christ, which strengtheneth me.
> I stopped by to tell somebody tonight.

If you've really been changed you have power to overcome,
If you've really been changed you have power to speak to your mountains.
If you've really been changed you can stand on the promises of Jesus.
If you've really been changed your latter days shall be greater than your past.
If you've really been changed greater is he that is in you than he that is in the world.
If you've really been changed you're holding to God's unchanging hand.
If you've really been changed you're building your hope on things eternal.
If you've really been changed your eyes have seen the glory of the coming of the Lord.

In a moment, in the twinkling of an eye, at the last trump: for the trumpet shall sound, and the dead shall be raised incorruptible, and we shall be changed.

For this corruptible must put on incorruption, and this mortal must put on immortality.

So when this corruptible shall have put on incorruption, and this mortal shall have put on immortality, then shall be brought to pass the saying that is written, Death is swallowed up in victory.

O death, where is thy sting? O grave, where is thy victory?

The sting of death is sin; and the strength of sin is the law.

But thanks be to God, which giveth us the victory through our Lord Jesus Christ.

Therefore, my beloved brethren, be ye steadfast, unmovable, always abounding in the work of the Lord, forasmuch as ye know that your labor is not in vain in the Lord.

Appendix M

Certificate of Achievement

Presented to

in recognition of your participation in the Paradise Baptist Church Women's Fellowship Summer and Bible School and the successful completion of the following:

Jesus' Relationships with Women
The Broken and Abused Woman
The Guilty Woman
The Labeled and Misunderstood Woman
The Stressed and Worried Woman
The Transformed and Triumphant Woman

Rev. Kim Yancey James, M. Div.   **Rev. Dr. Jethro C. James Jr.**
Facilitator

                                                    Pastor

August 3, 2007

Appendix N

Violence Against Women Community Awareness Day Flyer and Registration Form

Appendix N

Paradise Baptist Church
348-352 Fifteenth Avenue
Newark, New Jersey 07103
Rev. Dr. Jethro C. James Jr., Pastor
(973) 624-6614

*"Violence Against Women
Community Awareness Day"
Saturday, October 27, 2007
9:00 a.m.-12:00 p.m.
8:30 a.m.—Registration and Continental Breakfast Free!!!!!
All Persons Ages twelve Yrs. and up are Invited To Attend*

Break The Silence, Stop The Violence!!!

Confirmed Workshops and Facilitators

Carmen Diaz-Cuevas, M. A., LCSW—**The Effects of Violence and Abuse**
Pamela McCauley—**Essex County Prosecutor's Office—The Victim and The Law**
Linda Morales Dennis—**"I'm a Survivor"**

Rev. Kim Yancey James, M. Div., CSW—**Pastors and Clergy as Caregivers**

*The Essex County of Division of Welfare Mobile Office Van
will be present to take on-site applications for TANF,
General Assistance, Food Stamps and Medicaid*

*Seminar Hostess—Rev. Kim Yancey James, M.Div.
Please call 973-624-6614, option 3 to RSVP*

Appendix N

Paradise Baptist Church

348-352 Fifteenth Avenue~Newark, New Jersey 07103~(973) 624-6624~Fax (973) 624-8831

Violence Against Women
Community Awareness Day Registration Form

Name: _____

Address: _____ Daytime Phone: (___) _____

_____ Evening Phone: (___) _____

E-mail: _____

Church/Organization (if any) _____

Appendix O

Violence Against Women Community Awareness Day Donation Letter

Appendix O

Paradise Baptist Church

348-352 Fifteenth Avenue~Newark, New Jersey 07103~ Rev. Jethro C. James Jr., Pastor
(973) 624-6624~Fax (973) 624-8831

October 9, 2007

Honorable [Name of Council Member]
City Council
City of Newark
City Hall—920 Broad Street
Newark, NJ 07102

Dear Honorable [Name of Council Member]:

National statistics indicate that the major cause of injury to an adult female takes place in the home; four million American women experience a serious assault by a partner during an average twelve-month period and one in five female high school students report being sexually abused by a dating partner. Also, abused girls are significantly more likely to get involved in other risky behaviors, four to six times more likely to get pregnant and eight to nine times more likely to have tried to commit suicide. Therefore, the Paradise Baptist Church CDC, a 501(c) 3 non-profit corporation, in conjunction with the Women's Ministry of the Paradise Baptist Church, will sponsor its first Violence Against Women Community Awareness Day on Saturday, October 27, 2007, from 9:00 a.m.-12:00 p.m. Our theme, "**Break The Silence: Stop The Violence**" speaks to our commitment to make a difference in the lives of women in our church and community.

We are soliciting donations from local merchants, community leaders, and friends to help with expenses for refreshments, supplies, honorariums, etc. We have among our confirmed facilitators and service providers, mental health professionals, the Essex County Prosecutor's Office, and the Essex County Division of Welfare. We have enclosed a proposed budget indicating the estimated expenses associated with this endeavor.

Thank you so much for your consideration of our request. Should you decide to make a donation, please make checks payable to **Paradise Baptist Church, 348-358 Fifteenth Avenue, Newark, NJ 07103, Attn: Rev. Kim Yancey James**.

Please remember, your donation is tax-deductible and will be greatly appreciated. If you would like additional information, please feel free to call me at 973-624-6614, option 3.

Sincerely,

Kim Yancey James
Rev. Kim Yancey James, Executive Minister/Director of Women's Ministries

Appendix P

Violence Against Women Community Awareness Day Program

Paradise Baptist Church

348-352 Fifteenth Avenue
Newark, New Jersey 07103
Rev. Dr. Jethro C. James Jr., Pastor
Presents
Violence Against Women
Community Awareness Day

Break the Silence, Stop the Violence!
Rev. Kim Yancey James, M. Div.
Seminar Hostess

Saturday, October 27, 2007
9:00 a.m.-12:00 p.m.

The Facilitators

Carmen Diaz Cuevas—A licensed clinical social worker, she is a graduate of Montclair State University with a Bachelor of Arts in Psychology and Master of Arts in Counseling. Ms. Cuevas, who also has a private practice, has earned additional certifications in psychotherapy, hypnotherapy, and family counseling. Employed by the Passaic County Board of Social Services for twenty-six years, she is currently a senior training technician in the life skills/job readiness program.

Pamela McCauley—A graduate of St. Mary's College in Maryland earning a Bachelor of Arts with a triple major in Economics, Business Administration and Political Science. Ms. McCauley has been involved in victim assistance for twenty-one years. Employed by the Essex County Prosecutor's Office as director of victim advocacy for seventeen years, she is currently the victim witness coordinator. Ms. McCauley is a member actively involved in the ministries of Christ Church in Montclair, NJ, where Dr. David Ireland is the pastor.

Linda Morales Dennis—A graduate of Trenton Central High School, Ms. Dennis is a certified recovery counselor for New Jersey Access Initiative. She is a member of Paradise Baptist Church where she serves as president of the Missionary Ministry.

Rev. Kim Yancey James—An ordained minister and certified social worker, she has earned a Bachelor of Arts in political science from Howard University and Master of Divinity degree from New York Theological Seminary. She is currently a candidate for the Doctor of Ministry degree at United Theological Seminary in Dayton, Ohio, where the focus of her doctoral project involves a model of care for female victim-survivors of violence and abuse. Serving as executive minister of the Paradise Baptist Church, she is also the director of women's ministries. Employed by the Passaic County Board of Social Services for twenty-two years, she is currently a senior training technician in the life skills/job readiness program.

Program
Location—The Fellowship Hall

8:30-9:00 . . . . Registration and Continental Breakfast

Location—The Sanctuary

9:00-10:00 . . . . "The Effects of Violence and Abuse"
Carmen Diaz Cuevas, LCSW

10:00-11:00 . . . . "The Victim and The Law"
Pamela McCauley
Essex County Prosecutor's Office—Victim Witness Unit

11:00-11:20 . . . . "I'm a Survivor"
Linda Morales Dennis

11:20-12:00 . . . . Panel Discussion/Questions and Answers
Carmen Diaz Cuevas, LCSW
Pamela McCauley
Linda Morales Dennis

Location—The Fellowship Hall

11:20-12:00 . . . Clergy Only . . . . Clergy As Caregivers
Rev. Kim Yancey James, M. Div.

Location—The Sanctuary

12:00 . . . . Paradise Praise Dance Ministry

Closing Remarks and Benediction—Pastor Jethro C. James Jr.

Our Sincere Thanks To

The Essex County Division of Welfare
The Newark/ North Jersey
Committee of Black Churchmen, Inc.
The Committee to Reelect
Honorable Councilwoman Dana Rone
The Office of Newark City Council President,
Honorable Mildred Crump
The Office of Honorable Senator, Ronald Rice, Carmen Diaz Cuevas,
Pamela McCauley, Linda Morales Dennis
The Women's Ministry of Paradise Baptist Church
The Paradise Baptist Church Praise Dance Ministry
The Hospitality and Kitchen Committees

Appendix Q

The Interviews and Narratives

Participant A

Participant A is between thirty-six and fifty years old, is separated from her spouse, has a household size of two, rents her apartment, and has an annual family income of $20,000 to $30,000.

Participant A
Interview Questions

3. Prior to this interview, have you ever discussed the detail of your abuse with others? If yes, why? If no, why not?

   Yes—to share my experience for others who may be hurting and for my own freedom. I needed to get it out.

4. Why did you choose to tell your story?

   Because I'm a survivor and other people or women need to know they can make it. They need to know, especially if they were children, that they were victims.

3. How did you feel about telling or not telling your story?

   A lot more positive than before, I get freer and freer every time I tell it. It makes me feel good because I may have helped someone.

8. When you read literature about violence against women how do you feel?

   It still disturbs me to see women or especially children, whether it be physical or sexual. As a child, where was my protector? How does this happen in this day and age? It's disturbing. I don't feel rage, but it upsets me.

9. What do you think about sharing the story of your abuse with your children?

   I've shared it with my daughter. I was always trying to protect her, especially when she was three. I remember always saying that if I have a child I would always tell her what to look out for. I told her more as she was older. I visited my abuser, my stepfather, because he was my sisters' father and they lived with him. I would not leave my daughter alone with him. I told my daughter why I was in therapy. It made her uncomfortable because, for her, the man that she called Grandfather was my abuser. I never taught her to hate him.

10. How do you feel children can be better protected from abuse?

    Being told the truth about it by someone who has been abused. Being taught about their bodies.

11. How can the church serve as an instrument of healing for victim-survivors of abuse?

    Having a safe haven, a trusted contact person, someone who will not look down on them. Provide information—Maybe a hotline—I don't know. Someone they can talk to and it won't get around—pamphlets.

12. How do you define pastoral care and counseling?

    Comfort without criticism—a way of being able to get the spiritual guidance needed, hope, and encouragement.

13. If you had the opportunity to speak to your abuser(s) today what would you say?

    (Long pause) I would want to know why. What happened to him as a child? Something had to happen—Yeah—(Long Pause) that's about it. Yeah, that's cool.

14. How do you define healing?

    Healing is a process—it's growth—letting go.

15. How would you help to prevent other women and children from being abused?

What I'm doing right now. If someone needed me to speak I would tell my story leading them to where they can get help.

16. Why did you agree to be a part of this project?

    First of all, because you asked and because I'm a survivor still going through the process. I believe you see that some healing has taken place since I told you. To let people know. It's being hidden and we need to expose it.

17. What, if anything, have you gained from your participation in this project?

    More healing, better self-esteem, about myself. The way I carry myself is a lot different. Yeah, I carry myself better, I do.

This participant had difficulty with writing her narrative. She asked, if she could tell it if I would write it down for her. I agreed to do so. They documented the story just as the participant shared the information considering the significance of *how* one tells their story.

Participant A Narrative

My mom married my step-dad in 1969. They moved. I think I was about five years old when it began. He gave me a horseback ride on his leg . . . strange . . . very touchy. I was the stepdaughter. My sisters were his. He let me ride on his lap to drive the car. It was strange, a fun feeling for me.

Around age six, he would put his penis around the outside of my vagina. I was afraid because I didn't know if it was right or wrong. I started menstruating when I was in the eighth grade. He did not penetrate me and would not touch me during my menstruation. He abused my mom and I felt that he would abuse my mom more. I never told. I never told by my teachers. I was really good in school.

There were three girls in bed. I had twin sisters, but they were never abused. I have an eerie feeling about basements. He used to take me down to the basement. It was not finished. There were rats, a boiler, and a sump pump. He put me on a wooden table. He broke my hymen. After a while the sensation felt good because I didn't know any better. I never told. I was ashamed.

He was very sexual and would jerk off a lot. His sister implied that some abuse happened to him as a child.

When we went on vacations or rode in the car I rode in the front and my mom rode in the back. She was afraid of him—afraid to leave. She would pack and never leave. Before my mom died she told my aunt, her sister, who knew what he did to me, to tell me that I didn't have to stay. He was mean and would say to my mom "Look who's dying." I worked and gave my mom money for treatments and medication when I was seventeen.

Mom had a nervous breakdown. She went to the hospital after the twins were born. It could have been postpartum depression. She once came after me with a fork.

She worked 11:00 p.m. to 7:00 a.m. He worked from 4:00 a.m.-11:00 a.m. This caused him to abuse me around 1:00 a.m. or 2:00 a.m.

It messed me up spiritually. I thought if there is a God, why is my life so hard? I would pray and pray. I would call Oral Roberts. I stayed in Sunday school and church. I was a candy striper so I didn't have to stay at home.

He tried to keep me away from people. What made me leave was he hit me because a boy called. I asked him "why?" He step father [sic] was just a friend. At one point I was numb, like an out-of-body experience. He allowed me to have a boyfriend that he controlled. He did work around the house.

My mom died when she was forty-two. He apologized before he died. When my mom died, he really wanted me to be with him. I used to wear pads sometimes to pretend that I had my period.

I left home at eighteen and got married at nineteen. My husband was in the military and we drank together. My child was born in 1988 when I was into sniffing cocaine. My daughter's grandmother (mother-in-law) was the one who gave it to me. I could express myself when I was drinking. I finally let my mother go two years ago.

I don't feel for men who abuse children. I wish I could've gotten help. My husband knew and he used it against me.

My uncle also approached me. He said "be nice to me and I'll be nice to you." He gave me unusual hug and it's never been the same.

One night when we were getting high and drinking, my cousin's husband had oral sex with me while I was sleeping. I thought it was something wrong with me. He later had a child with his wife's niece. They (he and his wife) are still married.

This caused me to act out with men. I was very promiscuous. I didn't know anything about love.

I still called him Dad. I never treated him differently, but I never let my daughter stay with him. He later became a drinker. I took care of him somewhat when he became ill. His daughters didn't take care of him. I was shocked that he apologized.

I was in therapy for nine months, meeting weekly from October to July meeting every week, and then every other week when my insurance changed.

I spoke to Pastor about a year after joining church. I had just started recovery after using drugs for nineteen or twenty years. I had a miscarriage at four months pregnant when I used drugs. I can't remember if there was a second. I had three abortions. I know they would have been "drug babies." My first pregnancy did not tolerate drugs and alcohol so I didn't use. I didn't know I was pregnant until I sniffed and drank and vomited.

My drug of choice was cocaine. I was in and out of church. I brought it to pastor's attention what happened to me with my father. The day that I told you, you asked if pastor knew. You prayed with me and advised that I get professional counseling. I had been clean [from drugs] for about thirty days. I needed to forgive my biological father for leaving me. Pastor told me the same thing the therapist told me, but I didn't want to hear it.

I was never allowed, never had a relationship with a pastor. I didn't know what people would think. I had doubt about being a part of this. I kept thinking "I don't know why she picked me. I have no degree. What can I do?"

Participant B

Participant B is between the age of fifty and sixty-two years old, is married, has a household size of four, owns her home, and has an annual family income of $30,000 to $40,000.

Participant B
Interview Questions

1. Prior to this interview have you ever discussed the detail of your abuse with others? If yes, why? If no, why not?

   No, I didn't feel I had a problem.

2. Why did you choose to tell your story?

   I haven't told anyone. I didn't feel it was important, because it didn't happen to me.

3. How did you feel about telling or not telling your story?

Sometimes I feel crazy. It didn't happen to me. Why am I feeling like this? It shouldn't be bothering me. Why am I so emotional? It's crazy.

4. When you read literature about violence against women how do you feel?

   I feel upset because nobody should have to go through anything like that. I feel amazed that so many have gone through it.

5. What do you think about sharing the story of your abuse with your children?

   (Very long silence) I think it wouldn't be bad. It would enlighten them to be cautious. In my situation, I wouldn't want them to feel bad about their relationship with their relatives.

6. How do you feel children can be better protected from abuse?

   By knowing certain things they can look out for. They don't let themselves get in situations—tell somebody—don't feel that somebody would look at them crazy.

7. How can the church serve as an instrument of healing for victim-survivors of abuse?

   By being able to be there for them, not to feel that they are second-class citizens—having a heart for people and what they've gone through, listen and not spread what other people have been through. Some people need to share—not think they are crazy. Don't take it for granted just because it didn't happen to you.

8. How do you define pastoral care and counseling?

   The pastor is over a group of people, has a charge to guide people, may not have the answer, but can direct them to the proper people. Privacy and confidence is important, like a doctor.

14. If you had the opportunity to speak to your abuser(s) today what would you say?

In my situation, I don't think they realize and then again . . . they do. I would like to say "you have no idea what the devastating effect has been because of what you did. It not only hurt the person but others too."

15. How do you define healing?

    Healing is when you can address certain things, walk through it, and feel that you won't allow this to take over your life. You can refuse. You can't change anyone. You can go through being hurt expecting other people to fit your expectations. When you come to grips with all of that . . . it happened. You get to the point that you can rise above it . . . don't let it drag you down by dwelling on other people's actions. You don't think it had a drastic effect on someone else.

16. How would you help to prevent other women and children from being abused?

    I realize that I have protected my children all their lives, watching where they go, who they're with. There is a lack of trust with everybody. If they can turn, then anybody can. Women being second-class citizens, do as they are told. I really resent that.

17. Why did you agree to be a part of this project?

    I have compassion for people. I feel that I could be there to help troubled women.

18. What, if anything, have you gained from your participation in this project?

    Helped me to go deep . . . to see. Helped me to be more observant and compassionate about women who have been abused. When you see them do something I used to wonder, "Why are they doing that?" Now, I think something may have triggered something.

I added an additional question for this participant.

19. I notice that you are speaking in somewhat of a code language. If you were speaking with a professional counselor do you feel that you would be able to speak more freely?

Some of the details of the response have been omitted to protect the participant's anonymity.

I think I would be able to get it out with someone that I trust. I just think it's strange because it didn't happen to me. (I began to explain that her mother's was physical abuse may have affected her. It was at this point that the participant began to speak freely). My mother was a hard worker and she always sacrificed for her children. She always made sure we had what we needed. My father was not really there. I thought because I was younger that he was there for the older ones, but they told me that he wasn't there for them either. My mother wasn't afraid of him. She used to fight back. They think I don't remember but I do. She used to get up every morning and fix a full breakfast for us before she went to work. My father drove the car and she took the bus. They worked in the same place, but she had to be at work half an hour later than him. You would think that he would have gone to work earlier so she didn't have to take the bus, but he didn't. He left. He was a womanizer. My mother never told me anything bad about him. Every now and then she would tell me that I should go and see my father. When he got sick, she took him in and took care of him. She didn't want his children to have that responsibility.

I had a godfather who I used to spend a lot of time with. He was really good to me. I used to spend a lot of time with his family, but I was never really part of the family. He used to talk to me as teenager and give me good advice about men. When I became an adult there was a disagreement and the relationship changed. It really hurt me.

My sister . . . think that's why she is so angry and sometimes difficult. He (ex-husband) left her and he begged my mother to let him in to see my sister. When she let him in he held my sister at knifepoint. My mother tried to help her and he cut both of them. My brother was out of town at the time but was very angry. We had to beg him to stop looking for the man.

He was the protector, but now he seems to love money more than anything. He does things for his mother, but I think there is another motive.

Participant B Narrative

Prior to this interview, the participant called me stating that she was very upset and was unable to write her narrative. It is interesting that this participant had been identified as one who had not experienced abuse. She was asked to write because she had casually mentioned that her father was abusive to her mother. She was also the last of the five to be interviewed. This was initially due to scheduling. However, she may have been reluctant to share the information. This interview was done over the telephone.

I deemed it important to document the conversation with Participant B, during which she discussed her difficulty with writing the narrative. She left a message on a Friday evening requesting that I call her. Due to the lateness of the hour that I received the message, the call was not returned until the following morning. The participant answered the telephone and almost immediately began to cry. She stated that whenever she sits down to write she begins to cry and is unable to stop. She talked about witnessing the abuse of women in her family, but did not give any detail as to who they were or what had been done to them. It was as if she was speaking in code language.

She said that she always told her husband if he did any of those things that it would be over. She made the statement enough that her husband could finish the sentence and would often laugh about it.

I did not press her for the details and assured her that she should not anguish over her inability to complete the narrative. She stated that she is concerned that she may be depressed and is planning to be "checked out" by a doctor. She had recently received a monetary gift, which would allow her to purchase medical insurance, short term.

Participant C

Participant C is between the age of thirty-six and fifty years old, is married, has a household size of three, rents her home, and has annual family income of over $100,000.

Participant C
Interview Questions

1. Prior to this interview have you ever discussed the detail of your abuse with others? If yes, why? If no, why not?

   Yes. A family issue came up that we discussed. I told my husband before we were married. I needed to make sure that he knew about personal experiences that may affect our marriage. I trusted him enough to share.

2. Why did you choose to tell your story?

   I knew it would help my healing process

3. How did you feel about telling or not telling your story?

More comfortable than I had in the past, trying to tell it if I had to tell it.

4. When you read literature about violence against women how do you feel?

   I find myself in a defense mode for the victimized individual. I thought about Juanita Bynum. Reason—could I have prevented what happened to me? I watch Oprah. When I see things about women or children being abused I am always analyzing.

5. What do you think about sharing the story of your abuse with your children?

   I preferred to share with my daughter to let her know that she should not hold things in. I tell her to be careful how you carry yourself as a young lady. She may be able to help someone down the road. I didn't want her to feel sorry for me. I recently advised her to seek counseling concerning an experience that she was going through. She went to the counselor who had the book that we're reading, **Courage to Heal,** on her shelf. My daughter told her, "My mommy is teaching me from that book." It made her feel comfortable with the counselor. One of my co-workers has been a victim of domestic violence and I was finally able to get her to seek help. I went with her to the prosecutor's office today.

6. How do you feel children can be better protected from abuse?

   Parents should try to understand that the children should be with children, not left with adults in other rooms. Young ladies should not sit on men's laps. Monitoring them on a daily basis, school work, church, etc. You get to understand them more. If something is wrong you'd pick up on it.

7. How can the church serve as an instrument of healing for victim-survivors of abuse?

   Teaching—a group of individuals who could be trusted. We need a counseling group—a minister should be a part of the group, preferably female. Most of the time the abuser is a male.

8. How do you define pastoral care and counseling?

Open discussion—explaining my situation, looking for information to get assistance needed.

9. If you had the opportunity to speak to your abuser(s) today what would you say?

    I don't know. I think in my head. I don't know. I may run, cry, freeze up. I think about it a lot. (The main one/cousin). I wouldn't be violent unless provoked. I'd be too afraid.

10. How do you define healing?

    Discussing the situation—being able to speak freely about what happened, helping someone else. If I can tell the story it is a part of healing.

11. How would you help to prevent other women and children from being abused?

    Any of the things that happened to me—If I see something I would let the parent know.

12. Why did you agree to be a part of this project?

    It was a healing tool for me and I was able to tell the story. I didn't really deal with what happened to me to find out if I still had a problem.

13. What, if anything, have you gained from your participation in this project

    Peace—peace of mind—knowing my story is out there—I told it and I can move one.

Participant C Narrative

During my childhood life, I was abused several times by different people. During my childhood life, I enjoyed going to church and being around other children of my age. I also was a child who was around adults a lot during my childhood life.

One Sunday afternoon after church service was over I was asked to go get a soda from the deacon who sold them to us every Sunday afternoon after church was over. For some reason, this particular Sunday, it seemed as though I was the first one to approach him for a soda. As I gave him the money for the soda, he would squeeze my breast while he was handing me the soda. No one was around so I thought this was normal and I felt this was just something that was supposed to be done. From this point on I had no idea my childhood would be damaged for life. I was an innocent little girl that just wanted to get a soda after church. I made sure after this first incident I would of course bring backup with me, but he still would catch me off guard.

My father's side of the family enjoyed life with one another by always celebrating Christmas and Thanksgiving together. I really didn't look forward to Christmas and Thanksgiving dinner because this is when my abuse would take place. I knew that there was no chance I would escape my abuser because he was my cousin (but I addressed him as my uncle). My cousin would catch me on the stairwell while going up to join my other cousins who were playing in an adjacent room. Sometimes I would try to tiptoe up the stairs hoping he wouldn't hear me. But I had a blind Uncle who had a room also on that floor and when anybody would start up the stairs he would know you by your walk and call out your name and this would just give you away. I had no choice as a child but to go up the stairs because my parents, aunts, and uncles who were downstairs would tell us to go upstairs and play and stay out of grown folk's conversations. This was a losing battle.

Once I was noticed coming up the stairs by my cousin, he would threaten me and tell me to come into his room. Once I was in his room he would immediately padlock the door. The first time he took my hand and guided my hand toward his private parts, I immediately resisted. He told me that it was okay, but I still hesitated. There were times I wanted to run, but he had threatened me in so many ways that I felt my family would be in danger if I didn't do what he told me. I was threatened with a machete and gun. He also promised he would harm my family if I didn't do what he said. I was asked to perform oral sex. I did it. Once I thought I was done I would run into the bathroom across the hall and try to wash my mouth out with someone's toothbrush. After knowing that this would happen every holiday I would regret going over to their house and try to make believe I was sick. Sometimes I would give up making believe, because I wanted so much to be around my other cousins. There were times that he trapped me into his room where I would make believe I had passed out so that he wouldn't even ask me to do anything to him. He began to catch on that I was pretending.

Another incident was my father who asked me to touch his private parts. This happened because my mother left me in the house by myself after sending me to bed. My father had turned in early for the evening because I guess he was tipsy. Somehow he knew I was in my bedroom across from his room sleeping. He called out my name and I answered. He asked me to "come here." I slowly walked toward him with fear. He asked me to come closer and I hesitated. I finally got close enough to him not knowing in the dark he was naked. He then reached for my hand and placed it on him. I immediately thought "why me?" I just wanted to grow up.

Everyone has their reasons why they move from membership to membership. I chose to stay at my church despite what happened to me because I knew a comforter would come to help me. A member of the church was my first abuser. I thought I was safe in church. My cousin was my second abuser who I respected as a big brother. My final abuser was my father who was suppose to, I thought, protect me from violators. I just thank God that I am healed through our women's ministry in our church today. Without this women's ministry, I know, I would have lost my mind. My spiritual guidance has blessed my home and my life. I will never look back with guilt in my heart because I am a triumphant woman of God.

Participant D

Participant D is between the age of thirty-six and fifty years old, is single, has a household size of five, rents her home, and has an annual family income of between $40,000 and $50,000.

Participant D
Interview Questions

1. Prior to this interview have you ever discussed the detail of your abuse with others? If yes, why? If no, why not?

   Yes, the reason—I felt it was time to open up. It took over fifteen years because I was afraid of what people would think about me.

2. Why did you choose to tell your story?

   My children were going to school and there was a presentation given for parents by Cheryl Winters (pseudonym). The title was "Parents Are People Too." I was told that when you deal with things from your past it helps you to be a better person and a better parent.

3. How did you feel about telling or not telling your story?

   Dirty, disgusted at times.

4. When you read literature about violence against women how do you feel?

Sad, broken up—I realize [that] I wasn't alone. All the time I thought I was alone, I really wasn't.

5. What do you think about sharing the story of your abuse with your children?

   Afraid—more so with my daughter—I'm trying to protect her from my pain. She may be curious and do it anyway. You know how your parents tell you not to do something, but you do it anyway. Like our parents told us not to drink and we did it anyway. My sons are already overprotective and may just cut everybody off.

6. How do you feel children can be better protected from abuse?

   Whew! (deep sigh) Can we come back to this question later? (We came back to this at the end of the interview and the response was as follows). Being aware of where your children go, who they are in company with. That was the mistake that my grandmother made. She wasn't ready to take on the responsibility to raise four children after my mom died. I'm mindful of who my daughter plays with. No sitting on men's laps. I watch the boys, too. I recently called Ms. Winters (pseudonym) who did that presentation that caused me to open up. I needed to talk to her because my boys were asking me questions about feelings that they were having and I needed help to talk to them about sex.

7. How can the church serve as an instrument of healing for victim-survivors of abuse?

   Having workshops presented by people who have been abused. You're more comfortable with people who have gone through the same thing. It usually takes one person to open up.

8. How do you define pastoral care and counseling?

   When you can talk one on one with your pastor—feel comfortable about opening up. There's a comfort zone—one on one and you're looking for comfort. A lot of times I want to swing this door open (the interview took place in the pastor's office). Sometime [s] I dial his number in the midnight hour and hang up wondering why I didn't finish the call.

9. If you had the opportunity to speak to your abuser(s) today what would you say?

   I have confronted one. The other died. One day I ran into him while I was working. I gave him a strange look and he said, "I'm free." I said to him, "Are you really free?" He said he was sorry for what he and Darnell [pseudonym] did. I asked, "Why me?" He said, "I was going through a lot at the time and you were the first person walking down the hallway." I told him that they ruined my life and I have had problems with men. He asked me if we could talk. After all that was a long time ago and we're both different people now. I told him that I didn't want to talk to him, but he kept following me. I started screaming and telling him that if he didn't stop following me I would call the police. I was so afraid and shaken up that I stayed home from work for the next two days. When I went home that night I was standing at the kitchen washing dishes and my daughter's father came up behind me and touched my shoulder. I felt like I was being attacked and yelled out. He asked me what was wrong with me. I never told him, but I couldn't sleep with him. I slept alone and got dressed in the bathroom.

10. How do you define healing?

    Time—(Pause—sigh) and it's a process.

11. How would you help to prevent other women and children from being abused?

    I wouldn't even know. Sometimes I still feel like I need help.

12. Why did you agree to be a part of this project?

    'Cause I said it's gonna help and in time I'm gonna be able to help someone else. When I needed help there was no one there. Right now, I need help. I'm very emotional and would like to help, but I'm afraid that people will say "she's supposed to be helping me and she's falling apart."

13. What, if anything, have you gained from your participation in this project?

    That I was the victim and it wasn't my fault and in time I'm gonna be all right—sooner than I anticipated. Reading and writing has made me stronger, wiser, and aware. Meeting men, I felt vulnerable. I used to take whatever. For the past couple of years, I've been alone concentrating on me and my children. I didn't think I could do that. Studying and staying prayed up has brought me a long way.

Participant D Narrative

I lost my mother at the age of nine and moved in with my grandmother (my mother's mother) and step grandfather. She took a leave of absence from her job as a manager to raise four grandchildren. My grandmother applied for welfare and realized that there wasn't enough money to take care of four children. So she went back to work as a manager after two years. My grandmother worked during the day, but they didn't have a position on days anymore. She began to worry who would care for her four grandchildren if she had to work nights, 3:00 p.m.-11:00 p.m. Her husband, my step grandfather told my grandmother that he would care for us if she wanted to work those hours. So my grandmother took the position. Everything was fine until my brother was old enough to hang out with his friends, come in to eat, take a bath, and go to sleep.

My grandparents live on the second floor. We, the children, lived in the attic. My oldest brother didn't have the responsibility to care for us. He thought that he got a break. My step grandfather would give me and my sister money to do whatever we wanted to do. I thought this was good. First night, second night, third night he would go to sleep with us in the same bed; me and my sister under the cover/blankets and he lay on top of the blankets at the foot of the bed. The fourth, fifth, and sixth night he wanted a hug and kiss good night. From that point on it was on and popping. My grandmother worked her shift and he had either me or my sister. First, he just wanted to touch and smell me like I was fresh meat. As I began to squirm, he would tie my hands and put a sock in my mouth. Then he would suck on my breast and masturbate. This went on for several months. Between all of the months, gifts; money to me, my sister, and our friends. All of our friends loved him. They thought he was the best grandfather ever. He told me if I and my sister told he would kill our baby brother who was only two years old and didn't know what was going on.

I was chosen because my sister was light-skinned and reminded him of my grandmother. I was brown-skinned with beautiful skin, long hair and built for a twelve and a half-year-old. As time went on sex went on from two nights a week to four nights a week. As long as I sleep with him he would continue to give me money and take me, my sister, and our friends wherever we want to go. Now I am sick of this. I am trying to see who I can trust enough to tell them so they can save me and my sister.

I decided to join music and play the clarinet at school as an afternoon getaway. I went to music three days a week and my grandmother was off on the weekends. The school was close by so I was allowed to attend music from three fifteen to five forty-five, so by the time I got in and did homework, ate, and took a bath it was nine or nine thirty and my big brother was home and I was safe. My step grandfather was afraid of my brother. He was six feet and about three hundred pounds, solid.

I enjoyed playing the clarinet. I got pretty good at it. This boy named SR and his friend L was always picking on me every day for about two months. One day the music teacher paged me to come down to the music room in the basement. As I got close to the music room L and SR, covered my mouth and dragged me down to another part of the school under the music room so no one could hear me scream. Little did I know that angels were watching over me 'cause the kids were playing and practicing. The music was extremely loud. When the music stopped I knew I was about to be free. Just as L was finished his business with me SR thought it was his turn. L placed his penis in my mouth while he held my hands. SR took out his penis and I began to cry. They were laughing. I bit down on L's penis and he screamed so loud that the music teacher came out of the class to see what was going on. He heard me screaming, "Help me! They are raping me!" The music teacher came down and saved my life. I will never forget him. They got expelled from school pending their trial. My grandmother contacted the police. The two gentlemen wanted to go to trial saying that I wanted it just as much as they did. So we went to trial and they lost the case. They went to prison for fifteen years. They had four or five counts against them. L got more time because he actually penetrated inside of me. SR didn't. My step grandfather laid low for a little for a while 'cause I was having nightmares about all the things that were going on with me. I went to therapy. My aunt stepped in to help out by letting us stay with her every other week. So I went to my aunt's house for two weeks and stayed with my grandma for two weeks.

Around my sophomore year in high school stepfather started to get sick, having several problems. I was praying that I came home and he would be dead. As I went on I'm now a senior about to graduate, prom, class trip. I went to Virginia Beach for my class trip in June 1988. My big brother picked me up from school 'cause my grandmother was at the hospital. Her husband, HU, had a heart attack and died. I graduated. I was so happy I was free from this man.

My life as a woman was no picnic. I wouldn't wish what I been through in my worst enemy. Emotional, I'm still scared, scarred up. Every now and then I get into a shell and hibernate. I look into the mirror and cry for no reason. Afraid to take my clothes off in front of the men I have dated and slept with. In time I will get healed. Now that I'm saved I know what God said to me in His word. Philippians 4:13. It's more than anything I can imagine. I want to be able to help another young lady. If I can help one woman I'm satisfied. I wish I had one woman to save me. I want to make a difference. You have to watch for signs, be observant, and more importantly, listen to your children. Now that I'm a mother I talk to my children. I watch them and changes they go through. I'm mindful of who I have around them. I don't allow them to spend the night out. I'm so careful with my children that I'm too overprotective. I talk to my boys about touching and feeling on girls and "No" means "No."

Thank you in advance for the opportunity to share some of my life with you as a mid-teen.

Participant E

Participant E is between the age of thirty-six and fifty years old, is married, has a household size of three, rents her home, and has an annual family income of between $10,000 and $20,000.

Participant E
Interview Questions

1. Prior to this interview have you ever discussed the detail of your abuse with others? If yes, why? If no, why not?

   Yes—I was trying to heal myself. That's what I was told to do.

2. Why did you choose to tell your story?

   Purely selfish—it's for me to stay sober. It is to help, but it's purely selfish.

3. How did you feel about telling or not telling your story?

   Anxious, nervous.

4. When you read literature about violence against women how do you feel?

   Angry, sad, and sometimes helpless.

5. What do you think about sharing the story of your abuse with your children?

I've done that with my daughter. I've actually spoken with the youngest because I don't want her to go through it. When I was reunited with my oldest daughter I had to explain what was going on in my life. I felt the need to explain the child sex abuse. Her father was the physical abuser. My sister had her [daughter] since she was two. When I went to rehab she was sixteen. When I reunited with my father he gave her my number and she called me. Do you think it helped her? No (pause) not at all. She has a lot of issues with me, still. She wanted to get in touch with her father, but I haven't seen him in more than twenty years.

6. How do you feel children can be better protected from abuse?

    I don't know. I really don't. I am afraid for (named child). I don't know. Maybe it's me. I'm always watching and suspicious.

7. How can the church serve as an instrument of healing for victim-survivors of abuse?

    First, let it be known that there is abuse. Have some kind of therapy, a place to come, share, and be comfortable . . . a women's meeting, a survivor's meeting. That's what I'll call it.

8. How do you define pastoral care and counseling?

    You need help, you ask, they give it and that's usually how it works.

9. If you had the opportunity to speak to your abuser(s) today what would you say?

    Why would they do that? Why would they hurt somebody like that?

10. How do you define healing?

    I guess it would be learning how to live with what happened—just living with it. I guess, understand it. It's confusing. It's a fact that it happened. Just dealing with the fact that it happened. You have to accept it, then move on. You have to learn how to forgive.

11. How would you help to prevent other women and children from being abused?

Other than putting bells on their drawers, just recently I had an experience. This is different than the first time I told you about. I talked to your husband about it (pastor) and I asked him not to tell you. I woke up in the middle of the night and my husband was in the room where my daughter sleeps. He was leaning over the futon looking out of the window. She was sleeping on the futon. I asked him why he was out there and he said that it was too hot in our room. I told him to turn on the air-conditioner. I don't know if it's just me. (Begins to cry) I wonder why he gets so angry with her about boys. I wonder if he wants her for himself. I keep trying to set booby traps for him. I'm not sure if she would tell me if anything was going on. After all, she didn't even tell me that she had sex with that boy. She told your husband. I asked him (husband) to get some information for me concerning counseling for someone who was a victim of incest. I know because of the work that he does that, he can go right to that information but he didn't. I don't know. There's no foolproof way.

12. Why did you agree to be a part of this project?

Because you asked and people do need to know. Church people or people need to know it goes on and look how nutty you can end up—forty-four years later and I'm still nuts.

13. What, if anything, have you gained from your participation in this project?

Kinship, a little bit of understanding, some stress, relief. Sometimes it feels good to share not be judged. No matter how many time you tell it you feel like you're being judged from your past.

Participant E Narrative

I am a woman whose life has been molded by abuse; sexual, physical, and verbal. It started happening very early in my life, first by being sexually abused by my godfather at the age of five years old. This was a person who was supposed to protect me; instead he chose to use his trust to violate me. From the very beginning it was kept hush, hush by my mother and family. My mom did the best she could, but the damage was already done. I suppressed that traumatic occurrence until I was a grown woman. Because of that abuse, I can now see why I did some of the things I've done, why I always equated sex with love. My self-esteem was nonexistent so I became a person who was very promiscuous. In my house, growing up the youngest of three, me being the youngest and the only one at home. My brother was twenty-five years older and my sister was twenty years older. I was very spoiled. Today, I wonder if it was because of guilt by my mother and father. See, to this day, I don't know if he ever knew about the abuse by his friend. On the outside, our home life looked picture perfect . . . Mom, Dad, car, house, dog. It looked like we had it all. My dad was a respected man in the neighborhood, but the reality is we had a big secret and it was never to be talked about outside of the house. My dad was an alcoholic and a physical abuser of my mom. My mom was a verbal abuser toward me. My whole life my mom would say things that to this day still hurt my heart when I hear them. "You're stupid, you're good for nothing, you're a whore." When I hear someone say these things and it can be someone else saying it to be joking, I take it serious and it's not directed to me. She used to say, "Why can't you be like your sister?" Ms. Goody Good, one husband, good job, two kids, never in trouble, didn't drink, drug, followed all the rules. The more she said it, it seemed the more I did the opposite. I hung out with the people who did the cool stuff, and just to fit in I tended to do all the wrong things. I never felt like I fit in, not even with my own family. You see, all three of us had the same mom but different fathers, and mine being Hispanic, which was a no, no. My mom always told me if anybody ever asks what you are, don't tell them you're Puerto Rican. Tell them you're Italian. It was always a cover-up. I could never or should I say, I didn't know how to be myself.

    I tended to find guys who were just like what I thought was normal, like my first boyfriend. He was physically abusive. He would push and shove and yell and call me names, but to me that meant he loved me. At fourteen, what did I really know about love? At sixteen years old, I met someone who I thought loved me. In the beginning, he was great to me, a little controlling and a little jealous. I associated that with love, because he would tell me that he loved me. By this time drinking and drugging came into play. I got pregnant and married at seventeen. Then my life drastically changed. The control, verbal and physical abuse started very quickly. Being told what to wear, what to cook, who I could talk to, where I could go, and if the rules were not followed there would be hell to pay. At first, it would be a slap or I'd get yelled at. Eventually, it became torture and every day a beating . . . kicked, stomped, stabbed, punched, burned. I felt trapped and he had me believing it was all my fault and I really didn't know any better. I believed it was me, that I wasn't a good woman. I endured it for four years. It got to the point where my whole being was broken; spirit, mind, and body. If I had stayed any longer I would be dead. I could not breathe without being afraid. I was helpless and hopeless. I even thought of suicide, but I was too afraid to do that.

    The breaking point was when he hit my baby daughter and tried to hang me. I finally went through with it and had him arrested. I had him arrested plenty of times before, but always dropped the charges. This time, I went through it all the way. He got six months in the workhouse. So afraid he would get out and I knew he would kill me, I packed up everything and moved down south. I knew he wouldn't find me there.

Eventually, I moved back to my hometown. It was two years later that I ran into him. All the fear came back instantly, but this time I made a stand. He tried to intimidate me again, but I pulled a hatchet on him and he left me alone. But I was afraid. It took years of drug abuse and alcoholism to get me much needed emotional help. But besides that the scars are still there. Today, some situations send me right back to the abuse. I see something or hear something and my first thoughts are that physical or sexual abuse is going to happen again. Not to me, but to my daughter. It never leaves you, the fear. But now I am able to talk about it and make a stand, no matter what the outcome will be. I have to break the cycle. I'm sure it happened in the past history of my family, but they were not informed. It was kept quiet. Today, it's not. I can be more verbal and make a stand. I chose to break the silence.

Bibliography

Adams, Carol J. and Marie Fortune, eds. *Violence Against Women and Children.* New York: The Continuum Publishing Company, 1995.

Adkins, Winthrop R., Caroline Manuele Adkins, and Myriam Belloch-Cort. *Adkins Life Skill Program Career Development Series.* Vol. 1. 10 vols. 3rd ed. New York: Institute for Life coping Skills, Inc.

Alpha-Omega Ministries, Inc. *The Preacher's Outline & Sermon Bible* [Software Program]. Chattanooga, TN: Leadership Ministries Worldwide, 2007, 1992.

American Institute of. Stress. *America's No. 1 Health Problem.* Available from *www.stress.org/about.htm?AIS=6dd.* Accessed July 15, 2007.

Ammerman, Nancy T., Jackson W. Carroll, Carl. S. Dudley, and William McKinney, eds. *Studying Congregations.* Nashville, TN: Abingdon Press, 1993.

Anderson, Cheryl B. *Women, Ideology and Violence.* New York: T&T Clark International, 2004.

Associated Press. "Award Cut in Mormon Church Abuse Case." 15 Sept. 2007. Available from *http://www.rickross.com/reference/mormon/mormon431.html.* Accessed December 3, 2007.

Atwell, Mary Welek. *Equal Protection of the Law?* New York: Peter Lang, 2002.

Bader, Mary Ann. *Sexual Violation in the Hebrew Bible.* New York: Peter Lang, 2006.

Bellis, Agnes Ogden. *Helpmates, Harlots and Heroes.* Louisville, KY: Westminster/John Knox Press, 1994.

Benner, David G. *Strategic Pastoral Counseling: A Short-Term Structured Model*. 2nd ed. Grand Rapids, MI: Baker Academic, 2003.

Biblesoft's New Exhaustive Strong's Numbers and Concordance with Expanded Greek-Hebrew Dictionary. Seattle, WA: Biblesoft and International Bible Translators, Inc., 1994.

Black, Courtney and Maxine Hanks. *Mormon Women Must Be Heard* [Newspaper]. Boston, MA: Boston Globe. Available from *http://rickcross. com/reference/mormon/mormon/28.html. Accessed Dec. 8*, 2007.

Blumenthal. David R. *Facing the Abusing God A Theology of Protest*. Louisville, KY: Westminster/John Knox Press, 1993.

Bonhoeffer, Deitrich. *Life Together*. New York: HarperCollins, 1954.

Brandwein, Ruth A., ed. *Battered Women, Children and Welfare Reform*. Edited by Claire M. Renzitti and Jeffrey L. Edleson, Sage Series on Violence against Women. Thousand Oaks, TN: Sage Publications, 1999.

Brown, Sally A. and Patrick D. Miller, eds. *Lament*. Louisville, KY: Westminster John Knox Press, 2005.

Brown, Teresa L. Fry. *God Don't Like Ugly*. Nashville, TN: Abingdon Press, 2000.

Brueggemann, Walter. *The Prophetic Imagination*. Minneapolis, MN: Fortress Press, 2001.

Bullock, Cathy Ferrand. "Framing Domestic Violence Fatalities: Coverage by Utah Newspapers." *Journal of Interpersonal Violence*. 30 *Women's Studies in Communication*. (2007): 34.

Butler, Sandra. *Conspiracy of Silence: The Trauma of Incest*. Updated ed. Volcano, CA: Volcano Press, 1996.

Carruthers, Iva E., Frederick D. Haynes III and Jeremiah Wright, Jr., eds. *Blow the Trumpet in Zion: Global Vision and Action for the 21st Century Black Church*. Minnesota, MN: Fortress Press, 2005.

Cauthen, Kenneth. *An Essay on Using the Bible with Integrity*. Available from www.frontier.net/kenc/bibint.htm. Accessed November 15, 2003.

City-Data.com. *Newark, New Jersey.* Available from http:*www.city-data.com/city/Newark-New-Jersey-.html.* Accessed Dec. 3, 2007.

Classic Encyclopedia. *Newark, New Jersey.* Available from *http://www.1911encyclopedia.org/Newark%2C_New_Jersey.* Accessed December 3, 2007.

Clinebell, Howard. *Basic Types of Pastoral Care & Counseling.* Revised ed. Nashville, TN: Abingdon Press, 1984.

Coleman, Monica A. *The Dinah Project.* Cleveland, OH: The Pilgrim Press, 2004.

Collier-Thomas, Bettye and V.P. Franklin, ed. *Sisters in the Struggle.* New York: New York University Press, 2001.

Cone, James H. and Gayraud S. Wilmore, eds. *Black Theology a Documentary History Volume One.* Maryknoll, NY: Orbis Books, 1993.

_____, ed. *Black Theology a Documentary History Volume Two.* Maryknoll, NY: Orbis Books, 2003.

Cooper-White, Pamela. *The Cry of Tamar.* Minneapolis, MN: Fortress Press, 1995.

Cranton, Patricia. *Professional Development as Transformative Learning.* San Francisco, CA: Jossey-Bass, 1996.

Crawford, Vicki L., Jacqueline Anne Rouse and Barbara Woods, eds. *Women in the Civil Rights Movement.* Bloomington, IN: Indiana University Press, 1990.

Creswell, John W. *Research Design Qualitative, Quantitative, and Mixed Methods Approaches.* 2nd ed. Thousand Oaks, CA: Sage Publications, 2003.

Crowell, Nancy A., and Ann W. Burgess, eds. *Panel on Understanding Violence against Women: Committee on Law and Justice: Commission on Behavioral and Social Sciences and Education: National Research Council.* Washington, D.C.: National Academy Press, 1996

Culpepper, R. Alan. *The Gospel and Letters of John.* Nashville, TN: Abingdon Press, 1998.

Davies, Richard E. *Handbook for Doctor of Ministry Projects.* New York: University Press of America, 1984.

Davis, Laura. *The Courage to Heal Workbook.* New York: HarperCollins Publishers, 1990.

Davis, Sharon Ellis. Hear Our Cries: Breaking the Gender Entrapment of African American Battered Women. Ph.D. diss. The Chicago Theological Seminary, 2006.

Davis, W. Marshall. *Twisted Sister* Rochester, PA: Available from home.comcast.net/~wmarshalldavisjr/03-04-07.html. Accessed July 6, 2007.

Eastern Network and Central African Women in Development. *Violence against Women Trainers Manual.* Kenya: Paulines Publication, 1997.

Engel, Beverly. *The Emotionally Abused Woman.* New York: Fawcett Books, 1990.

Felder, Cain Hope. *Troubling Biblical Waters.* Maryknoll, NY: Orbis Books, 1989.

Fiorenza, Elizabeth Schussler and Mary Shawn Copeland, eds. *Violence Against Women.* Maryknoll, NY: Orbis Books, 1994.

Fitts, Bobb. *Alabaster Ministries* 2007. Available from *www.bobfitts.com/alabaster.html.* Accessed July 8, 2007.

Fortune, Marie M. *Sexual Violence the Sin Revisited.* Cleveland, OH: The Pilgrim Press, 2005.

Garfield, Gail. *Knowing What We Know.* New Brunswick, NJ: Rutgers University Press, 2005.

Gench, Frances Taylor. *Encounters with Jesus.* Louisville, KY: Westminster John Knox Press, 2007.

Gordon, Robert P. *1 & 2 Samuel a Commentary.* Grand Rapids, MI: Zondervan Publishing House, 1986.

Haberman, Clyde. "Back On The Air, Imus Vows to Play Fair." *The New York Times.* 4 Dec. 2007. http://www.nytimes.com/2007/12/04/nyregion/04nyc.html. Accessed Dec. 4, 2007.

Hampton, Henry and Steve Fayer. *Voices of Freedom: An Oral History of the Civil Rights Movement from the 1950s Through the 1980s.* New York: Bantam Books, 1991.

Hansen, Paul A. *Survivors & Partners: Healing the Relationships of Sexual Abuse Survivors.* Longmont, CO: Heron Hill Publishing Company, 1991.

Hardie, Elfreida. Church History. Newark, NJ: Paradise Baptist Church, 1993.

Harrington, Daniel J. ed. *Sacra Pagina The Gospel of John.* Collegeville, MN: The Liturgical Press, 1998.

Heaton, E. W. *Everyday Life in Old Testament Times.* New York: Charles Scribner's
Sons, 1956.

Hendricks, Obery. *Living Water.* New York: HarperCollins Publishers, Inc., 2003.

Herman, Judith. *Trauma and Recovery.* New York: Basic Books, 1997.

Hollies, Linda H. *Bodacious Womanist Wisdom.* Cleveland, OH: The Pilgrim Press, 2003.

Hopkins, Dwight N. *Shoes That Fit Our Feet.* Maryknoll, NY: Orbis Books, 1993.

Howard-Brook, Wes. *Becoming Children of God.* Eugene, OR: Wipf and Stock Publishers, 2003.

James, Jethro C. Church Mission Statement. Paradise Baptist Church, 1997.

Jones, Laura Beth. *Jesus, Ceo.* Reprinted ed. New York: Hyperion, 1993.

Jones, Major J. *The Color of God.* Macon, GA: Mercer University Press, 1987.

Justes, Emma J. *Hearing Beyond the Words.* Nashville, TN: Abingdon Press, 2006.

Kitzberger, Ingrid Rosa, ed. *Transformative Encounters Jesus & Women Re-Viewed.* Boston, MA: Brill, 2000.

Kroeger, Catherine Clark and James R. Beck, eds. *Women, Abuse, and the Bible*. Grand Rapids, MI: Baker Books, 1996.

Laatikainen, TJ. "Corticotropin-Releasing Hormone and Opioid Peptides in Reproduction and Stress." 23 *Ann Med*. (1991):489-96.

Lampman, Lisa Barnes, ed. *God and the Victim Theological Reflections on Evil, Victimization, Justice, and Forgiveness*. Grand Rapids, MI: William Eerdmans Publishing Company, 1999.

Lawless, Elaine J. *Women Escaping Violence*. Columbia, MO: University of Missouri Press, 2001.

Lencioni, Patrick. *The Five Dysfunctions of a Team: A Leadership Fable*. San Francisco, CA: Jossey-Bass, 2002.

Leslie, Kristen J. *When Violence Is No Stranger*. Minneapolis, MN: Fortress Press, 2003.

Lockyer, Herbert. *All the Women of the Bible*. reprint 1998 ed. Grand Rapids, MI: Zondervan Publishing House.

Lorin, Janet Frankston. "Shootings Renew Mayor's Sense of Purpose." *http://examiner.com/a-887966 _ Shootings _Renew _ Mayor _ s _ Sense _ of Purpose.html*. Accessed August 23, 2007.

Maxwell, John C. *Leadership 101*. Nashville, TN: Thomas Nelson Publishers, 2002.

Manlina, Bruce J. and Richard L. Rohrbaugh. *Social Science Commentary on the Gospel of John*. Minneapolis, MN: Fortress Press, 1998.

McBride, J. Lebron. *Spiritual Crisis: Surviving Trauma to the Soul*. New York: The Haworth Pastoral Press, 1998.

McCarter, P. Kyle. *The Anchor Bible 2 Samuel*. Garden City, NY: Doubleday & Company, 1984.

McNiff, Jean, Pamela Lomax and Jack Whitehead. *You and Your Action Research Project*. 2nd ed. New York: RoutledgeFalmer Taylor & Francis Group, 2003.

Meyer, Joyce. *Beauty for Ashes*. Revised and Expanded ed. New York: Warner Faith, 2003. Reprint, 2003.

Miller, Mary Susan. *No Visible Wounds*. New York: The Random House Publishing Group, 1995.

Miller, Patrick D. and Paul Achtemeier, eds. *Interpretation a Bible Commentary for Teaching and Preaching*. Edited by James L. Mays, First and Second Samuel. Louisville, KY: John Knox Press, 1990.

Myers, William R. *Research in Ministry: Primer for the Doctor of Ministry Program,* 3rd Edition. Chicago, IL: Exploration Press, 2000.

National Institute of Mental Health available at nimh.hih.gov/healthinformation/ ptsd/menu/cfm. Accessed July 16, 2007.

Niebuhr, Reinhold. *Faith and History*. Eugene, OR: Reprinted Wipf and Stock Publishers, 2001.

Omanson, Roger L. and John E. Ellington. *A Handbook on the First and Second Books of Samuel* United Handbook Series. New York: United Bible Societies, 2001.

Packer, J. I. and M.C. Tenney, eds. *Illustrated Manners and Customs of the Bible*. Nashville, TN: Thomas Nelson Publishers, 1980.

Park, Andrew Sung. *From Hurt to Healing*. Nashville, TN: Abingdon Press, 2004.

_____. *The Wounded Heart of God: The Asian Concept of Han and the Christian Doctrine of Sin*. Nashville, TN: Abingdon Press, 1993.

Parks, Brad. *Crossroads Pt.2: 5 Days That Changed a City* Newark: Newark Star Ledger, accessed Posted July 9, 2007 *http://blog.nj.com/ledger/2007/07/ crossroads _pt _ 2.html*. Accessed September 1, 2007.

_____. *Crossroads Pt.3: After the Riots, Change Is Slow to Come* [4 Part Series]. Newark: July 10, 2007 3:10AM Available from a _ pt _ 3.html. Accessed September 1, 2007.

Penn, Michael L. and Rahel Nardos. *Overcoming Violence Against Women and Girls The International Campaign to Eradicate a Worldwide Epidemic*. New York: Rowman & Littlefield Publishers, Inc., 2003.

Pierce-Baker, Charlotte. *Surviving the Silence*. New York: W.W. Norton & Company, 1998.

Pinn, Anthony B. *Why Lord?* New York: The Continuum International Publishing Group, Inc., 2006.

Pohly, Kenneth. *Transforming the Rough Places*. 2nd ed. Franklin, TN: Providence House Publishers, 2001.

MSN Encarta Premium. *Newark (New Jersey)* http://encarta.msn.com/encyclopedia _ 761566779/Newark_(New_Jersey).html. Accessed August 22, 2007.

Proctor, Samuel DeWitt. *The Substance of Things Hoped For*. Valley Forge, PA: Judson Press, 1995.

Leadership Ministries Worldwide. *The Preacher's Outline & Sermon Bible*. Chatanooga, TN: Leadership Ministries Worldwide.

Raphael, Jody. *Saving Bernice: Battered Women, Welfare and Poverty*. Boston, MA: Northeastern University Press, 2000.

Roberts, J. Deotis. *The Prophethood of Black Believers*. Louisville, KY: Westminster/John Knox Press, 1994.

Robinson, Lori S. *I Will Survive*. Emeryville, CA: Seal Press, 2002.

Sandomir, Richard. "Jury Finds Knicks and Coach Harassed a Former Executive". New York: *The New York Times*. 3 October 2007.

Schaberg, Jane, Alice Bach and Esther Fuchs, eds. *On the Cutting Edge*. New York: Continuum, 2004.

Scholz, Susanne. *Rape Plots*. New York: Peter Lang Publishing, Inc., 2000.

Sedmak, Clemens. *Doing Local Theology*. Maryknoll, NY: Orbis Books, 2002.

Sexual Harassment Support. *Sexual Harassment in the Workplace*. Available from *http://www.sexualharassmentsupport.org/SHworkplace.html*. Accessed December 4, 2007.

Simundson, Daniel J. *The Message of Job*. Lima, OH: Academic Renewal Press, 2001.

Sokoloff, Natalie J. and Christina Pratt, ed. *Domestic Violence at the Margins: Readings on Race, Class, Gender and Culture*. New Brunswick, NJ: Rutgers University Press.

Spence, H.D.M. and Joseph S. Excell, ed. *The Pulpit Commentary*. vol. 17. Peabody, MA: Hendrickson Publishers.

Steenson, Hal. *Useless Unless Broken*; Available from *www.3abn.org/devotional.cfm?id+1671*. Accessed July, 8, 2007.

Steinberg, Jacques. "Rutgers Player Withdraws Imus Lawsuit." *New York Times*. 12 Sept. 2007. Available from *http://www.nytimes.com/2007/09/12/sports/12rutgers.html*. Accessed December 3, 2007.

Stewart, Carlyle Fielding III. *Soul Survivors*. Louisville, KY: Westminster John Knox Press, 1997.

_____. *Effects of Stress* 2007; Available from *www.stress.org/topic-effects/* Accessed July 16, 2007.

Thomas, Linda E., ed. *Living Stones in the Household of God*. Minneapolis, MN: Fortress
Press, 2004.

Thomas, Owen C. and Ellen K. Wondra. *Introduction to Theology*. Harrisburg, PA: Morehouse Publishing, 2002.

Townes, Emilie M., ed. *A Troubling in My Soul: Womanist Perspectives on Evil and Suffering*. Maryknoll, NY: Orbis Books, 1993.

_____, ed. *Embracing the Spirit*. Edited by Dwight N. Hopkins. Vol. XIII, The Bishop Henry McNeal Turner/Sojourner Truth Series in Black Religion. Maryknoll, NY: Orbis, 1997.

Tracy, Steven R. *Mending the Soul*. Grand Rapids, MI: Zondervan, 2005.

Trible, Phyllis. *Texts of Terror*. Philadelphia, PA: Fortress Press, 1984.

Washington, James Melvin. *Conversations with God*. New York: HarperPerennial, 1994.

Weems, Renita J. *Battered Love*. Minneapolis, MN: Fortress Press, 1995.

West, Traci C. *Wounds of the Spirit*. New York: New York University Press, 1999.

White, Deborah Gray. *Ar'nt I a Woman? Slaves in the Plantation South*. New York, NY: Norton, 1999.

Williams, Dolores S. *Sisters in the Wilderness*. Maryknoll, NY: Orbis Books, 1993.

Wink, Walter. *Engaging the Powers*. Minneapolis, MN: Fortress Press, 1992.

Index

A

Abernathy, Ralph, 61
Abraham (husband of Sarah), 65, 150–51, 167
Absalom (brother of Tamar and Amnon), 63, 65–67, 152–53
abuse, xi, 20, 24, 35, 40, 81, 177–78
  child, 160–61
  drug, 20, 227
  neglect, 116
  nonphysical, vi, 22, 27
  physical, 5, 27, 116
  psychological, 6, 161
  sexual, 31, 54, 116, 160
    child, 18, 22, 28, 150
    clergy, 160
  spiritual, 116, 150
  verbal, 116
Adam (first man), 44, 49, 63, 82, 148
Adams, Abigail, 50
Adams, Carol J., 58
African Methodist Episcopal Church, 4, 35
American Institute of Stress (AIS), 175
Amnon (brother of Tamar and Absalom), 64–68, 152–53
Anderson, Cheryl B.
  Women, Ideology, and Violence, 49
Anna (prophetess), 137
assault, sexual, 18
Atwell, Mary Welek
  Equal Protection of the Law?, 51
Augustine, Saint, 44–45

B

Bader, Mary Anna, 65
Baker, Ella, 55–56, 61
Baraka, Amiri, 53
Bass, Ellen
  Courage to Heal, The, 31, 95
Bat-Dominiatus (physician), 141
Bates, Daisy, 55
battering, 18, 22, 27
Belenky, Mary
  Women's Ways of Knowing, 29
Bellis, Alice Ogden, 67, 153
Benner, David, 36
Between Voice and Silence (Taylor, Gilligan, and Sullivan), 31
Bird, Phyllis A., 43
Black Nationalist Movement, 53
Black Panther Party, 54–55
Blumenthal, David R., 49, 85
Bond, Julian, 56
Bonhoeffer, Dietrich, 21
Booker, Corey, 16
Book of the Covenant, 49
Brent, Linda. *See* Jacobs, Harriet
Brown, Elaine, 55
Brown, R. E.
  Community of the Beloved Disciple, The, 71
Brueggemann, Walter, 62, 64, 68, 230
Bullock, Cathy Ferrand, 50
Butts, Calvin, 59

C

Caldwell, J. W., 12
Callaway, Mary, 67, 153
Canaanite woman, 142–43, 145
Carter, Joe A., 41–42
Carter, Mae Bertha, 62
Cauthen, Kenneth, 46
civil rights movement, 55, 231
Clark, Septima, 55
classism, 46
Cleaver, Eldridge, 54
Clinebell, Howard, 36
Coleman, Monica A., 35, 38
Community of the Beloved Disciple, The (Brown), 71
Cone, James E., 74–76
confidentiality, 22, 28

Cooper-White, Pamela, 64, 231
Cotton, Dorothy, 62
Courage to Heal, The (Bass and Davis), 28, 31, 34
creation, 42, 46, 76
Creswell, John W., 90
Cuevas, Carmen Diaz, 39, 97, 203
Curcio, William, 20
Cyrus (emperor), 70–71

D

David, King, 66, 144, 152
Davis, Laura
  Courage to Heal, The, 31, 34, 95
Davis, Sharon Ellis, 24
Deborah (prophetess), 137
Devine, Annie, 61
diakonia, 36
didache, 36
Dinah (daughter of Jacob), 73, 94
Dinah Project, 35, 39
Doing Local Theology (Sedmak), 83
Douglas, Kelly Delaine Brown, 76
Dr. Flint (master of Harriet Jacobs), 53

E

Encounters with Jesus (Gench), 70
Equal Employment Opportunity Commission (EEOC), 57
equality, 45–46
Equal Protection of the Law? (Atwell), 51
Ess, Charles, 45
Eural, Wilbert Constance, 12
Eve (first woman), 44–45, 49, 63, 73, 79, 148
Evers, Medgar, 61

F

Faith Seeking Understanding: An Introduction to Christian Theology (Migliore), 145
Fanning, Patrick
  Self-Esteem, 31
Felder, Cain Hope, 43, 68, 71, 154
feminism, 19, 148
Flanagan, Beverly
  Forgiving the Unforgivable, 35

Fokkelman, J. P., 65
forgiveness, 35, 37, 46, 95, 158, 160, 162
Forgiving the Unforgivable (Flanagan), 35
Fortune, Marie M., 28, 61, 65, 150
From Hurt to Healing (Park), 21, 35, 158
Fuchs, Esther, 137

G

Gench, Frances Taylor, 71–73
  Encounters with Jesus, 70
Gilligan (author)
  Between Voice and Silence, 31
godliness, 189
Graham, Gadson L., 42
Grant, Jacqueline, 75
Guttierez, Gustavo, 83

H

Hagar (servant of Sarah), 73, 94, 96, 150
Hairston, Daryl, 79
Hamer, Fannie Lou, 55, 61
han, 33, 46, 160–61
Hansen, Paul, 26
Hendricks, Obery
  Living Water, 55
Hendricks, Obery M., Jr., 81
Herman, Judith, 33, 39, 54
hesed, 82
Higginbotham, Evelyn Brooks, 56
Hill, Anita, 57–58
holiness, 187
Hollies, Linda H., 70, 156
honor killings, 50
Hopkins, Dwight, 55, 62
Hudson, Winson, 62
Huldah (prophetess), 137

I

Ilan, Tal, 138–39
Imus, Don, 59–60
innah, 64

J

Jackson, Jessie, 16
Jacobs, Harriet, 53

Jairus (ruler), 168
Jakes, T. D., 166
James, Jethro C., Jr., 13, 41
James, Sharpe, 16
Jemison, T. J., 59
Jephthah's daughters, 156
Jesus, the Man Who Loved Women (Valcarcel), 96
Jesus Christ, 73, 75, 82, 86, 140–41, 156, 189–90
　belief in, 72
　healing ministry of, 141
　ministry of, 139
　relationship with women, 68, 137
Jezebel (prophetess), 45, 70, 155
Job, 83–85, 182
Job: A Theological Commentary (Simundson), 83
Johnson, John M., 60
Jones, Leroi. *See* Baraka, Amiri
Jones, Major J., 82
Jones, William R., 79

K

kerygma, 36
King, Martin Luther, 55, 61
koinonia, 36, 83
Kysar, Robert, 73

L

lament, 37, 74, 83–84, 230
Lampman, Lisa Barnes, 79
Lawless, Elaine J., 29
Law of Infinite Hermeneutical Adaptability, 46
laws
　Deuteronomic, 49
　Divine, 43
　Jewish, 69, 155, 163–64
　Levitical, 48
　Roman, 164
leadership, 39
Lee, Jarena, 148
Lewis, Margaret, 41, 95
Lincoln, Abraham, 51
Living Water (Hendricks), 55
Lorde, Audre, 86
Lot's daughters, 47, 73

M

MacKinnon, Catharine, 58
Malcolm X, 55
marginalization, 45, 71, 74
Martha (sister of Mary), 181–82
Martin, Clarice J., 79
Mary (sister of Martha), 65, 96, 181–82
Mary Callaway, 67, 153
Mary Magdalene, 185
McBride, J. Lebron, 67, 153
McCauley, Pamela, 97, 203
McWilliams, Weldon, Jr., xiii, 41
Mead, Robert, 12
Mending the Soul (Tracy), 77
Meyer, Joyce, 31
Migliore, Daniel
　Faith Seeking Understanding: An Introduction to Christian Theology, 145
Miller, Patrick L., 84
ministry project, xiii, 1–3, 18, 34, 37–38, 41, 89
　evaluation, 97–101
　goals, 93
　implementation, 94–97
　instrumentation, vii, 91
　intervention, 89
　measurement, 91
　research design, 89–90
　survey results, 102
　treatment hypothesis, vii, 89
Miriam (prophetess), 137
misogynism, 43
Mormon Church, 50
Morrison, Toni, 58
Mosby-Avery, Karen E., 86
Moss, Otis, Jr., 86

N

Nash, Diane, 55
National Baptist Convention, 59
Nelson, Jill, 59
Newark/North Jersey Committee of Black Churchmen, Inc., 97
New Community Corporation (NCC), 10
New Hope Baptist Church, 41, 95
New Hope Baptist Church Women's Connection, 41

Newton, Huey, 55
Niebuhr, Reinhold, 63
1967 race riots, 8, 10

O

Office of Violence Against Women, 19

P

Paradise Baptist Church, xi, xiii, 8, 10–12, 14–15
Paradise Community Development Corporation, Inc., 13
Park, Andrew Sung, 33, 46, 86, 160–62
From Hurt to Healing, 21, 35, 158
Passaic County Board of Social Services (PCBSS), 20
Pastoral Care and Counseling, 1, 3, 36–37, 109
patriarchy, 50
Patte, Daniel, 144
Peterson, Eugene H.
Under the Predictable Plant: An Exploration in Vocational Holiness, 17
Pierce-Baker, Charlotte, 30, 34
Surviving the Silence, 30
Pinn, Anthony
Why Lord?, 74
Pohly, Kenneth, 21
post-traumatic stress disorder (PTSD), 32–33, 67, 96, 153, 180
power and control wheel, 27
Proctor, Samuel DeWitt, 38

Q

Quateka-Means, RoyEtta, 70

R

Rahab (prostitute), 45, 70, 144, 155
Ransy, Barbara, 56
Richie, Beth E., 19
Roberts, J. Deotis, 45, 81
Russell, Diana
Secret Trauma, The, 31

S

Samaritan woman, 63, 69, 73, 96, 155
Sanders, Anucha Browne, 60
Sarah (wife of Abraham), 65, 68, 150–51, 154
Sarai. *See* Sarah (wife of Abraham)
Schneider, Sharon
Written That You May Believe, 71
Scholz, Susanne, 65
Secret Trauma, The (Russell), 31
Sedmak, Clemens
Doing Local Theology, 83
self-esteem, 64
Self-Esteem (Fanning), 31
sexism, 46, 51–52, 75, 149
sexual harassment, 18, 57
shamem, 66–67, 153
Sharpe, John, 13
Sharpton, Al, 59
Sholer, David M., 43
silence, xi–xii, 29–31, 33–34, 62, 87, 160
Simundson, Daniel J., 84
Job: A Theological Commentary, 83
Smith, John, 8
Stanton, Elizabeth Cady, 50, 148
Stephens, Steve
Wounded Woman, The, 96
Stewart, Maria, 74
stress, 175, 177, 180
Student Nonviolent Coordinating Committee (SNCC), 56
suffering, 74–75, 78–80, 86–87
Sullivan (author)
Between Voice and Silence, 31
Surviving the Silence (Pierce-Baker), 30

T

Tamar (sister of Absalom and Amnon), 45, 63–68, 73, 94, 96, 152, 231
Taylor (author)
Between Voice and Silence, 31
Thomas, Clarence, 57–58
Thomas, Isiah, 60
Tindley, Charles Albert, 87
Townes, Emilie M., 86

Tracy, Steven R.
  Mending the Soul, 77–78
Trible, Phyllis, 66
tribulation, 182–83
Trulear, Harold Dean, 86
Tyson, Mike, 58–59

U

Under the Predictable Plant: An Exploration in Vocational Holiness (Peterson), 17
United States Supreme Court, 57

V

Valcarcel, Dorothy
  Jesus, the Man Who Loved Women, 96
Vaughn, Kia, 59
victim-survivor, 21–24, 26, 32–33, 39
violence, 1, 18–19, 23, 27, 80
  domestic, 18, 80, 160
  nonphysical, 23, 149
  physical, 149
  sexual, 150
Violence Against Women Act (VAWA), 19, 21
Vredevelt, Pam
  Wounded Woman, The, 96

W

Walker, Alice, 76, 148
Walker, Lenore, 24
Walker, Wyatt Tee, 61
Washington, Desiree, 58
Weems, Renita, 77
West, Cornel, 60
West, Traci, 23, 53, 57
White, Deborah Gray, 51
Why Lord? (Pinn), 74
Williams, Dolores, 76
Williams, Hosea, 61
womanism, 76, 148
women
  battered, 25, 27, 230
  maltreatment of, 68–69, 155
  as slaves in United States, 51
  subjugation of, 1, 46, 60
  subordination of, 45, 138
Women, Ideology, and Violence (Anderson), 49, 229
Women of Divine Destiny, Inc., 3, 42
Women's Ways of Knowing (Belenky), 29
Wood, Francis E., 79
woundedness, 32, 36
Wounded Woman, The (Stephens and Vredevelt), 96
Wright, Jeremiah, 81
Wright, Marian, 55
Written That You May Believe (Schneider), 71

Y

Young, Andrew, 61

Z

Zehr, Howard, 85

CPSIA information can be obtained
at www.ICGtesting.com
Printed in the USA
BVOW06s2003040218
507193BV00001B/37/P